Mirage

THE FALSE PROMISE
OF DESERT AGRICULTURE

Russell Clemings

. . . .

SIERRA CLUB BOOKS • SAN FRANCISCO

Portions of this book first appeared in substantially different forms in *Longevity, Earthwatch,* and *The APF Reporter* magazines. This book is also based in part on the "Dust to Dust" series and related works originally written for the *Fresno Bee*. Portions of those works are reprinted here by permission of the *Fresno Bee*.

Library of Congress Cataloging-in-Publication Data
Clemings, Russell Allan, 1956–
    Mirage : the false promise of desert agriculture / Russell Allan Clemings.
        p.   cm.
    Includes bibliographical references (p. 221) and index.
    ISBN 0-87156-416-5 (alk. paper)
    1. Arid regions agriculture.   2. Arid regions agriculture—West (U.S.)   3. Arid regions agriculture—Environmental aspects.   4. Arid regions agriculture—Environmental aspects—West (U.S.)   I. Title.
S613.C64   1996
333.76'137'09154—dc20   95-38943

Production by Janet Vail
Jacket design by Amy Evans
Composition by Wilsted & Taylor

For Betsy and Elaine

Contents

Preface and Acknowledgments

In late 1984, when I abandoned humid Florida for the arid San Joaquin Valley of California, I knew nothing about the desert or the agriculture practiced there. My education was rapid. As soon as I arrived, I found myself writing about the historic wildlife disaster at the Kesterson National Wildlife Refuge, where drainage from nearby irrigated farms was dumped, poisoning ducks and other birds with selenium—an obscure trace element perhaps best known at that time as an anti-dandruff shampoo ingredient. In subsequent years, I wrote about identical problems at other locations in the valley, most notably in the Tulare basin's vast farm drainage evaporation ponds. During the next decade, through flood and drought and flood again, I covered California's ceaseless water wars and the struggle, largely unsuccessful so far, to repair some of the environmental damage that has resulted from the construction and operation of the state's big water projects. For giving me the chance to make a living by writing about this subject, I am extremely grateful to the *Fresno Bee* and its editors.

In 1988, I had the good fortune to receive a fellowship from the Alicia Patterson Foundation, a generous organization established by the founder of *Newsday* in New York. The foundation's money allowed me to transform the local Kesterson story into a global story about the sustainability of irrigated desert agriculture; its executive director, Margaret Engel, has been an unending source of encouragement from the fellowship year to the present. Later, when I turned the fellowship research into stories for various magazines and for the *Bee*, several editors helped to organize and clarify the results. Of these, I owe a special debt to Brenda Moore, then of the *Fresno Bee* and later of the *San Francisco Examiner*. I am also grateful to my agent, Barbara Bova, and my editors at Sierra Club Books, Barbara Ras and Scott Norton.

Many of the hundreds of people whom I interviewed during a decade of reporting are identified in the bibliography, but a few deserve special thanks for enduring endless questions on dozens of occasions. Joe Skorupa of the U.S. Fish and Wildlife Service is my idea of what a public servant ought to be, dedicated to serving what he sees as the public's interest regardless of the prevailing political and bureaucratic winds. Jim Oster of the University of California, Riverside, opened his Rolodex to me and helped line up appointments with experts in irrigation trouble spots all over the world. He also reviewed the manuscript; however, any errors that remain are mine alone, as are all unattributed opinions. Raul Fernandez of the University of California, Irvine, and Arturo Ranfla and Marta Stamatis of the Universidad Autónoma de Baja California were invaluable guides to the area around Mexicali in the Colorado River delta. E. J. Doering and Leo Busch helped me greatly in Pakistan; Clive Lyle and Bob Wildes did the same in Australia. Patrick Porgans is a walking encyclopedia of knowledge about the California State Water Project; his sense of the financial underpinnings of the project and San Joaquin Valley agriculture in general has inspired and guided my reporting for many years.

Among the many public information officers who gave me assistance, Louisa Beld and Bob Steele of the Bureau of Reclamation deserve special thanks, as do Lily Hahamy of the foreign ministry in Israel and Don Upton of the Westlands Water District. Because much of this book is based on archival research, I also am grateful to the staffs of the National Archives in Washington, D.C., and

Denver; the Dwight D. Eisenhower Presidential Library in Abilene, Kansas; the Nixon Presidential Materials Project in Alexandria, Virginia; the University of Wyoming's American Heritage Center; the University of California's Bancroft Library and Water Resources Center Archives; the Library of Congress; the library of the Colorado River Board of California in Los Angeles; and the Henry Madden Library at California State University, Fresno.

Piecing together the history of modern desert agriculture from so many far-flung sources was like trying to reassemble a broken dish, and I'm more than certain that I've left a few pieces lying on the floor. Some readers are likely to find this book too pessimistic; others, not pessimistic enough. Farmers may feel that they are portrayed as villains, but in most cases that is not my intent. If the practitioners of desert agriculture have failed to conserve their soils and water properly, they are culpable, but in many instances their actions are excusable when viewed in the context of the perverse incentives and penalties that our system of laws, subsidies, and business practices has produced. It will not be easy for society to maintain the gains it has made through a century of desert farming, but to do so will be one of the most important tasks to confront us in coming decades. This book, I hope, will show that we still have time to make the structural changes that are needed to set things right.

Clovis, California
September 1995

CHAPTER ONE

The Desert Farming Experiment

MAPS LIE.

This thought struck me on a broiling afternoon in March 1989 as I stood at the edge of an irrigated wheat field in the southwesternmost corner of Arizona, a mile west of the shabby border town of San Luis. A few yards to my left was an eight-foot chain-link fence, badly rusted and topped with triple strands of barbed wire. Beyond the fence lay the grimy streets and buildings of San Luis Río Colorado, the fourth largest city in the Mexican state of Sonora and exemplar of what makes the border the bleakest part of that otherwise picturesque country.

People walked along a street paralleling the fence. Some of them stared at this crazy Anglo standing in the brutal midday sun in the hottest, driest, most inhospitable desert in North America, but my attention was elsewhere. I was looking at a U.S. Geological Survey topographic map of the Gadsden quadrangle. According to the map, I was standing at the place where one of the world's most famous rivers, the Colorado, left the United States and entered Mexico.

The map marked the river with a thick blue line corresponding to a swath not more than a hundred feet from me. Yet when I looked in that direction, I saw only a narrow, concrete-lined ditch about twelve feet deep and filled with foaming, fast-flowing water the color of strong tea. Beyond that ditch, where the map said the river should be, there was only sand. To the south, an orange steel-and-concrete bridge carried Mexican traffic—trucks, mostly—across this wide, blindingly white barrier. Below the bridge, a half-dozen men trudged through the sand, adding their footprints to the hundreds of others snaking west across the translucent boundary from Sonora to Baja California.

In the nineteenth century, this place looked very different. For one thing, there was water—lots of it. In the winter of 1857–58, an army lieutenant named Joseph Christmas Ives brought a fifty-four-foot iron-hulled stern-wheeler up the river, steaming north from the Sea of Cortez to the foot of Black Canyon, not far from where Las Vegas presently sprawls. On his return, Ives filed a report saying that the lower Colorado River was suitable for year-round navigation and "would be found an economical avenue for the transportation of supplies to various military posts in New Mexico and Utah." The surrounding country, in contrast, struck him as worthless: "The region explored after leaving the navigable portion of the Colorado . . . is not of much value. Most of it is uninhabitable, and a great deal of it is impassable. . . . Ours was the first and will doubtless be the last party of whites to visit this profitless locality," Ives wrote. Few predictions have proved to be as far off the mark as that one; today, several million people live in the Sonoran desert in places like Las Vegas, San Luis Río Colorado, Phoenix, and Mexicali. They are the spiritual heirs of other men who, just a few years after Ives filed his report, began devising more ambitious plans for the storied Colorado.

In 1896, an eastern engineer named Charles Rockwood forded the Colorado above what is now Yuma, Arizona, and rode into southeastern California, quickly descending into a broiling basin a hundred feet below sea level. This was the same scorched and empty real estate that a Spanish explorer, Juan Bautista de Anza, had raced across a century earlier, desperate to reach the cool Pacific before his horses dropped dead from dehydration. Anza referred to his ordeal as "la jornada de los muertos"—"the journey of the dead." Rockwood, in contrast, looked at the broiling desert and saw only dollar signs. He cut a channel from the Colorado, let the water run downhill into the low desert, and started selling farmland in what his partner grandly christened the "Imperial Valley." Rockwood ended up losing his shirt—and his reputation— when the river flooded in 1905 and washed out a flimsy headgate. In the two years that followed, the Colorado carved a deep chasm in the soft desert alluvium as it emptied its entire flow onto the lowest part of the valley's floor, a desolate sink thereafter known as the Salton Sea. The breach was plugged only after President Roosevelt enlisted E. H. Harriman, owner of the Southern Pacific railroad, which had a spur to the new farming area, to send crews across the border—illegally, because the Mexican government's permission was never sought. Yet despite this false start, the valley eventually prospered, parlaying the imported river water and a twelve-month growing season into the kind of fortune that permitted dirt farmers to become gentlemen and move to La Jolla, where they could farm by telephone from hilltop offices with outstanding views of the Pacific.

The development of the Imperial Valley was a seminal event in U.S. history: it was the opening volley in a hundred years' war against the wild rivers of the arid West. One year after Rockwood finished his first canal, a Geological Survey engineer named Frederick Newell—a protégé of the survey's most influential early director, the legendary one-armed Colorado River explorer John Wesley Powell—persuaded President Roosevelt to champion a bill creating a U.S. Reclamation Service, the principal purposes of which would be to "reclaim" the nation's deserts for agriculture and to establish a beachhead for civilization in the vacant West. During the next century, the Reclamation Service, later renamed the Bureau of Reclamation, built 161 irrigation projects in seventeen western states at a cost of six billion dollars. Forty-one of those projects were on the Colorado River system, and the river paid dearly—by the early 1960s the combined diversions had dried it up completely.

Similar binges of dam- and canal-building began about the same time in other countries, most notably British India and Australia. In later decades, the gospel of desert reclamation spread to practically every nation with so much as an acre of arid land: China, Mexico, Israel, Italy, Peru, the Soviet Union, Syria, and dozens more. Today, the Food and Agriculture Organization of the United Nations calculates that 17 percent of the world's farmland is irrigated, but that figure tells only half the story. Because irrigation is generally practiced in warm climates with long growing seasons, irrigated land produces an average of twice the crop value of ordinary farmland. At present, one-third of the world's crops are produced by irrigation.

As with many achievements of twentieth-century civilization, this bounty is easily taken for granted, but its significance should not be doubted. Fifty years ago, our grandparents would have thought it quite odd to find fresh produce in the dead of winter in the frozen North. Today, thanks to irrigated farming in perpetually warm places like the Imperial Valley, modern Americans expect nothing less. More important, though, irrigation represents the difference between starvation and survival for much of the world, especially Asia. In Pakistan, for example, 80 percent of the gross agricultural product is grown on irrigated land: that desert nation's entire population of more than one hundred million people lives in a state of utter dependence on artificial rain.

At the same time, however, irrigation is fundamentally an experiment—easily the most ambitious experiment that humanity has ever performed on the natural environment, and possibly the most dangerous. When water is applied to historically arid land, it interacts with the sun and soil in ways that can poison the ground by lacing it with salt and other toxic contaminants, while producing mineral-rich runoff that poisons marshes and streams. If not managed correctly, irrigation can also set off a chemical reaction involving sodium that converts a porous clay soil into a mass of extremely fine, packed particles; the resulting powder is nearly impervious to water and completely hostile to life of any kind. In short, sustained desert irrigation can destroy the very prosperity it is supposed to create. And on at least one-quarter of the world's six hundred million acres of irrigated land—an area roughly as large as Texas—that is exactly what it is doing.

At present, the Colorado River's water irrigates two million acres of crops, including the Arizona wheat field I was standing near. Almost entirely as a result of federally funded Bureau of Reclamation projects, vast swaths of fierce desert as far north as Wyoming are routinely made green with water taken from the river. Some of that water eventually returns to the river, but when it does it is usually severely degraded, laced with dissolved salts and toxic minerals leached from desert soils laid down by Pleistocene seas— soils that, like the oceans, contain every element found in nature, good and bad alike. The cycle is repeated again and again as the river staggers southward—diversion, irrigation, return flow—until what little water is left is ill-suited for agricultural use because its salt content is so high that many crops irrigated with it will not germinate.

Mexico uses this water anyway. Just south of Algodones—a collection of sun-bleached shacks that sits atop a sand dune in northeastern Baja California opposite Yuma—the Mexican government has built a low concrete dam that backs up the river and forces its entire remaining flow into a wide "Grand Canal" heading west toward Mexicali. From that point south to San Luis, a twenty-three-mile stretch in which the river forms the international border, the only water that flows south is the flocculent broth that filled the narrow concrete ditch separating me from the dry riverbed.

The ditch contains salty return flows—or drainage, in the argot of irrigation engineers—from about 130 farms in the Wellton-Mohawk Valley on the lower Gila River northeast of Yuma. Though remote and desolate—travelers who pass through it on Interstate 8 might think it uninhabited—this valley has a long history of cultivation. For dozens of generations, the valley's Pima Indians irrigated crops with the Gila's annual floods. Then, in the 1950s, after white settlers had colonized the valley, Bureau of Reclamation engineers built a new canal to carry a vastly larger amount of water up from the Colorado. They did so hurriedly, with scant study of the valley's geology, and soon they regretted it. Just a few years after completing the canal, the bureau discovered to its dismay that the valley was becoming a giant saline bog. A dense plug of underground clay lay near the Gila's mouth, preventing excess irrigation water—the fraction that neither evaporates from the soil nor is transpired by growing plants—from seeping back into the Colorado. In no time at all, the influx of new water had turned the valley into a clogged bathtub of wet mud.

Again the bureau came to the rescue, drilling wells to pump the brackish water out of the ground and building another canal to carry the saline drainage out of the valley. That solved one problem but created another: what to do with a canal full of salty water. For that, the bureau came up with an audacious and cavalier solution. By treaty, the United States was supposed to set aside one-tenth of the Colorado's estimated natural flow for use downstream in Mexico. The bureau decided that the Wellton-Mohawk drainage, although one-fifth as salty as seawater, ought to count toward that requirement, so it dumped that drainage directly into the Colorado a few miles above the border, thereby rendering Mexico's entire share almost unusable. It was no different from tossing garbage over a fence into a neighbor's yard, but comity was not one of the bureau's priorities. Its commissioner at the time, Floyd Dominy, was reported to have bragged to Congress that, if it wanted to, the bureau could meet the terms of the treaty by giving Mexico raw sewage.

Mexico yowled, and threatened to haul the United States into the World Court. The State Department hastily did a study and concluded the obvious: that the court probably would be very sympathetic toward a developing nation that was being abused by the world's greatest military and economic power. The Nixon administration meanwhile had to weigh the risk of antagonizing Mexico at a time when student unrest was nudging its one-party government ever further to the left. Ultimately, on Labor Day weekend in 1972, Nixon appointed Herbert Brownell, a stalwart internationalist who had served as Thomas E. Dewey's campaign manager and as attorney general in the Eisenhower administration, to negotiate a compromise.

One result was construction of the concrete-lined ditch, which carried the Wellton-Mohawk drainage south past Mexico's Colorado River diversion. Another result was a water-desalting factory, to be built at the river's edge near Yuma. Once the plant was finished, a task that would take two decades to accomplish, the Wellton-Mohawk drainage would be desalted and delivered to Mexico. The concrete ditch would then be relegated to carrying only the briny reject stream from the desalting process—constituting about 20 percent of the original drainage volume but containing almost all of its impurities. The plant would enable the United States to squeeze the greatest possible use from the river before surrendering it to Mexico, but in the process it would increase contaminant levels in the remaining drainage by fivefold. Among other things, the plant would increase the effluent's level of selenium—a toxic trace element commonly found in desert soils—until it was high enough to kill ducks and other water-loving birds and deform their young. Via Brownell's concrete-lined canal, that poisonous residue would be dumped directly into the Colorado River delta, a verdant and fecund estuary—a saltwater Everglades—that the legendary naturalist Aldo Leopold called a "milk-and-honey wilderness."

Water has no natural place in a desert. It is foreign; the soil cannot accommodate it. On those rare occasions when rain does fall on the desert, the ground rejects it as though allergic. In humid regions, the soil is honeycombed with drainage channels of varying sizes. Formed by the action of countless roots, worms, and rodents over eons of time, these gaps permit whatever water falls on the surface to soak in and flow downward to nourish the roots of plants and trees or to emerge some distance away in a spring or stream, where it continues its leisurely journey to the sea, sustaining life along the way. In the desert, by contrast, the soil is dense and compacted, only slightly more porous than pavement. Water hits it and quickly runs off, coursing down rocky washes that are dry for all but a few hours each year, when they turn into deadly sluices of brown, frothing violence, producing flash floods that end as suddenly as they begin. The resulting runoff often settles into a low, enclosed basin called a sink. There the water sits, pooled atop watertight clays, until the dry atmosphere reclaims it, leaving only a shallow circle of white salt crusts.

Desert plants and animals are well adapted to this peculiar regime. To minimize the water they lose to evaporation, desert plants have tiny leaves or none at all. Their tissues are succulent and fleshy, capable of taking deep drinks when water is available and then doing without for weeks or months. Think of the saguaro, Arizona's statuesque state flower, the plant most people think of when they hear the word "cactus," standing ten to fifteen feet tall with two armlike branches curving skyward from its sides. The saguaro has no leaves, only sharp needles for defense. Its body is a tubular mass that swallows water like a sponge and stores it greedily. It is nature's version of a cistern, superbly adapted for life in a place where rain is scarce and infrequent. As for desert animals, the top of the food chain is populated mainly by reptiles— snakes, lizards, tortoises—whose leathery scales and cold-blooded metabolism help them to survive the desert's extremes of precipitation and temperature. Birds and mammals, for the most part, occupy only nooks and crannies in this reptilian world. They live burrowed below the ground, like voles, or on the fringes of the desert, in hills and mountains where the air is cooler and moister. Of all mammals, only one—man—has been drawn to live in the desert without benefit of special physiological adaptations.

Humans are poorly suited to aridity; their fragile skin relinquishes water like the petals of a delicate flower, and their kidneys operate inefficiently, purging wastes from the body by releasing them in a flood of urine. Except for oxygen, nothing is more necessary for human survival than a steady and copious supply of water. We can survive for weeks without food, but without water, on a hot day in an arid climate, we might not last for more than a few hours. It is simply astounding, then, that humans throughout history have not only managed to live in the desert but have often done so successfully. Most of the world's early civilizations—ancient Egypt; the successive waves of Assyrians, Sumerians, and Babylonians in the valley of the Tigris and Euphrates rivers; the civilizations of the Indus Valley—arose in deserts and flourished there. Still, those cultures did not live in the desert the way the saguaro does. They clustered in the desert's most humid parts, living in oases along the desert's few perennial rivers—streams that rose in faraway mountain ranges and crossed the desert only coincidentally before reaching the ocean. These cultures planted crops in the moist riverine plains after the floods, like the Egyptians, or they built simple diversions to tap into the run of the river, like the Tigris-Euphrates civilizations. They prospered as long as the river ran reliably and the soil did not turn sour—as happened in Sumeria—but they did not truly adapt themselves to the desert. They simply altered a small part of the desert to accommodate their presence.

Then, in the mid-nineteenth century, a breakthrough occurred that forever changed the relationship between humanity and the desert. In 1847, British civil engineers, full of hubris after lacing their homeland's isles with railways and barge canals, took their newly honed skills to the Crown's newest possession, the arid alluvial plain of the Punjab in northwestern India. A few years earlier, the British army had overrun the Punjab from the east, wresting control from the Sikhs who had governed for the previous half century. Among its other effects, the takeover idled a professional army of thirty thousand Sikh soldiers who had a well-deserved reputation for fierceness. The British quickly realized that a city-sized corps of restless, dispossessed men might prove difficult to govern, so they decided to turn the soldiers into farmers. The world's finest engineers immediately set to work diverting the Punjab's web of rivers, which included the Indus and five tributaries, the Jhelum, the Chenab, the Ravi, the Beas, and the Sutlej, starting several hundred miles north of the site of the ancient civilizations. Those rivers drained the western Himalayas and the Hindu Kush before crossing the Punjab en route to the sea. Turned out of their banks, they fed a canal system that could irrigate tens of thousands of acres, in some cases dozens of miles from the diversion point.

Suddenly, irrigation was transformed. No longer was it merely an ancient art that permitted resourceful interlopers to survive in a hostile climate; now it was a modern technology that could transform hot, arid deserts into farmlands of dazzling productivity, more fertile than all but the best soils of more humid regions. Within a few years, the Punjab became the subcontinent's breadbasket, a distinction it continues to hold today. Lessons learned there soon spread to other English-speaking nations. Delegations from the United States went to India to study what the British engineers had done, in hopes of applying similar techniques to the deserts of the American West. Australia's state of Victoria, a British colony at the time, passed a law in 1886 permitting private construction of irrigation systems. That set the stage for the creation of powerful irrigation bureaucracies in both Australia and the United States, and in the first half of the twentieth century, both nations plunged into dam-building with the zeal of the proselytized. After World War II, foreign aid took irrigation further still, into every arid corner of the world. Egypt built the Aswan High

Dam on the Nile; the Soviet Union diverted the rivers that drained into the Aral Sea. In the Punjab, divided between India and Pakistan in 1947 by the now-retreating British, the two new nations built still more dams and canals to extend the reach of the Indus and its tributaries. Meanwhile, Turkey dammed the Euphrates, and Israel tapped into Yam Kinneret, the biblical Sea of Galilee. Today, because of irrigation, one-third of the world's agricultural output is produced on 17 percent of its farmland. But the transformation may prove to be temporary, even in its Punjab birthplace. Of fifty-five thousand square miles of irrigated land in Pakistan, most of it in the Punjab, one-fifth is now severely damaged by waterlogging or salinity.

Almost as soon as the first flood of water washes into the furrows of a "reclaimed" field, the soil starts to change. Delicate states of equilibrium that took eons to achieve are upset in a few weeks or months. The water deposits some substances into the soil and dissolves others, moving them around. It changes the soil both chemically and physically. The soil's pores fill with water; the clays expand; the fine silts and sands migrate downward into the subsoil.

Most important, the water brings in salt. When rain and snow hit the ground, they unlock cations of sodium, calcium, and magnesium and anions of chloride, sulfate, and carbonate from the rocks of the earth's crust. These substances—the chemical building blocks of salts—gradually wash downstream, making their way toward the planet's great reservoirs of salt, its oceans. Then along come humans, taking water from the rivers to irrigate the land, and taking the salts as well. The cations and anions combine into several types of salt: ordinary table salt, or sodium chloride; gypsum, or calcium sulfate; and others, less well known, like sodium sulfate and magnesium chloride. These salts tend to precipitate in the slightly moist soil that extends as much as several feet upward from the water table—the zone where water wicks toward the surface by capillary action in defiance of gravity. Sometimes, if the water table is high, the moist soil may reach all the way to the surface. But even if it stops short, the sun's evaporative powers eventually reach down and extract the water, leaving behind salty brine.

Whether dissolved in the soil's water or returned to solution when a dry soil containing precipitated salts is wetted, salt is death to plants. It robs cells of their nourishment, even their water, poisoning them from within. Sometimes it does its work directly, as when chloride and other constituents infiltrate the plant's tissues, interfering with metabolism, the chemical process by which the plant makes its food. Other times, the salt is more insidious, dehydrating plants by osmosis, the process by which water passes back and forth between solutions of different concentrations via a semipermeable membrane, such as a cell wall. Osmosis is why a stalk of celery left to soak in a dish of fresh water becomes crisper; molecules of water migrate from the surrounding pure water into the somewhat saltier plant cells. The opposite happens when a plant's external water supply is saltier than its own cells; water moves from the plant cells to the saltier water outside. The process continues until both solutions have roughly the same salt concentration—or until the plant has no more water to give up.

Some plants can muster a limited defense against salt, but to do so leaves less energy available for growth. The most common defense plants employ is to manufacture alcohols and amino acids to raise the osmotic pressure inside their cells. Other plants deal with the problem more directly—they let the salt in and store it inside their cells in special structures called vacuoles. It takes less energy to store the salt than to exclude it, so plants that store salt in vacuoles tend to be more salt-tolerant. Many desert plants fall into that class.

A few plants even have special glands on their leaves that secrete excess salt. The red mangrove, a tree common in tropical tidal flats, won't grow unless its roots are standing in salt water. But few crop plants have such specialized defenses; most crops deal with salinity in the most costly way, by diverting energy from growth. Even if a crop shows no outward sign of distress, it may betray salt damage by a drop in yield. If the drop is subtle, farmers may never know what hit them. Higher levels of salt do more obvious damage, causing plants to wilt, turn brown, or die—or, more likely, never live in the first place. Significantly, though, the growth stages most sensitive to salt are a plant's germination and the period immediately following; if they survive those delicate few weeks, many plants can get by with water of somewhat higher salinity for the rest of their lives.

For all the damage that salt does to crops, a good drink of low-salinity water can set everything right. The same, unfortunately, is not true of salt-damaged soil. When water with high levels of sodium percolates through the soil, a chemical change occurs that permanently damages the soil's ability to produce a crop. Sodium is a fairly common element, but an odd one; highly unstable because it is missing an electron, it is almost never found in isolation in nature. When water containing sodium salts evaporates from the soil, the sodium is left behind to cast about for an electron to share. Usually, it attaches itself to the nearest particle of clay it can find, and therein lies the trouble. Ordinarily, soil particles cling to each other in tiny clumps, but when there is excess sodium around, the soil particles release their grip on each other to combine with the sodium. The structure of the soil thus collapses as each particle surrounds itself in a blanket of sodium. Coarse soils become fine, even powdery. The spaces between the soil particles shrink, leaving no room for air, water, nutrients, or roots. Water doesn't penetrate; it just sits there until it evaporates.

Repairing a sodic soil is possible, but sometimes the only way to do it is to plow truckloads of expensive gypsum (calcium sulfate) into the soil before irrigating. Then, when the water hits the soil, it can rinse away the sodium, leaving calcium in its place. But gypsum isn't cheap, and even if a farmer can afford it, he may have an underlying drainage problem that will cause a recurrence if left un-corrected. Sodic soils most often develop where the ground is constantly moist because of high water tables, which occur frequently on irrigated desert lands and are caused by subterranean layers of clay or hardpan that impede the downward percolation of water. And fixing a drainage problem is usually much more expensive than buying gypsum. There are three basic ways to do it: install buried, perforated pipelines to extract water from the subsoil and carry it to a sump for disposal; dig shallow ditches to intercept the rising groundwater and carry it away, which means sacrificing some land to build the ditches; or drill wells and pump the groundwater out.

Each method involves large cash outlays for materials and labor, and each poses an identical dilemma: how to dispose of the salt-laden water after it is drained from the soil. Dumping it back into the river merely transfers the problem to another irrigator downstream. Sequestering it away from the river—for example, in a low-lying marsh or an artificial pond—raises the specter of a different nightmare, the poisoning of wildlife by toxic trace elements like selenium, released from the desert's soil by the unprecedented application of water.

Selenium is the second great Achilles' heel of desert agriculture. Occupying a place toward the right of the fourth row of the periodic table—between arsenic, a metal, and bromine, a corrosive nonmetallic liquid—selenium is an odd element that has some properties of both metals and nonmetals, much like sulfur, which occupies the position directly above it. Selenium's role in nature is similarly confused: an essential nutrient in small doses, it becomes a deadly poison in amounts only slightly greater. Cattle in some parts of North America are fed selenium-enriched grain to ward off deficiencies; at the same time, in much of the arid West, ranchers must worry about their steers grazing on selenium accumulators such as *Astragalus bisulcatus,* the plant commonly called locoweed.

In irrigated desert agriculture, however, selenium is an unambiguous villain. Leached out of old seabed soils by the application of water in extremely arid regions, selenium hitchhikes in saline drainage flows, sometimes for many miles. The results can be calamitous. At the Kesterson National Wildlife Refuge near Los Banos, California, in 1983, thousands of migratory birds were killed or crippled by feeding in marshes where selenium-rich drainage was dumped. The same thing happened in subsequent years at other nesting grounds in the western states: embryonic chicks developed hideous deformities such as missing or shrunken wings, legs, and beaks, and grotesquely swollen brains. The carnage inflamed public opinion, especially in places like the San Francisco Bay Area, a few dozen miles from Kesterson, where the vox populi had never been enthusiastic about the desert agriculture experiment in the first place. And it raised new questions about whether that experiment, so successful in its first century, could persist for very long into its second.

What if it doesn't? Then the future of our desert gardens might look like the present in southern Iraq, where a vast salt flat between the Tigris and Euphrates rivers provides the most telling evidence of the environmental costs of poorly managed irrigation projects. About 3000 B.C., engineers diverted water from the Tigris and Euphrates to the low-lying plain between them. For a few centuries, the land gave them ample crops of wheat and barley. Then, over-irrigation made their fields waterlogged, and the soggy soil drew salt to the surface like a sponge. With that, the place that modern schoolchildren know as the Fertile Crescent began an unrelenting decline.

Today, on 150 million acres of irrigated land around the world, the same thing is happening, magnified many times because of the delayed side effects of the twentieth century's explosion in irrigation projects. According to a 1989 report by the Worldwatch Institute, an environmental think tank, 15 percent of China's 117 million acres of irrigated land is being destroyed by poor drainage;

the United Nations Environment Programme places the figure at 20 percent. In Pakistan, Worldwatch says 20 percent; in India, 36 percent. In parts of Africa, the numbers are even more dismal. For a time in the 1970s, until a massive rescue project was begun, Egypt had severe drainage problems on 90 percent of its farmland—an unintended but perfectly predictable consequence of the Aswan High Dam. Time and time again, shortsighted project designers have built their dams and canals and distribution systems and then walked away without attending to the corollary business of providing a way for the excess water—and salt—to drain away. They got away with it for a while, simply because it takes a few years or decades for the effects of poor drainage to surface. Now, however, civilization faces a difficult choice: either abandon the global irrigation experiment—and risk losing one-third of the world's crop-producing ability—or find a way to deal with the environmental side effects.

"One of the big issues that keeps coming up is best summarized in the question 'Is irrigated agriculture sustainable?' " says Jan van Schilfgaarde, a U.S. Department of Agriculture administrator and one of the world's most experienced drainage engineers—a member, in fact, of something called the Drainage Hall of Fame.

"The answer is a very clear-cut yes, but with a hedge, and the hedge is: 'If you're willing to pay the price.' We know enough about how to manage irrigated land so that we can keep it productive indefinitely. But we're kidding ourselves if we say we can do that without some environmental insult. And whether we're willing to pay that price is a political decision, not an engineering decision."

Much of what humanity does in the name of technological progress bears a hidden cost.

In the 1970s, we learned that the chlorofluorocarbons that kept our cars cool and our underarms dry were also destroying the ozone layer that protects us from the sun's ultraviolet light. In the

1980s, we found that our habit of burning fossil fuels for energy was cloaking the globe in a blanket of carbon dioxide, raising its temperature ever so slightly, but with potentially cataclysmic effects.

In the 1990s, we may finally begin to understand that what we have done to our deserts in the quest for ever-greater quantities of food carries a hidden cost as well. Irrigation can poison the land and water, it can cripple birds and make fish toxic, and worst of all, its undeniable benefits may prove to be fleeting. Like spring, the blooming of the desert may be temporary: evanescent, like a mirage.

CHAPTER TWO

Manifest Destiny

IN 1994, HUNDREDS OF small boats rode the Colorado River through the Grand Canyon. In 1869, only two boats made that trip, and as far as anyone knows they carried the first group of men ever to float down that violent stretch of river and survive. Their leader was a one-armed Civil War major, an amateur scientist with a strong yen for exploring unknown territories—John Wesley Powell.

Today, Powell's name is blazoned across the West and elsewhere: the largest reservoir on the Colorado and a prominent peak in the Rockies both bear his name. So does the headquarters of the Geological Survey in Washington, D.C., attesting to Powell's place in the history of U.S. science. But in 1868, Powell was an obscure geology professor at Illinois Normal College. To the extent that he was known at all, it was mainly as a collector of shells and for his record of service on Grant's staff at Vicksburg and Shiloh, where his right arm was amputated below the elbow after being smashed by a Confederate minié ball. His expedition, which the novelist and historian Wallace Stegner has called "the last great exploration within the continental United States," was undertaken with no significant government support and little money. Three members of his crew of nine were killed by Indians when they climbed out of the canyon after abandoning the others three days from the end of their ninety-nine-day ordeal. Two of the expedition's four boats were wrecked. Frequent swampings and other disasters destroyed much of the group's food, many of Powell's notes, and all of the barometers and sextants he had borrowed from the Smithsonian Institution for the trip.

When the seven surviving crew members and two surviving boats reached the mouth of the Virgin River, they were weeks overdue. The first people they saw were three Mormons and an Indian seining for fish. The Mormons told Powell that a messenger from Brigham Young in Salt Lake City had come by weeks earlier, asking them to watch for fragments of boats or other signs of Powell's expedition, which was presumed lost. The press had already published premature reports of Powell's demise; he had been eulogized as a hero. "In my supposed death," Powell later wrote, "I had attained to a glory which I fear my continued life has not fully vindicated." On his unexpected return, the same press was filled with accounts of the trip and its terrors, and Powell became a celebrity. He shrewdly parlayed the publicity into a series of meager appropriations from Congress for a scientific study of the West: "The United States Geographical and Geological Survey of the Rocky Mountain Region, J. W. Powell in charge."

Today, historians trace the birth of the federal irrigation program to that shoestring survey of Powell's, but at the time it wasn't much of an operation. In fact, it was just one of four competing surveys of the unsettled West. The largest was under the Department of the Interior and was directed by Dr. Ferdinand Vandeveer Hayden, a medical doctor and geologist. One of the most thoroughly educated Americans of his time, Hayden was nevertheless sufficiently ambitious to gauge the prevailing political winds and adjust his science accordingly. It was his survey more than anything else that was responsible for spreading the quaint but destructive notion that "rain follows the plow"—the idea that settlers on the Great Plains, by breaking up the ancient sod that generations of buffalo had grazed, would somehow set off a climate change that would produce sufficient rainfall for crops. (To Powell,

such thinking was worse than laughable; it was unscientific.) Two
other competing surveys were in the War Department: one, under
Lieutenant George M. Wheeler, consisted mainly of topographic
mapping; the other, led by Clarence King, concentrated on mapping deposits of important minerals. Impressed with Powell's Colorado River explorations, but apparently not overly impressed,
Congress in July 1870 appropriated a paltry ten thousand dollars
and instructed Powell to explore and map the region around the
river.

Powell's survey spent the better part of a decade quietly crisscrossing the West, studying its geology, hydrology, biology, and
human habitation in loving detail. The survey crews paid close attention to the handful of fledgling farm colonies that already dotted
the Great Basin. Some, mostly established by Mormons, struck
Powell as well run and appropriately located; others seemed
doomed to failure because of poor siting, poor management, or
other flaws. But Powell's careful approach did not win him many
admirers. By 1876, his annual appropriation had reached forty-five
thousand dollars, but the next year, amid a push for new funding
by the Hayden and Wheeler surveys, Congress cut his budget by
a third, to thirty thousand dollars. The reduction was openly attributed to rising frustration in Congress over Powell's failure to
produce much from his survey, unlike Hayden, who was churning
out hundreds of flatulent pages a year. The cut may also have been
because of Powell's failure to produce results that were useful to
the mining, land speculation, and railroading industries, which
found much to like in the work of the other surveys, especially
Hayden's. Only a fierce lobbying campaign by Powell, who called
in favors from dozens of fellow scientists and got them to write
letters to members of Congress on his behalf, rescued his survey
from extinction.

Powell concluded that he needed to produce a major work to
shore up support for his foundering survey. The only thing he had
in preparation that even remotely fit the bill was a report on the

public domain that had been incubating for several years. It would take time to finish, but Powell believed there was good reason to hurry. A new president, the reform-minded Rutherford B. Hayes, had been elected, and he had appointed a new secretary of the interior, the reform-minded Carl Schurz. While Hayes tried to clean up the civil service after the Grant years, Schurz aimed to shield public lands from pillage. Reformist elements were gaining strength in Congress as well, and in that climate a voice like Powell's seemed likely to get at least a sympathetic hearing. So in one of those acts that only in retrospect turns out to be a turning point in U.S. history, Powell rushed into print a volume based on his decade of research in the West. Starting with a thorough report on his survey's work in Utah, he spliced on an ambitious—even revolutionary—program for western development, a program rooted in his commonsense understanding of the nature of the West and relying on his keen understanding of what would and would not work, an understanding based largely on the experiences of the Mormons. This document, the *Report on the Lands of the Arid Region of the United States,* set the stage for two decades of debate that culminated in the primary piece of legislation shaping the West today, the Reclamation Act of 1902—a law based in spirit, though not in every detail, on Powell's prescriptions.

The seeds of this remarkable report—this "manifesto," as some of its contemporary detractors called it—had been germinating in Powell's mind for much of the previous decade. As he traveled through the Colorado River basin with his survey team, mapping the land, measuring stream flows, admiring successful Mormon irrigation projects, picking the bones of unsuccessful non-Mormon irrigation projects, and watching settlers from the humid East migrate naïvely to the arid West, Powell came to two rather profound (for the times) conclusions: first, land without water is next to useless to a settler; and second, there is almost no water anywhere in the West, except along the Pacific coast.

In 1874, when Powell was preparing a long statement for the

House Committee on Public Lands, he let himself muse for a few paragraphs on the essential aridity of the West, providing the first public glimpse of the thinking that later flowered in the arid lands report. Two-fifths of the country, Powell said, was too dry for agriculture without irrigation, and within that arid region there was only enough water to irrigate a small amount of land, "perhaps from one to three per cent." The few rivers that could easily be diverted by small groups of settlers, such as those in the Great Salt Lake Valley, had for the most part already been appropriated; any future irrigation works would have to be run "by cooperative organizations, great capitalists, or by the general or state governments." As a first step, Powell advised, the government should do a survey of the western regions to find the most suitable places for irrigation projects. (The ideal person to be in charge of the survey, he added, would be John Wesley Powell.)

Powell continued to refine his philosophy in speeches and testimony over the next few years. In 1877, he gave a speech to the National Academy of Sciences on the "public domain," and for once he got the attention of the eastern press—even Horace Greeley's *New York Tribune,* which boiled down Powell's remarks to a few words: "In the whole region, land as mere land is of no value; what is really valuable is the water privilege." Homesteads consisting of 160-acre rectangles—the basic unit of settlement that the government had been using to distribute land since it began carving up the old Northwest Territories—were useless in the West, Powell said, unless they lay along a stream, and all of the streams had already been appropriated by stockmen and speculators.

The report on arid lands, when it came out the following year, added no new themes to the ones Powell had been developing for the past decade; it simply applied Powell's thinking to the realities of the arid West and came up with what he considered to be a logical system for western settlement. Conceptually, Powell divided the nation into two parts, separated by the hundredth meridian, a line running from the Dakotas to Texas. East of that line, rainfall was generally greater than twenty inches per year; west of the line, it was generally less. In Powell's opinion, the only thing that was certain west of the hundredth meridian was drought: "The limit of successful agriculture without irrigation," he wrote, "has been set at 20 inches, that the extent of the Arid Region should by no means be exaggerated; but at 20 inches agriculture will not be uniformly successful from season to season. Many droughts will occur; many seasons in a long series will be fruitless; and it may be doubted whether, on the whole, agriculture will prove remunerative." At the time Powell's report was released, western land settlement was one of the nation's most aggressive industries. Newly established railroads were longing for business transporting migrants and their cargoes, and state legislatures and western merchants resorted to puffery and worse in their efforts to increase the flow to the frontier. While Powell issued dire warnings, men like William Gilpin, a Colorado promoter, enticed settlers to the arid Great Plains with platitudes about gentle spring rains and freshly flowing artesian waters. If what Powell was saying were true, then those settlers would probably starve.

Powell's report went on to propose a revolutionary approach to settling the arid West that called for careful evaluation and classification of the western lands according to the kinds of uses that made the most sense for them: irrigated agriculture in the low, warm alluvial plains along the rivers; grazing in the foothills and other elevated lands where frost was a greater danger; and timbering at the highest elevations, where moisture was more plentiful but summers were short. At the same time, Powell urged the undertaking of a survey of the West's mineral resources, with the most valuable mining areas to be noted and set aside.

The reception that Powell's report received when it was published was about what might have been expected for a document so rigorous in logic, so heedless of the conventional wisdom, and so independent of the prevailing political and economic winds. It was ignored. About the only notable result was the reorganization of the four competing surveys of the West, as Powell recommended, into one—the U.S. Geological Survey. President Hayes put Clarence King, a Powell ally, in charge of the new agency, with Powell going to the Bureau of Ethnology to study Indians, another of his passions. But in 1881, King vacated the office and Powell replaced him. Finally given a chance to put his theories into practice, Powell decided his initial goal would be to catalog the lands of the West as a first step toward rationalizing their settlement in accordance with his arid lands report—a project for which he needed a generous appropriation from Congress. For most of the next decade Powell wrote, spoke, and twisted arms toward that end, but mostly he simply waited for the times to catch up with him.

By 1888, with the sun wringing every last drop of moisture out of the sky and leaving none of it for the plains, opportunity presented itself in the person of William Morris Stewart, who represented Nevada in the Senate from 1865 to 1875 and returned to it in 1885. Nevada's economy was a shambles then; the Comstock lode was playing out and the state was plunging into depression. As a candidate, Stewart hung his hat on two remedies—the coining of silver to boost its value, and irrigation to diversify the state's economy. Once in Washington, Stewart and other western senators formed a committee on irrigation, and in March 1888, Congress passed and President Cleveland signed a joint resolution calling on the secretary of the interior to do a survey of sites for irrigation projects in the western states. The job was quite naturally given to the Geological Survey, and Powell, its director, set to work the following October.

What he set to work on was not exactly what Stewart had in mind. Instead of putting together a quick list of reservoir sites using existing data—which was what Stewart wanted—Powell outlined a plan of study that would take seven years and cost seven million dollars to finish, and in the process would accomplish most of what he had proposed ten years earlier in the arid lands report.

Grumblings were heard. Then, in August 1889, something happened that turned the grumblings into shrill cries of outrage. The survey's appropriation had provided that all lands "made susceptible of irrigation" be withdrawn from public entry, but with speculators trailing Powell's survey parties, the acting commissioner of the General Land Office, William M. Stone, decided that virtually the entire public domain should remain off-limits until the survey was finished. Powell was gleeful; Stone's action gave him enough breathing room to do the kind of careful, scientific study that he considered necessary before any irrigable lands were designated. But Stewart, who only two years before had embraced Powell, calling him "competent, energetic and enthusiastic," began shrieking for his hide.

Stewart's opposition was more than enough to derail the survey. That August, the land withdrawal provision was repealed and the irrigation survey's separate funding eliminated. Powell had asked for $720,000 for the irrigation survey alone that year; instead, his entire agency got only $350,000. A year later, the figure was whittled down even more, and although Geological Survey parties continued to gather hydrographical data in the West, Powell was finished as a force in Washington for all practical purposes. He retired from the Geological Survey in 1893, retreating into ethnology and speechmaking, but he left behind a cadre of engineers who a decade later would form the nucleus of an irrigation program that would dwarf anything the world had seen until then.

Egyptians invented irrigation, Sumerians improved it, and various other cultures practiced it for seven millennia. But it took the British in India to perfect it, and it took the Americans to set about remaking the earth with it. Yet until the twentieth century, irrigation in North America was little different from irrigation in Babylonia.

Typical practitioners were the Hohokam, an Indian civilization that irrigated the Arizona desert for a millennium. Today, jets gliding into Sky Harbor Airport in Phoenix cast fleeting shadows across two of the most prominent artifacts of this extinct race, the Pueblo Grande ruins and the adjacent Park of Four Waters. Archeologists say the Hohokam met their demise sometime around 1450, a generation before Columbus. At their peak in the eleventh century, they numbered sixty thousand people, maybe more, distributed across ten thousand square miles of the continent's hottest real estate.

The Hohokam extended as far south as modern Tucson, as far north as Prescott, as far west as Gila Bend, and as far east as Safford. They shared two key characteristics with the Anglo civilization that has developed in Arizona in the past century. First, their world was centered in the Salt River Valley, a broiling basin now occupied by the metropolitan sprawl of Phoenix, Mesa, Tempe, and Scottsdale. Second, the Hohokam, like modern Anglos, achieved their prosperity by manipulating the meager flows of the Salt River. That tiny stream, fed by winter rains in the San Francisco Mountains of eastern Arizona and western New Mexico, carries less water in a year than the Mississippi carries in a morning. Today, most of its flows are dammed and diverted long before they reach the metropolitan areas. Yet in prehistory, the Salt River was the foundation of an irrigated agriculture more advanced than any other in North America before the present century.

Hohokam canals laced the desert basins like strands of glistening pearls. There were more than two hundred miles of them in all, some measuring eighty feet wide and twenty feet deep. And because there is no evidence that the Hohokam used domesticated animals, archeologists have concluded that every last mile of the canals was scratched out of the earth by humans using a few simple tools, such as sharpened sticks and stone hoes.

The Hohokam grew corn, beans, and squash, but they probably suffered some lean years; elaborate as it was, the Hohokam canal system lacked any way to store water from one season to another, so a dry year meant having less water for irrigation than they were accustomed to. In fact, archeologists theorize that what finally finished off the Hohokam may have been a long series of dry years—a sudden change in climate that sharply and permanently reduced the flows of the Salt River. They also theorize that with water scarce, the Hohokam may have tried to stretch their supply further than they should have, triggering a fatal buildup of salt in the underwatered soil. Having managed to irrigate with success for so long, the Hohokam might not have realized that their prosperity rested on a fragile balance of water, sun, and soil.

North America's next successful band of irrigators did not irrigate by choice; rather, they were refugees from the Midwest, outcasts driven into the desert by persecution. Today, the Mormons regard it as an article of faith that their ancestors were the first people to practice irrigation in North America. Though the Hohokam would give them an argument on that point—and so, for that matter, might the padres at some of the old Spanish missions in California—in a sense Anglo-American irrigation as we now know it was born a few hours after Brigham Young led his first bedraggled group of pilgrims over the crest of the Wasatch Range on July 23, 1847.

There is no evidence that the Mormons practiced irrigation before moving to the valley of the Great Salt Lake, but it is obvious that they had studied its techniques because once they arrived they wasted no time in setting to work. During the migration, the settlers organized themselves into committees of ten, fifty, and a hundred. On their arrival in the valley, one group was sent to lay out a townsite, another to look for timber in the nearby canyons, and yet another to plow, plant, and irrigate a thirty-five-acre plot of land. The last group built a simple dam in City Creek, one of the dozens of snowmelt streams that tumbled out of the Wasatch into the Great Salt Lake, and dug rudimentary ditches to carry the water to fields that would be planted in potatoes, beans, turnips, and grains. One pioneer, Orson Pratt, recorded the first day's work in his diary: "In about two hours after our arrival, we began to plow, and the same afternoon built a dam to irrigate the soil, which at the spot where we were plowing was exceedingly dry." The next day, Pratt wrote, the Mormons "commenced planting our potatoes, after which we turned the water upon them and gave the ground a good soaking."

In that first year, the ever-growing settlement of Mormons suffered through shortages of food, largely because too many people came too soon. (A second migration, larger than the first, arrived in September 1847.) A late frost the following spring and a plague of crickets the next summer only made things more desperate. Until vast flocks of seagulls arrived and devoured the crickets—a sign from God, in the eyes of the Mormons, who later erected a seagull monument in Salt Lake City—the future of the new Zion looked dismal indeed. But somehow they survived, and in the years that followed, the Mormons systematically explored the Great Basin. They established settlements throughout the basin: cities as far-flung as Carson City; Las Vegas; San Bernardino; Mesa, Arizona; and Sugar City, Idaho, have Mormon roots.

Yet nowhere in their explorations did the Mormons see a site they liked better than the one Brigham Young had chosen for them. Possibly by chance, but more likely by design (there is evidence that before making the last leg of the migration Young talked extensively with western explorers and trappers such as Jim Bridger and Fr. Pierre Jean DeSmet), the Mormons had managed to settle in one of the few places in the western United States that was ideally suited to irrigation. There was a reliable source of water —the twelve-thousand-foot snow-capped Wasatch Range, which drained into dozens of streams on a gentle sloping plain twenty miles wide and two hundred miles long. Unlike many of the West's rivers, the streams had not buried themselves in deep canyons; they could easily be turned out of their beds and onto the land. Drainage was not a problem because the entire plain drained into the Great Salt Lake, a splendid natural sump. The only problem was the altitude; at forty-five hundred feet, the valley was susceptible to late frosts in the spring and early frosts in the fall. After substantial crop losses the first few years, the Mormons learned to confined their agriculture to the warm, dry summer months, relying solely on irrigation to supply the needed moisture.

There were not many places in the West—or in the world for that matter—that were as forgiving of irrigation as the Great Salt Lake Valley. Other places had poor drainage or high levels of sodium in the soil. If the soil was all right and the drainage was good, then the nearest source of water might be hundreds of miles away—a distance that could be crossed only by huge canals built at great public expense. Or the altitude might be so high that the growing season was only two or three months long, ruling out pretty much any crop other than cattle grass.

Nevertheless, for more than a century after the Mormon migration, Americans tried to duplicate their success in every corner of the West. Any creek deserving of a name was given a dam, and any piece of ground that a plow could penetrate was declared suitable for irrigation, often with only the briefest of studies. Fortunes were made; great cities like Los Angeles and Phoenix and Reno sprang into being almost overnight. Irrigated farming changed the way the nation ate. Chicago got fresh lettuce in winter; Cleveland got fresh fruit whenever it wanted. For a while, it seemed as if all of it was going to work just fine. But then, as the end of the twentieth century approached, Americans suddenly had second thoughts. Horrified by the escalating costs of building irrigation projects, and by the environmental damage they caused, the nation simply stopped building them sometime around 1980. Moreover, it soon found itself scrambling just to keep the desert from reclaiming what had already been built.

Notwithstanding Powell's initial failure, by the 1890s so many forces were conspiring in favor of a federal irrigation program that it had assumed the inevitability of a mudslide. For one thing, there was the growing political power of the western states. In 1888, the map of the West contained only seven states: Kansas, Nebraska, Colorado, Texas, California, Nevada, and Oregon. In the two years that followed, six more were admitted: North and South Dakota, Washington, Montana, Idaho, and Wyoming. Utah joined in 1896. Instead of fourteen senators, the West suddenly had twenty-eight—an instant lobby for irrigation. All these politicians lacked was a viable plan. In the vacuum left by the ending of Powell's irrigation survey, leadership of the irrigation movement fell to William Ellsworth Smythe, an Omaha newspaperman who was converted to the cause by a series of stories he wrote on irrigation in 1891. Smythe helped to organize the first National Irrigation Congress in Salt Lake City in September 1891, at which the delegates —including land agents, railroaders, businessmen, and journalists—declared that the federal government ought to cede the entire public domain to the states, the better to get some serious irrigation development under way.

That idea wasn't new. Cession of public lands had been proposed by a long line of western politicians for the previous half century. The idea soon got a trial, but it failed miserably. The Carey Act of 1894 authorized the secretary of the interior to cede up to a million acres of land to each of the arid states if the states would irrigate it, sell it, and return the proceeds to the federal treasury. The act's sponsor, Senator Joseph M. Carey of Wyoming, seemed to believe that the mere transfer of ownership would remove whatever obstacles there were to irrigation development, but the truth proved different. Eight years after its passage, fewer than twelve thousand acres had been patented under the Carey Act. The legislation offered no incentive to states to undertake the difficult job of irrigation development. And because only the land that was actually reclaimed could be used as security, borrowing money for construction was next to impossible.

Meanwhile, California was making a halfhearted attempt to implement Powell's plan for irrigation districts. In 1887, the state legislature passed the Irrigation District Act, commonly known as the

Wright Act after its sponsor, a state senator named C. C. Wright. The Wright Act had a simple answer to the question of what role the state would play in irrigation development—none at all. It simply threw the whole problem into the laps of prospective irrigators, who were encouraged to form districts. There was no provision for making sure the districts were viable; all that had to be done was organize them and elect a board of directors, but then the districts were on their own. Virtually all of them collapsed. They built dams on rivers that had too little water, issued bonds that nobody wanted to buy, and argued endlessly over the allocation of what little water they could manage to make available. Although the Wright Act was supposed to bring about the transformation of two million acres, less than a hundred thousand acres were ever irrigated.

Across the West, private irrigation ventures were failing with stunning regularity. Those that didn't collapse of their own dead weight were given a fatal nudge by the panic of 1893. Thus, by the mid-1890s, Congress, the state legislatures, and entrepreneurs had pretty much made a mess of every irrigation development program they had tried. The only approach that remained untried was direct federal aid. By 1893, even Smythe's Irrigation Congress began calling for a federal irrigation program; at first it was hesitant, but by 1900, its official position was that irrigation was an obligation of the federal government. In 1897, George H. Maxwell, a California lawyer, set up the National Irrigation Association, a Washington-based lobbying arm of the Irrigation Congress. For the next five years, with grants from the railroads, he churned out press releases and periodicals to drum up support for a federal irrigation program. Meanwhile, several members of Congress, including Nevada's sole representative, a wealthy Californian named Francis G. Newlands, introduced bills.

Newlands had learned about the shortcomings of private irrigation ventures the hard way—by taking a bath in one. A Yale-educated lawyer, Newlands set up shop in San Francisco in 1870

and soon thereafter wooed and married the daughter of a former
Nevada senator, William P. Sharon. His bride died within a few
years, but Newlands maintained his relationship with his father-
in-law, eventually becoming the manager of the old man's Comstock fortune. After Sharon died in 1885, Newlands moved to Nevada and within six months of his arrival was making plans for an
ambitious irrigation project on the Truckee and Carson rivers,
which flowed into Nevada from the mountains around Lake Tahoe
and ended in saline desert lakes. Between 1889 and 1891, Newlands sunk $250,000 of the Sharon fortune into dams, ditches, and
canals. Speculators plopped down along the river between Newlands's dam sites and his farmland and refused to sell him their
river frontage; then, once the first dam was built, they diverted all
of the water before it could get downstream to the farms. Newlands
tried to salvage the project by offering it at cost to the state, which
could condemn the speculators' land and thereby protect the
stream flow. But at that moment, the state irrigation program,
which Newlands had prodded the legislature to create in 1889,
was falling apart as politicians squabbled over whose district
would get the first project, so his offer was spurned. Newlands was
utterly dejected, but with his reputation oddly enhanced by the
failed venture, he won election to Congress in 1892.

Chastened, Newlands lay low on the irrigation issue for most of
the decade. Stewart, his fellow Nevadan, and Wyoming's Senator
Francis E. Warren developed a series of bills calling for the federal
government to build storage reservoirs and turn them over to the
states. Newlands believed, based on his Nevada experience, that
such a program would be a recipe for further disaster because state
politicians would fall to bickering over who would get the water.
But Newlands's was the minority view. In 1901, when Newlands
finally introduced a bill to create a strong federal irrigation program, it languished; a Warren bill calling for federal construction
of reservoirs under the control of the states was passed instead by
the Senate. The House seemed likely to follow, and President

McKinley, an easterner who was apathetic about irrigation, probably would have signed it. But fate intervened.

On September 6, 1901, an anarchist named Leon Czolgosz shot McKinley and made Theodore Roosevelt the youngest president in the nation's history. Though he was from a wealthy New York Huguenot family, Roosevelt was western in outlook and decidedly in favor of an irrigation program. That he was in favor of a program that resembled Newlands's more than Warren's complicated things considerably. But in March 1902, Warren was called away from Washington by the death of his wife, and Roosevelt took advantage of the vacuum to tell the House leadership that he would gladly support the Warren bill with a few changes in "phraseology"— changes that amounted to substituting Newlands's entire bill for Warren's. Roosevelt dispensed flattery and favors to get the bill onto the House floor, where the Democratic leadership let it pass with little debate. When he returned from Nevada, Warren gave up any hope of blocking the measure; he simply spoke briefly against it in Senate debate and pledged to offer some "modifications" in future sessions.

The bill that became the Reclamation Act of 1902 (the idea being to "reclaim" the desert wastelands) and established the Geological Survey's Reclamation Service (later removed from the survey and renamed the Bureau of Reclamation) was born of the lingering mistrust Newlands had for state governments after his failed Truckee-Carson venture. It called for irrigation projects that would be federally run and, because he trusted his fellow members of Congress even less than he did the states, financed not by appropriations but by a revolving fund fueled by the sale of public lands. Thus insulated from politics, the new program was closer in spirit to Powell's proposals than anything before it, and for good reason: in drafting the bill, Newlands had relied heavily on the advice of some of the engineers that Powell had recruited to his abortive irrigation survey in 1888, especially Frederick Newell. (For good measure, Newell was working the White House angle simultaneously; when Roosevelt, in his first message to Congress, called for a federal irrigation program, the words he spoke were for the most part written by Newell.)

Appropriately, Newell became the first director of the new Reclamation Service. For the first few years that followed, the new bureaucracy conducted itself in a Powell-like manner, trying to build modest projects on eminently sensible sites. But like Powell, Newell felt the pressures of politics, and he was no more successful at deflecting them than his mentor was. To fend off hostile inquiries from congressmen whose states had been passed over for projects, Newlands resolved to try to build at least one in each eligible state immediately. As a result, the infant service was overwhelmed; it simply tried to build too many projects too fast, twenty-five in the first five years. The undue haste prompted numerous mistakes: projects were built on streams that had scarcely been studied; reservoirs leaked. In New Mexico, a reservoir on the Carlsbad project was built over strata of soluble gypsum, which, when the dam's gates were closed and the water began to pool, melted like butter, causing an investment of $375,000 to disappear into the earth.

Worst of all, the engineers of the Reclamation Service found themselves utterly at a loss to cope with the "soft" side of irrigation, namely, human relations and education. Faced with the delicate task of teaching neophyte settlers how to irrigate without destroying the land through waterlogging and salinity, the engineers contented themselves instead with the more easily understood problems of construction. It was a decidedly un-Powell-like way of doing things, but Powell had been an intuitive expert in economics and social problems, as well as geology and hydrology; his successors, too often, were mere engineers.

It took the new Bureau of Reclamation until the late 1920s to recover from its early missteps, but when it did, the result was Hoover Dam. That graceful concrete monolith, wedged into a Colorado River canyon by a Depression-era workforce, was designed in large part to rescue California's Imperial Valley from its unending quarrels with Mexico over the diversions and canals that Charles Rockwood and his successors had built and to prevent another flood like the one that nearly ruined the valley between 1905 and 1907. But the dam accomplished far more than that. It yielded enough electrical power to trigger runaway growth in cities like Los Angeles and Las Vegas, inspired Bugsy Siegel to build the Flamingo Hotel and ignite the Nevada gambling boom, and like any success, attracted hordes of imitators. In fact, a case could be made that it was Hoover Dam, even more than the early British successes in the Punjab, that was responsible for the twentieth century's worldwide binge of water development and irrigation. If so, the dam may have been built just in time.

When Christ walked the earth, the planet contained no more than a few hundred million people, fewer than those in Europe alone today. By the beginning of the nineteenth century, the world population reached one billion, then doubled in the next century, and when the last third of the twentieth century began, doubled again. Now, with the twenty-first century upon us, the human race has more than five billion people. By 2050, the United Nations predicts that the world population will level off somewhere between ten and twelve billion—but only if hoped-for progress in reducing birth rates in underdeveloped countries actually comes to pass. Miraculously, world food production has more or less kept pace with this recent population surge. Especially in the past two decades, famine has become increasingly rare, except in cases in which normal food distribution is disrupted by war, as in the Horn of Africa. In the 1950s, about 23 percent of the world's people were hungry; today, only 9 percent are. In short, the world now produces enough food, thanks mainly to a dramatic increase in average yields—not in planted acreage, but in the amount of food produced per acre.

Until the present century, most gains in world food supplies were achieved by bringing new lands (in some cases, new continents) into agricultural production. But since 1900, the needed increase has come principally from applying modern technology— chemical pesticides and fertilizers, mechanized equipment, and irrigation—to lands previously farmed by more primitive methods. As populations doubled and redoubled during the twentieth century, so did the yields produced by an average acre of farmland. Precisely how much of the yield increase is attributable to irrigation is hard to calculate, but in 1989 the Worldwatch Institute, an environmental think tank, estimated that the amount of irrigated farmland worldwide increased from 120 million acres in 1900 to 235 million acres in 1950 and 625 million acres today, while the amounts of nonirrigated cropland shrank by a similar amount, and that the average irrigated acre produces twice the yield of the average unirrigated acre. Some of the greatest gains in productivity have come in nations like Mexico, Pakistan, and India, where irrigation and chemicals were coupled with new high-yielding seeds of wheat and rice to produce what came to be called the Green Revolution. Between 1964 and 1968, the high-yielding strains were planted on more than thirty-four million acres, almost all of them irrigated; the new seeds were so successful that world food prices actually dropped by 20 percent in the 1980s. Without irrigation, this achievement would have been impossible.

Unfortunately, this increase may not be enough. The ceaseless growth in world population is expected to increase food needs to three times current levels by 2050. Already, fully 40 percent of the photosynthesis that occurs on this planet is put to use, one way or another, by humans. Clearly, this figure will have to rise substantially in the decades to come, but the real trick may be to prevent it from falling. Irrigation is by no means the only weak spot in the global food system; despite advances in nonchemical pest controls, the problem of insect resistance to pesticides remains urgent as well. Yet one other figure stands out from the Worldwatch report—the estimate that, worldwide, one of every four acres of irrigated farmland may already have been damaged by salt.

CHAPTER THREE

An Early Warning

THE ENGINEERS THAT John Wesley Powell had recruited to his short-lived irrigation survey formed a ready nucleus for the new Reclamation Service after it was created by the Reclamation Act of 1902. In its early decades, the new agency was led first by Powell's protégé, Frederick Newell, who held the title of chief engineer of the Reclamation Service from 1902 to 1907 and became the first director of the Bureau of Reclamation when the service underwent its metamorphosis in 1907; then, on Newell's retirement, by Arthur Powell Davis, who was not only a student of Powell's but his nephew. Both men, as well as other early leaders of the reclamation agency, were steeped in the lessons of the arid lands report and the aborted irrigation survey, but somehow, after Powell's death in 1902, they managed to forget much of what the master had taught them. As a result, at the end of its first twenty years, the infant agency was in serious trouble, and many of the projects that it had erected—too hastily, in too many cases—were perched on the brink of collapse.

Eager even then to please their congressional patrons in the lightly populated western states—and conscious of the act's requirement that they allocate their spending in roughly the same geographical distribution as their receipts from public land sales, the source of the reclamation fund's revenues—reclamation's early leaders built projects all over the map, often in places that had received only the most perfunctory of hydrological and geological studies. Sometimes, as with the doomed Carlsbad project and its disappearing reservoir, the results were comical, albeit costly in economic terms; other times, they were tragic, as innocent settlers struggled to grow crops on ground that was too alkaline, with a water supply that was too unreliable, and with a drainage system that often existed only on paper. Reclamation's early engineers built projects on windy, high-altitude plateaus where growing seasons were too short to produce anything more remunerative than pasture grass; they erected dams on streams that produced far less water than their rosy scenarios had projected; and worst of all, they scarcely bothered to investigate the need for drainage before starting work on dams and canals. "Right from the start," said Floyd Dominy, the eventual commissioner, "they didn't pay enough attention to the fact that when you put water on the land, you've also got to figure out how to get it off the land."

In its first two decades, the bureau erected more than two dozen irrigation projects, at least one in every western state except Texas. By the early 1920s, low-lying portions of virtually all of the projects were suffering from waterlogging, salinity, or both. On New Mexico's Rio Grande project, thirty-seven thousand of the project's two hundred thousand acres were waterlogged by 1917, nine years after the first deliveries of water were made. In the next four years, the bureau spent $1.5 million digging drainage ditches to bring the water table down to manageable levels. Nevada's Newlands project required the same treatment not long after the bureau brought water down from Lake Tahoe in 1905 to irrigate seventy-three thousand acres of land around Fallon; costs escalated to such an extent that Congress ended up eating more than half the project's bills in 1926. Colorado's Uncompahgre project had fifteen thousand waterlogged acres in 1915; that same year, the Boise project in Idaho had eleven thousand.

By 1923, 103,000 acres of bureau-irrigated land was water-logged—almost one-tenth of all the desert acreage the agency had managed to bring into agricultural production in twenty-one years of feverish construction. Partly as a result, costs for most of the projects were running double the original estimates, and the luck-less settlers the bureau had lured to the projects were agitating for relief from their ballooning repayment obligations. The same year, Elwood Mead, an irrigation expert from the rival Department of Agriculture, was assigned to head a commission that surveyed the wreckage. "The situation that has developed on the federal recla-mation projects is serious," Mead began his report to Interior Sec-retary Hubert Work. "Three projects have been abandoned, and unless remedial measures of a permanent character are applied, several more of the projects will fail, and the federal reclamation experiment, conceived in a spirit of wise and lofty statesmanship, will become discredited."

Mead's report gave several causes, all related, for the problems plaguing the reclamation projects. Their hurried construction was at the top of the list; at one time, just a few years after the Recla-mation Act's passage, the government tried to build twenty proj-ects at once, when a more reasoned approach would have been to build two or three and apply the lessons learned from them toward planning and building future projects. Also, construction costs on many of the early projects turned out to be several times larger than estimated, which bankrupted the revolving fund that paid for them—Congress had to make a twenty million dollar loan to bail out the fund—and saddled farmers with repayment bills that were far higher than they had been led to expect. "This has become a source of constant attack upon the reclamation service and of dis-content among water users," the report said.

But Mead reserved his harshest criticism for the way Powell's heirs had focused solely on engineering at the expense of the equally important job of helping the settlers use the federal water to turn deserts into farms. Instead of rushing to assist struggling

neophytes with technical advice and access to needed capital, the
government had been content to simply finish construction, then
sit back and wait for the payments to start coming in:

> A fundamental error was made in believing that the construction of
> irrigation works would of itself create irrigated agriculture. . . . Atten-
> tion has been centered almost entirely on engineering features. Settlers
> were accepted without capital or experience. They were not organized
> to work together, but were left to struggle without sufficient aid or
> direction to complete what the government has only begun. . . . The
> inexperienced farmer should have been given more and better infor-
> mation and advice; the poor farmer, with honest courage but little or
> no capital, should have been provided with proper credit facilities; the
> farm with a rough, rolling surface should have been leveled; the greedy
> owner of private lands, ready to trade upon the natural desire of vig-
> orous hard-working men for independent homes, should have been
> squelched; the good farmer with small business capacity should have
> been given the assistance of cooperative organizations for buying and
> selling; all should have been supplied with intimate advice from com-
> petent official advisors on all farm matters; and by every effort, the way
> should have been made easier for the water user, who not only profits
> by the labor and skill of the engineer but who also absorbs engineering
> mistakes and pays engineering bills.

Mead concluded his report with a long list of recommendations,
many of them focused on relieving settlers from the crushing burden of the huge debt they owed the government for project construction costs. He proposed, for example, basing repayment
obligations on the productivity of the land, so that high-altitude
farms on poor soils would not have the same debts as fertile, highly
productive farms. He also counseled the bureau on how to prevent
the same mistakes from happening again: "New projects . . .
should be authorized only after full information has been secured
concerning the water supply, engineering features, soil, climate,
transportation, markets, land prices" and other factors. Estimates
of the need for drainage works should be made before the start of
project construction, he said, and their costs should be figured into

the overall costs and repayment obligations of the projects. Settlers should be chosen according to their ability, rather than being accepted almost at random. And those who had been settled on infertile lands should be given the privilege of exchanging them for different farms at the same or another project.

The same year his committee's report came out, Mead was appointed to the newly renamed post of commissioner of reclamation, replacing an interim commissioner who had supplanted Arthur Powell Davis a few months before. During Mead's tenure, which lasted from 1924 to 1936, the bureau logged its greatest achievement—the construction of Hoover Dam on the Colorado River at the height of the Great Depression. The dam transformed the bureau from a middling government engineering outfit into a powerful shaper of the West—and a leading engine in the New Deal public works job machine. But, somehow, in spite of the warnings contained in Mead's 1923 report, the agency's failings persisted through the era of its greatest success.

Take, for example, the Kendrick project in Wyoming, authorized a year before the completion of Hoover Dam. Floyd Dominy described what happened in characteristically blunt fashion: "The Kendrick project was a bastard project from the very beginning. In the first place, the water supply was dependent on flood flows above what was already appropriated in the North Platte River. So you could only divert water in an occasional year. Fortunately, we ran into so many soil problems that we never did try to develop it to the full extent of the original proposal."

Dominy blamed the unexpected soil problems on a series of "inadequate" soil surveys dating back to 1922. Not until 1947, a year after the first delivery of water to the Kendrick project lands, did the bureau get around to doing a complete study of the project's soils, and what the survey found was extremely disturbing. There was, in fact, irrigable land within the project's boundaries, the soil experts reported, but it was mostly on the higher ground, where the topography was rolling rather than flat. Irrigating that land would mean a lot of costly grading and leveling. Down below, on the plains along the North Platte River and Casper Creek, the soil was dense and full of sodium-based salts—exactly the type of soil that would be transformed into an impermeable mass by sustained irrigation. Irrigating there would mean spending a fortune on gypsum and a system of perforated underground pipelines for drainage. And then there was the selenium. About 75 percent of the Kendrick project's grayish soils were derived from marine shales of the Cretaceous period, and those shales were rich in selenium. Already, the new flood of irrigation water had started leaching selenium out of the soil and into the groundwater. Early Kendrick settlers tried to drill wells on their farms, but the water was undrinkable: besides being one-fourth as salty as sea water, it had more than fifty times as much selenium as was considered safe for human consumption.

Between the sodium problem and the selenium problem, the bureau ultimately abandoned thirteen thousand acres of the Kendrick project, leaving only twenty-two thousand acres of farms scattered around on the area's better soils. The project never came close to being economically viable. A 1988 report on Kendrick's selenium problems said that more than half of the project's 252 farmers were moonlighting at other jobs. The project's high altitude limited the growing season to three months, and farmers' average income, before expenses, was less than one hundred dollars per acre. Most of what they grew was alfalfa and pasture for their livestock. And selenium remained a problem. Studies by the Fish and Wildlife Service turned up severe deformities among Canada geese and avocets that nested on shallow lakes of selenium-rich water within the project's boundaries.

Still, Kendrick wasn't the most misbegotten of the bureau's high-altitude projects. It wasn't even the biggest lemon in Wyoming. That distinction belongs to the Riverton project, perched on a windswept Rocky Mountain plateau in west-central Wyoming. Beginning in 1925, World War I veterans were lured to the Riverton project by the promise of 160 free acres of high desert land and enough federally subsidized water to turn it into a farm. Some of those pioneers made a go of it, but a sizable proportion didn't, being defeated by soil that drained at a snail's pace and collected so much salt in the meantime that nothing worthwhile would grow. By the 1940s, the Bureau of Reclamation estimated that eleven thousand of the project's forty-eight thousand acres were severely affected by salinity or waterlogging, and sixty-five hundred acres had been taken completely out of production. But the worst was yet to come.

For the returning veterans of World War II, the bureau and Congress decided to expand the misbegotten project by fifty thousand acres, creating a whole new Third Division on some higher, colder, scrubby ground north of the original project. This time it took less than a year for the land to go sour. In some places, the water would just sit there, turning newly plowed fields into swamps. In others, it pushed salts to the surface, especially the dreaded sodium salts, which turned the ground into a hard, packed powder that repelled water. Convinced the fault must have lain with the settlers and not the engineers, the bureau set aside a hundred and sixty acres of the Third Division as a demonstration farm, which Dominy, then a midlevel bureau functionary, was assigned to oversee. In 1951, the farm's workers tried to grow oats, legumes, grass, potatoes, and winter rye, but they failed; in 1952, they gave up. "We proved you couldn't farm the Third Division," Dominy said. "That sodium content in the soil just tied it up, and the root zone was just like a rock. Water wouldn't penetrate. It was almost concrete."

Had it been a warmer climate, where higher yields and longer growing seasons give farmers a greater per-acre income, the Riverton project might have been salvaged. Its farmers might have spent thousands of dollars installing drain lines under their fields, plowing gypsum into the ground to dislodge the sodium from the clay particles, and rinsing the last traces of salt from the soil. But

on the chilly Wyoming steppes where spring and fall frosts are separated by three months at most, such an expensive bailout was out
of the question. Ultimately, the bureau simply wrote off the rest of
the Third Division, abandoning it in midconstruction and selling
the land. The unlucky settlers were offered land on other bureau
projects in Washington and Arizona.

Dominy blamed the bureau's soil scientists for the Riverton de-
bacle, saying that they should have predicted the sodium problems
that crippled the Third Division. But he blamed Congress as well,
saying that the bureau's slipshod soil survey was caused in part by
pressure from Congress to build new reclamation projects for the
returning soldiers, and to build them in a hurry. He said as much
to the House Interior Committee in 1963, when, as commissioner,
he was being grilled yet again on the failings of the Riverton project. "I won't say to you that we did not make mistakes on the Riverton project," Dominy testified. "I will say that they were not
made on the basis of lack of technical experience, judgment and
knowledge on the part of the Bureau of Reclamation. I say that mistakes made in constructing the Riverton project on an untimely
basis could have resulted from pressures not solely originating in
the Department of the Interior and the Bureau of Reclamation."

The wind whipped up white dust devils as Ron Anglin, manager
of the Stillwater National Wildlife Refuge near Fallon, Nevada,
stood in the middle of what the official refuge map persisted in
calling Tule Lake. Once the spot where Anglin stood had been surrounded by eighty thousand acres of healthy marshes, fed by an
annual torrent of snowmelt from the eastern Sierra—a Serengeti
in the middle of the arid Great Basin. But in 1907 federal reclamation engineers began diverting most of the water to farmers on
the Newlands irrigation project, which it was building a few miles
upstream on the Carson River.

By the early 1990s, almost all the marshes were gone. Instead,
windswept salt flats like Tule Lake dominated the landscape. Only

two hundred and fifty acres of wetlands remained, but they were fed mainly by a trickle of fetid Newlands drainage—a toxic soup that contained selenium and a long list of other naturally occurring trace elements. "We're dealing with high concentrations of boron, high concentrations of molybdenum, arsenic, lithium," Anglin said, wearily reciting the list from memory. "Depending on the water sample there's cadmium, beryllium—it just goes on and on. It's like the periodic table."

In short, it was exactly the type of water that Anglin didn't want in his marshes. But he had no choice. Drainage from the Newlands project was running unavoidably into Stillwater for the simple reason that Stillwater was slightly lower than most of the farms. Even so, the contaminated water might not have been a problem if Stillwater could get a big surge of fresh Sierra snowmelt every year to dilute the drainage and purge the marshes of pollutants. Unfortunately, however, there was no fresh water. Every drop was already called for by upstream users. "We're working with drain water, because that's all the water we get," Anglin said.

It is Stillwater's misfortune to lie at the very end of a river system that is one of the most heavily developed and most litigated in North America. The system starts in the high Sierra, in the headwaters of the Truckee River, which spills out of the northwest corner of Lake Tahoe, and the Carson River, which rises just beyond a ridge to the south of the lake. As they leave the mountains, the two rivers flow through steep canyons into the desert, where they support most of northern Nevada's human population. Reno and Sparks siphon water from the Truckee as it passes by; Carson City and Minden do the same on the Carson. Farmers along both rivers water crops. Downstream of Reno, Pyramid Lake, the sole habitat of an endangered fish called the *cui-ui,* and the Paiute reservation get a portion of the Truckee's remaining flow. The rest is diverted through a long tunnel into the Carson, where it is stored for use by the Newlands farmers—a group that includes the agrarian Fallon Paiute tribe. Only after all these other users have satisfied their thirst does the remainder of the two rivers' combined flows reach the Stillwater marshes. Historically, that has meant that in most years Stillwater gets nothing at all, other than drainage siphoned off the Newlands project via a network of ditches. "We get salt loads on our marshes now that are twice as salty as sea water," said Norman Saake, a biologist at the Nevada Department of Wildlife office in Fallon. "Some of them, the meters and stuff I have won't even measure it. They go right off the scale."

Stillwater isn't the only victim of Newlands, nor is it even the first. Before the Truckee was diverted, Pyramid Lake would regularly overflow into an adjacent valley, where it formed a sixty-thousand-acre marsh called Winnemucca Lake. Great clouds of white pelicans, nesting on an island in the middle of Pyramid Lake, would fly over the ridge every day to feed at Winnemucca. But not any more. When the Bureau of Reclamation diverted the Truckee to irrigate the Newlands farms, it deprived Pyramid Lake of its excess water. As a result, Winnemucca dried up completely in 1938. Today the Pyramid Lake pelicans must fly a round-trip of 120 miles to feed in the only remaining wetlands in the region—the Stillwater marshes. Meanwhile, the declining level of Pyramid Lake has threatened the survival of the *cui-ui* fish.

Yet for all the havoc it was wreaking on the environment, the Newlands project in the late 1980s was not much better from the farmers' point of view. Handicapped by high altitude, poor soils, and a short growing season, the Newlands farmers were able to grow only low-value crops such as alfalfa. They fought a constant battle against poor drainage in their fields, a battle that began almost as soon as the project was opened to settlement. And they fought a constant battle in the courts to keep their water—mainly because the federal government didn't bother securing water rights to the Truckee and Carson rivers until after it built the project.

But in the struggles of the Newlands farmers lay the seeds of a solution that Anglin and other wildlife advocates devised for Stillwater—buy water. Or, more specifically, buy marginal farmland

and let it revert to desert—or let the farmers spend the money to improve their irrigation efficiency and divert the unused water to Stillwater. Anglin calculated that it would take an annual commitment of fifty-four thousand acre-feet of fresh water to fix what was wrong with Stillwater—enough water to put eighty-four square miles of land under twelve inches of water. But that quantity is only a fraction of the 320,000 acre-feet that the Newlands farmers use every year. "It's a simple problem," Anglin said. "There's not enough water for everybody to continue to do what they did in the past. And it's a simple solution. It takes money. You have to come up with the money, tighten up the efficiency of the irrigation district, buy up marginal lands and put the water in the marshes."

A survey done in 1988 showed that there was no shortage of willing sellers among the Newlands farmers, but their water broker, the Truckee-Carson Irrigation District, was dead set against the idea. "The question is, what do you do? Do you completely ruin the agricultural economy for the sake of the wetlands?" asked Lyman McConnell, the district's manager. Still, the idea won converts. In 1990, Congress authorized the Fish and Wildlife Service to buy enough water to restore twenty-five thousand acres of the Stillwater marshes and other dried-up wetlands in the nearby Carson Lake bed. Restoring both of those areas would require an estimated 125,000 acre-feet of water per year, but if enough willing sellers could be found, most of the needed water could be bought from Truckee-Carson farmers. The law authorized the government to buy up to half the district's water and transfer the water rights to the Fish and Wildlife Service, and set aside $10.5 million per year for three years to make the buys. Meanwhile, The Nature Conservancy and other environmental groups raised funds for additional purchases. It is only a start; Anglin estimates that the eventual need may be fifty million dollars for Stillwater alone, and at least that much more for the Carson Lake wetlands. But he is heartened by the progress.

The situation at Stillwater has its echoes all over the western

United States—high-altitude, low-value irrigation projects that simultaneously steal water from wetlands and pollute the little water that is left. At Utah's Stewart Lake Waterfowl Management Area, the Bureau of Reclamation first deprived the marsh of its water source—flood flows of the Green River—by building Flaming Gorge Dam upstream in southwest Wyoming. Then it began to dump drainage from nearby Central Utah Project farms into the dwindling marsh. At other western wildlife areas—including the Ouray National Wildlife Refuge in northeastern Utah, the Benton Lake National Wildlife Refuge in north-central Montana, and the Salton Sea in southern California's Imperial Valley—biologists have found deformed bird embryos, or toxic levels of drainage-related pollution, or both. In some of these places, selenium is believed to be the primary culprit. In some, elements such as boron, molybdenum, and arsenic may play a role. But in every case, the pollutants were unlocked from the arid soil not by nature but by human works of irrigation. And now, only humans can provide solutions.

Drainage problems respect no boundaries. The challenges posed by the threefold explosion in worldwide irrigated acreage since World War II affect nations around the world; almost everywhere where desert agriculture is practiced it is prey to the ravages of poor drainage, waterlogging, and salinity. And now, an upsurge in drainage problems is seen by many experts as being not just possible but probable.

Asia, the most populous of the continents, has some of the world's largest irrigated areas, nourished by the great rivers of the East—the Indus, the Ganges, the Brahmaputra, the Yangtze Kiang, and the Hwang Ho—and some of the world's worst drainage problems. In China, where 250 million acres are irrigated, the United Nations estimates that 20 percent is salinized to some extent, including nineteen million acres in northern China alone. Pakistan's

Indus basin contains the single largest expanse of irrigated land in the world, fifty-five thousand square miles, roughly the size of Wisconsin or Florida; in 1988, the National Commission on Agriculture estimated that one-fifth was damaged by waterlogging or salinity. To the east, where the Ganges drains a large portion of northern India, irrigation has helped bring an end to a once-perennial state of famine, yet in one Indian state alone, Uttar Pradesh, more than four thousand square miles of irrigated farms have become salty wastelands.

The Soviet Union dried up the Aral Sea to irrigate its central Asian republics, but now two of its former republics, Uzbekistan and Tadzhikistan, are battling salinization, and the Aral Sea itself has become one of the world's leading ecological disaster zones, prone to violent climatic shifts and dust storms of salt. Even land-locked, mountainous Afghanistan has not been exempted: its Helmand Valley Project was so plagued by waterlogging in the 1960s that the government called in the Bureau of Reclamation to install a system of drains. In the Middle East, the worst problems are in Syria, Iran, Iraq, and most notably Egypt, where the Aswan High Dam, completed in 1971, triggered a binge of over-irrigation that just four years later had left 90 percent of Egypt's irrigated land waterlogged. Farmers were not the only ones affected: some of Egypt's most familiar monuments, such as the Sphinx, are slowly being destroyed by salt water seeping into their stone from the newly elevated water table. The nation is gradually making amends by putting in drainage systems at a cost of eighty dollars an acre, paid by the landowners in installments over twenty years. And even in places where irrigated desert agriculture is scarcely practiced, such as in Europe and South America, waterlogging and salinity can be a problem in isolated areas. The Incas in Peru had seven thousand square miles under irrigation when the conquistadores arrived; today, the country waters only about one-fifth of that amount, but there are severe drainage problems on 375,000 acres, about 15 percent of the total. Spain has similar problems; the area affected is small, but to farmers on those lands, it is serious.

Everywhere, the fundamental causes are essentially the same as those identified by Elwood Mead in 1923. From the days when the British first subjugated the tributaries of the Indus, engineers have understood how to catch and store runoff in great reservoirs, and how to deliver it efficiently through canals to faraway lands. The physics of concrete and earth could be captured in simple yet elegant equations by the engineers and their new science; but the details of what to do with their magnificent edifices, of how to turn raw water and raw land into life under the desert sun, were not so easily captured. The elements were predictable; humans were not. And so the true challenge of modern desert agriculture, as Powell had suggested, lay not in building dams and canals, but in building agrarian civilizations where before there had been only the desert.

CHAPTER FOUR

Of Drainage and Baby Ducks

G ARY ZAHM REMEMBERS the feeling he had, the vague impression that something was terribly wrong at California's Kesterson National Wildlife Refuge, which he had just been put in charge of. Mostly, it was the smell that bothered him. "I've worked in alkaline marshes all my career," Zahm said. "And this was an alkaline marsh, but it didn't smell right. It was like nothing I'd ever smelled before." There were other signs of trouble, too. The tips of the cattails were turning brown; huge, flocculent mats of algae were floating in the water; and, eeriest of all, the place was utterly quiet. The noises one would normally expect to hear in a marsh— the croaking of frogs, the splashing of muskrats—were noticeably absent from Kesterson. "It just wasn't a healthy place," Zahm said. "There were things missing that should have been there."

Zahm made his initial observations in October 1980. During the next four summers, his concerns prompted one of the leading avian biologists in the Fish and Wildlife Service, Harry Ohlendorf, to stubbornly uncover a wildlife disaster at this obscure little refuge in a low-lying portion of the San Joaquin Valley about a hundred miles southeast of San Francisco. Ultimately, thousands of migratory birds were found dead, poisoned by selenium, a toxic trace element. Its source: subsurface drainage from irrigated farms, dumped at the refuge in willful ignorance by the service's sister agency, the Bureau of Reclamation.

Some have referred to the Kesterson episode as the Three Mile Island of irrigated desert agriculture. That may be an overstatement, but in the eyes of irrigators and wildlife advocates alike, Kesterson and similar incidents in subsequent years have brought desert farmers in the United States to a crossroads. The nation's taxpayers have already spent more than eleven billion dollars in the past century to build the world's most extensive irrigation systems. Now they may have to shell out tens of billions of dollars more to rescue those same systems from disastrous side effects such as the ones at Kesterson.

It takes Harry Ohlendorf more than an hour to tell the story from start to finish. Chief of the Pacific field station of the Fish and Wildlife Service's Patuxent Wildlife Research Center when the Kesterson episode began, Ohlendorf tells his stories the same way he approaches his science, first gathering the appropriate facts with painstaking care, then assembling them in logical order and setting them forth utterly without emotion, letting the facts speak for themselves and leaving his audience to draw its own conclusions. When you work for the federal government, especially in an agency as highly politicized and beset by external pressures as the Fish and Wildlife Service, it pays to keep your head down. Scientists and bureaucrats who speak out tend to be slapped down; sent to Alaska, as the agency's biologists grimly joke; or stuck in a windowless office with no work to do until their civil service pensions kick in.

Quiet and unassuming, Ohlendorf speaks in the slightly nervous, high-pitched voice of a high school algebra teacher who knows his material but isn't quite sure of his delivery and hopes none of his students will notice. This demeanor had served Ohlendorf well in his Fish and Wildlife Service career, which so far had spanned more than a decade, enabling him to move up the organizational chart in a flash. He spent only two years in the field—as an ecological biologist specializing in fish-eating birds—before being named, in 1973, to be assistant director of the Patuxent center at its headquarters in Maryland. He kept that job for seven years, handling administrative details like office space and budgets but also keeping a hand in research, both by supervising the work of other scientists and by writing up some previous research he had done on the thinning effects on eggshells of DDT and other organochlorine chemicals.

Eventually, however, he was confronted with a choice:

> I was at a point where either I needed to go on to a higher-level administrative job or think about going back to research. I could have moved into the Washington office, where I'd probably be in some staff position for three or four years until some other administrative job opened up. But I was on a detail into the Washington office for six weeks while I was stationed at the Maryland research center, and I decided that wasn't what I wanted to do.

So when the Patuxent center decided in 1979 to set up a Pacific field station in California, Ohlendorf jumped at the chance to take charge of it. At that time, the station existed only on paper, its location undetermined. Ohlendorf inspected both Davis and Santa Barbara and chose the former; both cities had University of California campuses that could play host, but Davis had the added advantage of being close to state and federal government offices in Sacramento, fifteen miles east.

With three full-time scientists and a half-dozen assistants wedged into a single portable building and two Quonset huts on a dusty back lot on the western edge of the UC Davis campus, the field station seemed an unlikely flash point for a controversy that would shake the foundations of California's powerful agribusiness establishment. But from the very beginning, Ohlendorf's little laboratory had a full plate of contentious work. It was responsible for monitoring the effects of offshore oil exploration and production on the state's coastal kelp forests and endangered sea otters. It kept tabs on the ecological condition of the San Francisco Bay system, the largest estuary on the West Coast and one of the most belea-guered, facing threats as varied as urban runoff, shipping, dredg-ing, oil refining, and massive diversions of fresh water from inland tributaries. The station was also responsible for research on what were called agricultural return flows—wastewater from irrigated farm fields. What was unusual about this research, however, was that the Fish and Wildlife Service was looking at this wastewater not as a problem but as a resource, something that could amelio-rate what the agency viewed as the single greatest challenge facing it in the western United States: procuring water for wildlife.

Most of the San Joaquin Valley fits the climatologist's definition of a desert—less than ten inches of rain falls there in an average year. This is a startlingly small amount of precipitation, especially in a place where the sun can evaporate a half inch of standing water on a typical summer's day. When all ten inches fall during the winter, as is the case in most of California, they produce a sudden green carpet of grass in February and March, but by May the grass is brown and tinder-dry, and a discarded cigarette can scorch forty acres in a matter of minutes.

Yet when the first Anglo settlers came to the San Joaquin Valley in the middle of the nineteenth century, they found a landscape decidedly undesertlike, even in the dead of summer. What they found was an immense marsh, blanketing millions of acres of the flat valley floor and fed every spring by a tremendous torrent of snowmelt from the Sierra Nevada on the valley's eastern edge. Each winter, the fourteen-thousand-foot mountains wrung sixty inches or more of Pacific moisture from passing weather fronts in the form of snow, as much as twenty-five to thirty feet of it in a normal year. As the weather warmed, that thick mantle of snow melted. Rivulets of cold, clear water in the mountains joined to form small streams, then larger ones, then still larger ones, until finally they created violent rivers that crashed over boulders and sliced through steep, narrow canyons. The rivers coursed through the foothills and spilled out onto the flat plains of the San Joaquin Valley, then slowed considerably, spreading out into a sheet of barely moving water twenty to thirty miles wide and as much as several feet deep, migrating ever so slowly northward toward the San Francisco Bay. Flocks of waterfowl numbering in the millions fed and nested in the resulting marshes every year. Hundreds of thousands of tule elk and pronghorn antelope grazed on the marsh fringes; grizzlies came down from the mountains to feast.

That picture was altered dramatically in 1942 when the Bureau of Reclamation, in the first phase of the Central Valley Project, put a giant concrete plug in the biggest of the Sierra rivers, the San Joaquin, and stopped the annual flood in its tracks. Today, instead of making its way naturally from the mountains to the bay, most of the San Joaquin's snowmelt is trapped and stored behind Friant Dam for irrigation. Some of it is later shipped north in the Madera Canal; some goes south to Bakersfield in the Friant-Kern Canal. Virtually none of it gets downstream, and in most years the San Joaquin River is mainly a dry bed until it is joined downstream by its relatively undammed tributary, the Merced. In a matter of a couple of years after its gates were closed, Friant Dam wiped out the southernmost winter run of chinook salmon in North America. In a few more years, it dried up virtually every marsh in the valley.

Once Friant was built and the water was gone from the valley marshes—after all of the damage was done, in other words—the Fish and Wildlife Service began trying to set up a network of valley wildlife refuges. Despite the explosion in agriculture that followed the dam's completion, finding land was not as big a problem as finding water; by that time, most of the water in the valley had been locked up by the bureau or by farmers and irrigation districts. The Pixley National Wildlife Refuge was established in 1959 on eighty-eight hundred acres of land in the valley's southern tip, but to this day it has no guaranteed supply of water. It gets no water at all except in wet years, when a nearby irrigation district lets some leftover water run down to the refuge. Pixley is not alone; of the nine major wildlife areas in the San Joaquin Valley, four have no guaranteed water and, except in flood years, none gets all of what it needs to keep its marshes wet.

This history helps to explain why the Fish and Wildlife Service decided in the early 1970s to strike a deal with the devil, in the form of the Bureau of Reclamation, which had a problem of its own. In 1960, in an attempt to rescue a handful of big western San Joaquin Valley landowners whose irrigation wells were running dry, the bureau had gotten authorization from Congress to build a new system of dams and canals called the San Luis Unit of the Central Valley Project. The San Luis service area had a warm, sunny climate and friable soil, perfect for farming. But it also had one of the world's worst drainage problems, thanks to a buried layer of clay called the Corcoran formation. For thirty years, growers had been pumping millions of gallons of water from their wells—many of which tapped an aquifer beneath the Corcoran clay—and dumping the water over their land to grow cotton. Some of the water evaporated, and some was used by the thirsty crops, but as much as half of it simply trickled back down to the Corcoran clay and parked there, creating a vast new brackish aquifer that was slowly creeping toward the surface. In some places, the growers had already driven the shallow water table up to within ten feet of the surface. Now the bureau was preparing to put more than a million acre-feet per year of new water on the same soggy ground.

The plan to take care of this problem involved pouring still more concrete. The bureau was going to build a 188-mile drainage canal from the San Luis service area to the Sacramento–San Joaquin delta, at the upper end of the San Francisco Bay system. Farmers would be able to extract the shallow groundwater from their fields with buried drainage lines and dump the salty wastewater into the canal, which would be called the San Luis Drain. But halfway between the start and finish, the drain plan got hung up. People in

Contra Costa County, the delta county that would be on the receiving end of the drain, got wind of the plans and were understandably incensed at the idea of a bunch of farmers dumping millions of gallons of dirty water into their backyard. Their congressman, John Baldwin, had a rider inserted in the 1965 public works appropriations act that effectively barred the bureau from finishing the drain to the delta.

At that point, a more prudent group of bureaucrats might have held off on delivering water to the San Luis service area to avoid making the drainage problems there any worse. Instead, the bureau decided in 1967 to deliver the water and then wait, hoping the opposition in Contra Costa County would somehow go away. In the meantime it built the first part of the drain, an 82-mile section from Mendota to Los Banos, where a set of holding ponds would even out the seasonal variations in flows in the drain. The Fish and Wildlife Service decided that these ponds could pass muster as a wildlife refuge, at least in the dewatered San Joaquin Valley. So, under a law allowing the service to operate wildlife refuges at some of the bureau's installations, the service and the bureau signed an agreement on July 23, 1970, to make the holding ponds into the Kesterson National Wildlife Refuge. The Fish and Wildlife Service acquired the free use of fifty-nine hundred acres of land—though no water, except the bureau's drainage—and the bureau was able to write off more than one million dollars of the cost of the San Luis Unit to "wildlife enhancement," which made the government's subsidy to the unit's growers appear somewhat less extravagant than it actually was.

For the first few years, the deal seemed fabulously good. The service worked out an agreement with a neighboring irrigation district to buy a few thousand acre-feet a year of water to put on Kesterson, and tens of thousands of ducks and other waterfowl began to move in. Multitudes of fish populated Kesterson's pools, including channel catfish, carp, sunfish, and silversides. Some of them inhabited the newly completed San Luis Drain as well; since the drainage water wasn't flowing yet, the bureau was forced to keep the channel full of fresh water to keep its concrete lining from collapsing under the pressure of the surrounding groundwater. Birds were drawn to all that fresh water as though the ground were covered in suet. It looked, Gary Zahm said, as though Kesterson was going to be some of the best bird habitat in the valley.

But over the next few years, the bureau watched the Contra Costa County forces grow stronger. Baldwin died and his seat in Congress was taken by Jerome Waldie, an antagonist of the bureau. In 1974, Waldie gave up the seat to run unsuccessfully for governor and was replaced by George Miller, who was not only antagonistic to the bureau but savvy enough to eventually take over the House committee overseeing the bureau's operations and have his staff chief installed as the commissioner of reclamation. Each of the three congressmen supported his constituents' opposition to the drain, and each had the political skill to make that opposition stick. Meanwhile, farmers in the Westlands Water District, the largest of the irrigation districts in the San Luis service area, kept dumping reservoirs full of water on their land, doubling and redoubling their pace after the bureau started delivering their San Luis water. As a result, the regional water table shot up like a missile. By the late 1970s, the farmers had two choices—go out of business or put drain lines under their fields and dump the excess groundwater into the half-finished San Luis Drain, where it would become the bureau's problem. Not surprisingly, they chose the second option.

Thus, in 1978, the bureau had an 82-mile drain, 1280 acres of shallow ponds where the drain ended at Kesterson, and a rising flood of salty drain water coming from Westlands. The bureau then did the only thing it could do, under the circumstances—it dumped all of the rotten water into Kesterson and left it there to evaporate in the sun. Slowly, the salt content of the ponds began to rise. Gary Zahm was assigned to the refuge two years later; by then, the flow into Kesterson consisted almost entirely of drain water. Its effects were painfully obvious. "When I first got here, I noticed there weren't any fish in the reservoir, other than mosquito fish," he said. "There weren't carp; there weren't anything, and there should have been. I just assumed—and I'm not sure it was a good assumption—that it was just from the salts. But a striped bass should have been able to live in there; it's a goddamn ocean fish, you know?"

Zahm mentioned his concerns to his supervisors but otherwise kept them to himself until 1982, when he talked to Michael Saiki, a Fish and Wildlife Service fisheries biologist. Saiki was in the area to study the effects on the lower San Joaquin River of drain water dumped by irrigators elsewhere in the valley. His interest in Kesterson and the San Luis Drain had already been piqued by a meeting he had attended with people from the Bureau of Reclamation and the state Water Resources Control Board. At that time, the bureau was getting ready for another futile attempt at finishing the drain to the delta and was doing some tests on the drain water to find out what chemicals were in it. One of the chemicals was selenium; it looked as if there was quite a lot. Saiki didn't know much about selenium at the time, but it was one of those details that he filed away in his mind for future reference.

In the spring, Saiki went down to Kesterson to tour the refuge and talk to Zahm in more detail. He took along Harry Ohlendorf because of his expertise in birds. Later, Saiki netted some tiny mosquito fish from the Kesterson ponds and sent them off to be tested, along with fish from the nearby Volta Wildlife Area, a small refuge that was usually flooded with spillovers of clean water from the bureau's Delta-Mendota Canal. The results, when they came back from the lab, showed that selenium levels in the Kesterson and San Luis Drain fish were astronomical—seventy to a hundred times higher than in the Volta fish. Saiki called Ohlendorf with the results, and Ohlendorf went to the library. After a couple of hours

of research, Ohlendorf decided that selenium might be a big deal
indeed.

His calm, measured speech belying the enormity of the discov-
ery, Ohlendorf said:

> The levels of selenium in the mosquito fish at Kesterson were roughly
> ten times the levels that had caused reproductive effects in chickens in
> studies that were done in the mid-thirties in South Dakota. In the
> South Dakota studies, what happened was that at many of the farms,
> the farmers were unable to feed grain they grew on their farms to their
> chickens. The eggs wouldn't hatch. They'd have either dead embryos
> or severely deformed embryos. They found that the selenium levels
> were very high in the grain, and this was causing monstrosities, as they
> called them then, in the eggs and the embryos. There was a whole se-
> ries of papers published on this in the *Journal of Poultry Science* back
> in the mid-1930s.

Saiki and Ohlendorf proposed a major study on the effects of
drain water at Kesterson. This happened in a roundabout way.
Ohlendorf was supposed to be working on a similar study at the
Kern National Wildlife Refuge about a hundred miles to the south;
there was no drainage going into that refuge at the time, but some
neighboring farmers had more drainage than they knew what to
do with, so the service, still desperate for new marshlands, was
planning to shunt some of that drainage onto the Kern refuge and
watch what happened. But this was during the first years of the
Reagan administration in Washington, and at the Office of Management and Budget David Stockman was slashing the budgets of
domestic government agencies almost at random. One casualty
was the Kern study. But not every agency felt the knife to the same
extent. Over at the Bureau of Reclamation, plans to finish the San
Luis Drain were barreling ahead, and as part of that effort the bureau was doing its own studies of the chemical makeup of drainage. Its laboratories and biologists were overwhelmed, so the
bureau approached the Fish and Wildlife Service to see if it would
be interested in contracting to do some research on drain water

toxicity. Though the mosquito fish results were still incomplete, Saiki and Ohlendorf quickly put together a set of brief study proposals and sent them to the bureau. Soon, the two scientists went to Sacramento to discuss their proposals with the bureau's regional water quality branch chief, Don Swain, and the engineer he had just hired to bird-dog the San Luis Drain permit application, Ted Roefs.

The reception they got was their first clue that they had picked up a hot potato. In a memo written later "to the record," Saiki said, "Even if money was available, [the bureau] has decided not to fund our research at Kesterson Reservoir because the data would not immediately help [the bureau] to obtain the [drain water discharge] permit for the bay-delta. . . . Thus, our study plans to (a) evaluate fish production and bioaccumulation of contaminants, and (b) examine the potential for biomagnification of contaminants through the food chains of migratory waterfowl have both been shelved." In other words, the bureau was saying, we want data that will help us get a permit to finish the drain; if you won't give us that data, we'll give our contracts to someone who will.

Once the mosquito fish results came in, the bureau's attitude didn't change; by Swain's own subsequent admission, he did not "appreciate the significance" of the service's data. In an interview several years later, Swain offered the excuse that he had been "strung out" at the time from overwork. But Dave Lenhart, a contaminants specialist in the service's regional office in Portland, later told a federal investigator that the bureau challenged the service's results and questioned its expertise to test for selenium. (A few months later, the service engaged a geologist, Ivan Barnes, and a chemist, Theresa Presser, from the Geological Survey to check on its results. The two quickly determined that the service's results were correct and the bureau's wrong. "We found out the Bureau of Reclamation didn't know how to analyze for selenium, and the Fish and Wildlife Service did," Barnes said later.)

By early 1983, the service's brass had become concerned enough about the selenium levels in the mosquito fish to pay for Ohlendorf's and Saiki's proposed studies out of the agency's own budget. For most of April, May, and July of that year, Ohlendorf collected eggs and hatchlings of ducks, shorebirds, coots, and grebes from Kesterson, while Saiki gathered food-chain items—water, sediments, plankton, algae, midge larvae, dragonfly nymphs, and plants. The birds, Ohlendorf soon discovered, had selenium levels ten to twenty times higher than the same species at the cleaner Volta Wildlife Area. They also had the same kinds of "monstrous" deformities that had been found in the South Dakota poultry studies of the 1930s.

Early one morning that spring, Ohlendorf went to Kesterson with Felix Smith, an ecological specialist from the service's Sacramento office. They paddled a canoe to the far edge of the marsh and started examining nests. From one, Smith picked up a coot's egg; the bird inside was trying to hatch. Smith held the egg in his hand so that Ohlendorf could take a picture. It was an emotional moment for both men. "Here were these birds hatching out," Ohlendorf said. "They had no eyes, no legs, no beaks. . . . Some of them couldn't hatch because the deformities were so severe. Then there were also these embryos that just died before hatching. Mostly it seemed to be related to selenium."

Smith had been aware of Ohlendorf's and Saiki's results from the start. An atypical bureaucrat who went to work for the Fish and Wildlife Service in 1956, Smith received almost as many official scoldings as awards during his career, and the awards were so numerous that they threatened to pull down his office walls. In 1978, he received a special conservation merit award from American Motors; two months later he was kicked out of his job as field supervisor in the service's Sacramento office. He attributed his demotion to his unwillingness to sacrifice natural resources for economic gain. "I did not know when to compromise," Smith said, his agitated manner of speech sounding more of Brooklyn than his native

San Francisco. "I held my ground. So they said, 'Well, we'll get somebody in there who's different.'"

After he went to Kesterson and watched the deformed coot struggle to hatch in his hands, Smith became the service's noisiest voice on Kesterson. In doing so, he was forced to give up any hope of career advancement and fight a constant rearguard action even to hang onto the job he had. In 1986, he beat the service brass when they tried to abolish his job and ship him up to the regional office in Portland, more than six hundred miles from Kesterson; on his return to Sacramento, he was placed in a windowless office and given no assignments. After a few years of that torture, he took early retirement and joined the board of directors of the Bay Institute of San Francisco, an environmental group. But all of that came later; when the Kesterson episode began, Smith simply set about trying to figure out what selenium was doing in the drain water in the first place.

"I went to the University of California at Davis, I went to the state Division of Mines and Geology, and I started picking brains. 'Where in the hell is it? Where is this stuff on that side of the valley? Where are the selenium-based soils? Where is the selenium in the substrate?'" Smith said. "Pesticides came as a quick answer, but then the group kind of chatted and said, 'No, there's just too goddamn much of it.'" Ultimately, Smith found himself rummaging through an old Geological Survey soils report. "I was just about to give up, and there was a little paragraph in there where it talks about the same material being found in South Dakota." That, of course, was the same region where "monstrosities" attributable to selenium had been found in baby chicks in the 1930s, according to the papers Ohlendorf had found in the library. Gradually, the pieces were falling into place: like the soils in South Dakota, soils in the San Luis service area were naturally seleniferous; irrigation water was picking up the selenium as it trickled down through the soil; and subsurface drain lines were taking it out of the soil and carrying it up to Kesterson, where it was moving up through the food chain, bioconcentrating, and triggering highly unnatural rates of deformities in the birds at the top of the food chain.

Up in Portland, Dave Lenhart wrote a brief summary of the service's findings, labeled it "Concern Alert," and sent a copy to the bureau. Swain immediately went apoplectic. The "Concern Alert," he wrote in an internal bureau memo, contained "several inflammatory statements which concern me and which . . . would lead one to an inaccurate conclusion as to the facts surrounding the abnormality of the young-of-the-year at Kesterson Reservoir." In the future, he grumbled, such documents needed to be worded more carefully "to prevent misunderstanding and unnecessary opposition to a water resource project which is essential to the continued farming of lands throughout the west side of the San Joaquin Valley"—in other words, the extension of the San Luis Drain to the delta.

The bureau started scrambling to keep a lid on things. Ohlendorf later told an investigator from the Department of the Interior that the bureau "seemingly did not believe that selenium was responsible for the waterfowl problem" and "questioned [the Fish and Wildlife Service's] ability to analyze for selenium throughout the remainder of 1983." Individuals came under attack as well. Ohlendorf, who by then had almost twenty years of experience and impeccable credentials as a scientist, was almost immune from criticism, but Saiki had been with the service only five years. "The bureau people wanted to tackle Mike Saiki because they thought he was the weakest one," Felix Smith said. Saiki later spoke only reluctantly of the experience: "Well, it made me very cautious. I believed my chemists, let's put it that way."

Meanwhile, the service's Sacramento office put together a meeting with a group of state water quality officials to disclose the Kesterson findings. Simultaneously, it prepared a press release and sent it up the chain of command to Washington for approval. "The press release never came out," Ohlendorf said. "It went as far up as the assistant secretary's office in Washington. I guess it came back with questions, and somebody didn't want to take the trouble to answer the questions, but the press release never came out." Smith, who had a copy of the release on his desk, said he was told by Joe Blum, the service's deputy regional director, to "tear it up." Instead, he gave it to a writer from the Audubon Society's magazine, winning himself another reprimand. The meeting with the state went ahead, however, and within a week Ohlendorf got a call from a reporter at the *Fresno Bee,* which had been tipped by a state official who was angry over the appearance of a coverup. Ohlendorf got permission from the service's public affairs office "to state whatever we know to be fact, and avoid anything that is speculation," and on September 21, 1983, the *Bee*'s story brought the deformed birds at Kesterson to public attention.

Over the next year and a half, conferences on the Kesterson issue became something of a cottage industry in California. For leaking the press release, Smith was officially scolded by the service's regional director and told to "use extreme discretion" in what information he provided outside the service. A short time later, he was issued his transfer to Portland, after relating to several reporters and congressional staff members a conversation he had overheard in which Don Swain had told another bureau official and some irrigation district people that "there had to be a way to muzzle [the service] in regard to statements [the service] was making about the Kesterson issue." Swain denied that he had said any such thing.

Harry Ohlendorf spent the summer of 1984 looking for more bird eggs from Kesterson. He narrowed his focus to just two species, coots and stilts, both of which had been nesting plentifully at Kesterson the summer before. It wasn't long before he noticed that something else had changed since the previous summer:

> We searched all the same places where we found coot nests in 1983, but we found ninety-two nests in 1983 and in 1984 we found nothing. What we were seeing instead were dead birds, adult birds—dead

coots lying around in the ponds. So we picked up some of those birds that were pretty fresh and shipped them off to our wildlife health lab in Madison, Wisconsin, and they were necropsied there. The pathologists looked at all kinds of things, and there wasn't anything they could find in the way of a disease problem. What they were finding was that the birds were emaciated; they were below normal body weight. They saved some tissues for us so that we could get chemical analyses of them. This led to a diagnosis of selenium poisoning.

First the fish had died, then the birds had hatched deformed chicks, and now adult birds were dying in the ponds. In less than four years, Kesterson had gone from a thriving wildlife refuge to a death trap, and it wasn't long before somebody in the Fish and Wildlife Service opined that the bureau was probably violating the Migratory Bird Treaty Act, which makes it a crime to "pursue, hunt, take, capture or kill any migratory bird, nest or eggs" except as authorized by law.

The act had been applied only to illegal hunting until the early 1970s, when prosecutors began using it in cases of pollution—birds killed by illegal pesticide use, drowned in open pits of oil, or poisoned in lagoons of chemical-laced wastewater. Could the bureau, by dumping selenium-laden drainage at Kesterson, be violating the Migratory Bird Treaty Act? Could its top officials be prosecuted? David Lindgren, the regional solicitor of the Department of the Interior, thought not; but just in case, the bureau and the service decided to attack the problem—not by cleaning up the refuge, but by getting rid of the birds. Crews were stationed at the refuge with shotguns and propane-fueled noisemakers; scarecrows were planted in the ponds. It was a bizarre sight: the workers scooted around the refuge on three- and four-wheeled ATVs and amphibious vehicles, wearing Fish and Wildlife Service uniforms with goggles and particle masks to protect them from seleniferous dust. Every now and then they stopped and fired off a shell or two, or set off a cannonlike blast from the propane guns, and a flock of sickly coots would start flapping their wings furiously, trying to get airborne. The "hazing" program, as it was called, was expensive—$180,000 per year for more than three years—and it was also an utter waste of time. Other than the coots, which were too sick from selenium poisoning to start nesting anyway, few birds were scared away or discouraged from nesting. "We found pretty much the same numbers of birds nesting in 1985 as we'd seen in 1984 prior to the hazing program," Ohlendorf said.

Eventually, a neighboring landowner, Jim Claus, who had a combination duck hunting club and cattle ranch just to the south of the refuge, decided that he'd had enough. In April 1984, Claus petitioned the regional water quality board to order the flow of drain water stopped, not just to Kesterson but to the entire Grasslands area, which encompassed fifty-one thousand acres of duck clubs like Claus's. When the regional board turned him down, Claus appealed to the state Water Resources Control Board, which was still waiting for the bureau to send in the rest of its data on extending the drain to the delta. Claus was a big man with a booming voice and a passion for western clothing; he was also quixotic, litigious, and angry enough to spend every cent of his considerable fortune fighting the government over Kesterson. He quickly made it clear that he was going to force the issue, regardless of what it cost him, so in the fall of 1984 the state board held two evidentiary hearings on his petition. On February 5, 1985, the board issued an order giving the bureau three years to stop the flow of drainage into Kesterson and to purge the refuge of selenium. The bureau momentarily considered ignoring the board's order—how could a state agency get away with telling the federal government what to do?—but on March 7, Secretary of the Interior Donald Hodel said the feds would comply.

By this time, a flood of reporters and camera crews was descending on Kesterson. On March 10, 60 Minutes aired a segment about Kesterson in which the bureau's regional director, David Houston, tossed off an estimate that cleaning up Kesterson could cost the government as much as thirteen billion dollars, a figure that seemed intended to shock but had no basis in reality. The following Friday, George Miller, the Contra Costa congressman who had just become chairman of the House Subcommittee on Water and Power Resources—the bureau's overseer—called a field hearing on Kesterson at the Los Banos fairgrounds. Three of the San Joaquin Valley's congressmen were there—Tony Coelho, Richard Lehman, and Chip Pashayan. So was Bernie Sisk, Coelho's predecessor and mentor, who had first introduced the bill authorizing the San Luis Unit as a freshman congressman in 1956 and shepherded it to passage four years later. Sisk testified first, saying that although no one in the late 1950s knew that there would be a selenium problem in the valley in the mid-1980s, everyone knew that the San Luis Unit would require a drain, and wasn't it just too bad that none had been built. Then a panel from the Department of the Interior sat down to testify: Houston, Joe Blum, Marc Sylvester from the Geological Survey, and Carol Hallett, a former minority leader in the state assembly who had just taken a job as special assistant to Hodel, who himself had been in office only a few weeks. Miller begged the audience to be quiet, and not for the first time; the barnlike building echoed with the voices of several hundred farmers, politicians, environmentalists, and journalists.

Then Hallett began, and the room became quiet eleven sentences into her testimony:

> Policy-level officials in Washington have concluded that because the hazing program at Kesterson has not proven to be as effective as was hoped, and because of the prohibitions of the Migratory Bird Treaty Act, immediate action must be taken. That act appears to create the possibility of violation of criminal laws without regard to intent or knowledge. Therefore, the secretary has instructed the Bureau of Reclamation and the Fish and Wildlife Service to begin the process of shutting down the Kesterson Reservoir. This process will result in plugging the San Luis Drain and stopping the delivery of irrigation water to the lands which drain into the reservoir.

When Hallett finished speaking, Houston testified that, yes, everyone had heard right: the flow of irrigation water would be stopped to the farms that drained into Kesterson—about forty-two thousand acres in all—probably immediately. The three valley congressmen, whose constituents and campaign chests had grown wealthy as a result of the irrigation of the San Luis Unit, were more than surprised at Hallett's announcement; they had been blind-sided, and they were livid. "What is so damn secret about what you just announced that you couldn't discuss it with the congress-man who represents the area, or you couldn't discuss it with anybody involved?" Coelho fumed. Hallett replied that she had been kept in the dark herself—at five o'clock that morning, she and Houston had received phone calls from Washington informing them that a decision had been made to shut down the drain and turn off the water. "We were not involved in those discussions," Hallett said. "We had no idea yesterday afternoon that this was going to be a decision reached last night in Washington, D.C., and early this morning. Had we known that, we might indeed have contacted some of you."

As the details emerged, both in the hearing and during suc-ceeding weeks, it became clear that plans for the Los Banos hearing had provoked something of a panic in Washington, leading to weeks of debate within the Department of the Interior over whether the Migratory Bird Treaty Act would apply to Kesterson. Hallett, Houston, Blum, David Lindgren, and a few others from Interior's regional offices met the afternoon before the hearing to go over their testimony and to rehearse some answers to the ques-tions they thought would come up. As he had done at least twice before, Blum brought up the Migratory Bird Treaty Act. At first, the discussion fell into a familiar pattern: Blum, from the Fish and Wildlife Service, argued that the act applied to Kesterson and that the government was in violation; Lindgren, the regional solicitor and an ally of the bureau's Houston, said the act did not apply, as long as the government used "due care" to avoid harm to birds—a requirement that was satisfied, he said, by the hazing effort. Even-tually, the question got turned around a little bit: if the government were challenged, how would a court rule? At that point, Hallett decided to bump the question up to Washington, and the group made a conference call to Interior's chief solicitor, Frank Richardson. After a few minutes of discussion, Richardson said he'd get back to them.

By then it was late afternoon in Washington. Richardson quickly called a meeting of his own: Robert Broadbent, assistant secretary for water and science, who was Houston's boss; some people from the Bureau of Reclamation; a representative of Hodel's; and a whole gaggle of lawyers from Richardson's shop. The discussion started with Hallett's question—what would a court rule?—but quickly moved to a more pressing corollary: could a government employee, Dave Houston specifically, be sent to jail for what was happening at Kesterson? "Then somebody said that we should look at whether we should begin to get some kind of representation for the people involved," Broadbent later testified to Miller's subcommittee. "I thought, well, that's the craziest way I ever saw to run government, candidly. A guy acting in good faith, doing a job on what he considered good faith, and then telling him he might have to go get an attorney to defend himself."

Early in the evening, the group sent a delegation downstairs in the Interior building to Hodel's office. After hearing the problem, Hodel ordered the solicitor's staff to work overnight on the question of whether a court might rule against the government. The next morning, Hodel got his answer: it might, depending on the court. All right then, Hodel said, just to be safe, let's shut down Kesterson. Broadbent called Houston in California to let him know of the decision, and Houston, Broadbent's protégé and fellow Nevadan, was beside himself. Legions of driven, conservative young men like Houston, who turned thirty-three in 1985, had joined the federal bureaucracy during the Reagan revolution. Most of them were ironically hostile, like Reagan himself, to the institutions that they were taking control of, but Houston made an effort to keep up appearances, at least: he put a vanity license plate reading "DAM BLDR" on his car. But more important, Houston was acutely pained at the idea of backing down from a good fight. As the bureau's regional director, he had just spent the last few months denying that the bureau was violating the Migratory Bird Treaty Act, and now he was supposed to say it might be in violation after all? He refused. "I told Broadbent that was testimony that I couldn't give," Houston said in a later interview. "I said, 'I won't be employed here tomorrow if you guys make me do this.'" So instead, Carol Hallett, who hadn't planned to attend the hearing, was recruited to deliver the news.

The bombshell couldn't have come at a worse time for the several dozen farmers on the forty-two thousand acres of irrigated land that drained into Kesterson. Spring comes early in the San Joaquin Valley, and by mid-March most of the year's crops were already in the ground, or about to be. The idea of having their water cut off after they had already borrowed to plant their seeds set off a fierce panic in these farmers. Suddenly, the prosperous growers of the valley, usually portrayed as the villains in California's perennial water wars, looked like victims.

"My name is Jim Gramis, ex-farmer, as of about an hour and a half ago," one grower testified after Hallett was finished. "We are in the middle of production, or in preparation for production, for planting. We have tomatoes that have emerged. We will never bring those crops to harvest. We are not only bankrupt; we are devastated."

Darrell Silveira, who farmed a few miles away from Gramis, spoke next:

> We have some very difficult decisions facing us. Number one, what are we going to tell our employees when we get back to the ranch? We have about twenty-five people working for us full time. Several of those have been with us for ten years or more. Unless we have an awful lot of understanding from our financial institution—which I cannot understand how we can have after this order—those people are all going to have to go home today or tomorrow. We will not be able to meet

payroll this coming Friday. Am I supposed to call the bank when I get back and tell the bank, "We spent over one million dollars of borrowed money to start this crop, and we have no means of repaying that money, but we want you to keep giving us money so we can continue to operate until we can find out exactly what the bureau is going to do?"

Not surprisingly, Westlands Water District immediately threatened to take Hodel to court over the irrigation shutoff. That action could have put the Kesterson closure and everything else on hold for months if not years; as a practical matter, it forced Interior to back down. During the next two weeks, officials of Westlands, the bureau, the service, Interior's solicitor's office, and the Justice Department worked out a compromise. Water would continue to flow to the forty-two thousand acres; Westlands would cut back the flow of drainage in five stages, starting in September; and by June 30, 1986, the subsurface drain lines emptying into the San Luis Drain would be plugged, stopping all flows of drainage to Kesterson. Then it would be up to Westlands to find another way of dealing with its rising water table before the affected farms were driven out of production. To buy time, the district began recycling its drainage by mixing it with fresh irrigation water and putting it back on the crops.

The deal to close Kesterson was a bittersweet one: Westlands guaranteed that it would stop the drainage flow on a definite date, rather than letting a judge decide. But in return, Interior had to accept that Kesterson would remain polluted by drain water through two more nesting seasons—1985 and 1986. The Fish and Wildlife Service found dead and deformed birds at Kesterson in each of those years, and in 1987 as well. Finally, in the summer of 1988, after the state board vetoed a bureau plan to sequester Kesterson's selenium by keeping its ponds flooded with fresh water, the bureau spent $3.4 million trucking 1.1 million cubic yards of earth into Kesterson and buried the selenium.

By the end of 1988, Kesterson was no longer a marsh but an

arid grassland. In the spring of 1989, wildflowers sprouted by the thousands. Field mice and their predators moved into the old ponds; killdeer, eagles, and hawks hunted there. The poisoning of birds by selenium, which had been a fact of life at Kesterson every spring for most of the past decade, was now a thing of the past. Or was it? Harry Ohlendorf testified before the state board again on June 28, 1989. New data from Kesterson, he said, showed that killdeer and meadowlarks—dryland birds—had levels of selenium in their bodies that were ten times the normal level and were probably high enough to cause deaths or deformities. Continued monitoring of the site over the next few years produced similar findings. Roots of dryland plants were reaching down into the buried reservoir of selenium and bringing it up to the surface. Mushrooms growing in the detritus of selenium-rich cattails had astronomical concentrations of the element. Meanwhile, the threat that pools of selenium-rich groundwater would form in winter despite the raised elevation was still very real; the only reason it hadn't already happened, it appeared, was that California had been in the grip of a severe drought since the marsh was filled. The selenium problem at Kesterson hadn't been solved at all, it turned out. It was only waiting for a chance to strike again.

There was no reason to believe that Kesterson was unique. In most places where there is irrigation, there is subsurface drainage. In most places where there is subsurface drainage, there is a river or lake or marsh into which that drainage ultimately seeps or is dumped. And in most of those bodies of water, there are fish and birds and amphibians. The only question at the time of the Kesterson shutdown was whether any of those other drainage projects would contain selenium, and there was plenty of reason to believe that at least some of them would.

Eight days after the Los Banos hearing, most of the scientists who were working on the Kesterson issue met in Berkeley for a symposium held by the University of California, the Fish and

Wildlife Service, and the Bay Institute of San Francisco. Ivan Barnes, the Geological Survey geologist who had straightened out the bureau on its selenium lab work, talked about the sources of selenium in the San Joaquin Valley—marine shales in the Diablo Range above the valley floor—and described how the chemical moved from the mountains to the farms below. Afterward, Barnes was asked why there wasn't a similar selenium problem in the Sacramento Valley; too much rain, he answered. "If you want some generalizations, I'll give them to you," he said. "If there is a continental climate with marine pyrite and less than twenty inches of precipitation a year, there will be a selenium problem. If there is a Mediterranean climate with marine pyrite and less than twelve inches of precipitation a year, there will be a selenium problem." What Barnes was saying, in essence, was that more Kestersons were inevitable. Marine soils are common in the western United States; those soils and the rocks they come from often contain pyrites; and virtually the entire region gets less than twenty inches of rain. It was a cinch that there was much more selenium out there, and many places where it could cause trouble.

Somebody higher up in the Department of the Interior must have been whispering the same thing in Donald Hodel's ear. Carol Hallett's statement to the subcommittee in Los Banos said that Hodel had already told the Fish and Wildlife Service, the bureau, and the solicitor's office to look for other irrigation projects that might be violating the Migratory Bird Treaty Act. Hodel repeated those instructions at least twice in the next two months; the last time, he pointedly asked Broadbent and Craig Potter, the acting assistant secretary for fish, wildlife, and parks, to brief him on what they had done to identify projects "at which there is any reason to believe the drainage water transported by facilities for which the department is responsible has caused some harm to wildlife."

On the face of it, the assistant secretaries had done quite a bit. Broadbent had already put together a task force of Geological Survey and bureau officials to come up with a study plan; at the same time, both the bureau and the Fish and Wildlife Service had or-dered their regional staffs to check around for drainage-related problems in their geographical areas. But in the end, the burst of activity came to nothing. The bureau produced a report stating that, aside from Kesterson, the only place where drainage seemed to be harming wildlife was the Imperial Valley, where there was a problem with residues of the pesticide DDT. The Fish and Wildlife Service rehashed a 1983 study on contaminants at wildlife refuges but didn't do any new testing. As for the task force, it sent its report to Broadbent's office, where the document just sat. Broadbent later admitted sheepishly to George Miller's subcommittee that shelving the report was his idea.

"I guess the determination was largely made by myself," he said. "I was worried about a lot of the legal problems. . . ." Perhaps the biggest legal problem would have been the lawsuits the govern-ment would have faced if more Kestersons were found; Broadbent had fired off a memorandum to the department's solicitor on that question. But there were other problems, too, Broadbent contin-ued: "To begin a monitoring study of the scope that we were going to do on agricultural drainage . . . you ought to start it at the be-ginning of a drainage season, which is spring, and . . . carry it through the drainage year. We did not think that we could possibly be ready to start it this year and do a [good] job. First of all, we did not know where we would get the funds. We did not think we had time to get to Congress to get the money."

Broadbent had reason to be chagrined during his testimony; he was being called on the carpet. Five days before the hearing, the *Sacramento Bee* had beaten the government to the punch when it published the results of tests it did showing high levels of sele-nium—in many cases higher than were found at Kesterson—at wildlife areas throughout the western United States. The list of poi-soned refuges read like a roster of the West's most popular water-fowl watering holes: the Salton Sea in California; the Imperial refuge on the lower Colorado River in Arizona; Bosque del Apache in New Mexico; Desert Lake and Stewart Lake wildlife areas in Utah; Bowdoin Lake, Benton Lake, and Freezeout Lake in Montana; Deer Flat in Idaho; and the Belle Fourche and Cheyenne rivers in South Dakota. Within a few weeks the Department of the Interior approved money for a series of reconnaissance studies of the areas named by the newspaper; by the following spring nearly all of the high selenium levels had been officially confirmed and a few new ones added: the Kendrick reclamation project in Wyoming; the Stillwater National Wildlife Refuge in Nevada; the Tulare Lake basin in California. Over the following months and years, more names were added to the list: the Malheur refuge in Oregon; Sweitzer Lake in Colorado; the Arkansas River in eastern Colorado and western Kansas. Biologists began looking at some of the sites and found deformed birds in the Tulare basin and at Kendrick and Stillwater. In early 1992, when tens of thousands of eared grebes died at the Salton Sea, tests on some of the carcasses showed elevated levels of selenium. More substances joined selenium on the list of chemicals being found in drainage water at levels high enough to be toxic to wildlife—arsenic, molybdenum, lithium, boron, chromium, mercury: a virtual periodic table of contaminants. They had been there all along, apparently, but until Kesterson, nobody had bothered to look.

CHAPTER FIVE

A Prophet Without Honor

IT WAS THE FATE OF Cassandra, daughter of Priam, the king of Troy, to be endowed with the gift of prophecy but saddled with the curse of never being believed. Apollo bestowed the gift on Cassandra because he was smitten with her, but then spit in her mouth to establish the curse when she resisted his advances. Something similar happened to Harvey O. Banks, a retired California engineer. In the late 1950s, when Congress was debating whether to build the San Luis Unit, the California irrigation development that led to the Kesterson disaster, Banks correctly predicted that unless it was designed with proper drainage—which it wasn't—the new project would leave the western San Joaquin Valley wallowing in the saline effluent of desert irrigation.

The evidence of Banks's prophecy lies in the transcript of a March 1958 hearing of the U.S. Senate Interior Subcommittee on Irrigation and Reclamation. Banks, then director of California's Department of Water Resources, was testifying on a bill that would authorize construction of the San Luis Unit, which would bring canal water for the first time to more than one million acres of the valley's arid west side. He issued a warning: the influx of water would turn farms into salt-choked swamps unless the government also built a drainage canal to carry off the excess groundwater. And

he offered a remedy: amend the San Luis bill to forbid water deliveries until a drain was built.

"Well, that's what should have been done," Banks said in an
interview thirty-two years after he lost that debate, twenty-three
years after the first water deliveries were made from the San Luis
Unit, and six years after long-delayed plans to build a valley drain
were put on the shelf, possibly forever. Long since retired from
state service but still working as an engineering consultant, the oc-
togenarian Banks could afford to be philosophical. True, his advice
had been disregarded, and as a result a seven-billion-dollar-per-
year farm economy was in slow decline, but that really wasn't his
problem anymore. He had tried and failed, and the state water resources directors who succeeded him had tossed the drain project
around like a hot potato but never built it. Absent the sense of ur-
gency that Banks had tried to instill, his successors didn't think it
necessary to get the drainage system built during their tenures.
They thought delay would make the job easier, but what happened
was the exact opposite. Drain opponents raised objections on environmental grounds, fearing contamination of drinking-water
supplies and wildlife areas in the downstream Sacramento–San
Joaquin delta. As years became decades, the opposition became or-
thodoxy, and the options grew ever fewer. In desperation, the Bureau of Reclamation, which began delivering water to the San Luis
Unit in 1967 even though there was still no way to drain it,
dumped its drainage from 1978 to 1986 into the Kesterson National Wildlife Refuge and created a holocaust for migratory birds.
Now the salt-laden effluent that went to Kesterson for eight years
is mostly just accumulating in the ground, a quietly ticking time
bomb for farmers on a million acres of San Joaquin Valley cropland. And, like Cassandra, Harvey Banks is looking more and more
like an unheeded prophet.

Since at least the early 1930s, it has been no secret that the San
Joaquin Valley's irrigated farms could not stay in production in-

definitely without some way to drain away excess water—the portion beyond what is lost to evaporation and plant uptake—along with the crop-killing salts dissolved in it. The valley's friable soils, level ground, plentiful sunshine, minimal rain, and imported irrigation water make it one of the world's most lucrative farming regions, but they also carry the seeds of eventual ruin. Bringing vast amounts of water into a desert environment of fierce sun and poorly drained soils is never a simple task, but in parts of the San Joaquin Valley it is virtually a suicidal one.

With its thick layers of gravel, sand, and silt eroded from the surrounding Sierra Nevada, Coast Ranges, and Tehachapis, the valley is a giant bathtub that quickly filled when Anglo settlers built canals a hundred years ago and began irrigating. Its meager natural drains—principally the San Joaquin River and the Tulare basin's terminal lake beds—were soon overwhelmed. The first problems appeared on the valley's east side in the late nineteenth century, when newly minted fields at places like Traver and Kerman became waterlogged or saline after neophyte farmers applied too much water at once. By 1915 in Fresno County alone, some eighty thousand acres of irrigated land had groundwater less than fifteen feet below the surface. Farms failed by the dozen—then, completely by accident, the affected farmers were rescued by their own neighbors. Seeking ever-larger quantities of water to irrigate ever-larger acreages, the surviving east side farmers began sinking wells into the region's deep aquifer, which was directly connected to the water table, with no intervening clay layers to block the downward movement of water. The increased pumping relieved the waterlogging, and the sodden fields, in many cases, were rejuvenated.

On the west side, agricultural development proceeded at a slower pace, which was fortunate, because a similarly easy fix was not possible there. While the east side's water table was directly connected to the deep aquifer tapped by the wells, the west side's deep aquifer was segregated from the water table by a dense geological layer called the Corcoran clay. In the early twentieth century, when west side farmers began drilling wells to irrigate new ground, the excess water trickled back down to the Corcoran and slowly accumulated there. Later, after completion of the big west side water projects—the original Central Valley Project in the 1950s and the San Luis Unit and State Water Project in the 1960s—the water table began to rise much faster as the new canals came into service and more new land was farmed. The trickle of water to the Corcoran clay became a flood, and the west side's water table shot up rapidly. The groundwater also grew more and more saline, because along with its irrigation water the valley was importing 1.6 million tons per year of dissolved salt from the delta—the equivalent of forty-three fully loaded railroad cars arriving every day.

By 1990, when state and federal scientists completed a fifty million dollar study of the problem, saline groundwater lay less than five feet below the surface of a Yosemite-size chunk of western San Joaquin Valley farmland—roughly 850,000 acres, mainly in the valley's low-lying trough and the Tulare and Buena Vista lake beds. The massive study made a dire prediction: if drastic steps were not taken in the next few years, the San Joaquin Valley would be in danger of losing as much farmland as was brought under irrigation by the two biggest water projects built in twentieth-century California: the federal San Luis Unit and the State Water Project, which together irrigated one million acres in the valley's western and southwestern reaches.

It seems fitting that the valley's growing drainage problems may soon negate the gains achieved by those two projects. Building the drain—a 276-mile canal that was to start at the valley's southern tip and run north to an outlet in the Sacramento–San Joaquin delta—was considered an integral part of the two projects from the moment they were conceived; there is really no excuse for its not having been built. The need for a drain was first noted as early as the late nineteenth century, and in the early 1950s, when the state first began to draw up plans for the State Water Project, the drain was included in the planning. The same was true in 1955, when the Bureau of Reclamation issued a feasibility study on the San Luis Unit (which later was redesigned to share some of its dams and canals with the state project). Laws authorizing both projects spoke of the need to build a drain to serve the area they would irrigate, yet except for the ill-fated 85-mile section that ran to Kesterson from the Westlands Water District south of Mendota, the drain was never built.

It may be just as well: the environmental awakening that began in the late 1960s created a consensus that dumping saline, nutrient-rich drainage into the delta was not a very good idea. Still, the fact remains that although canal water continues to come into the valley, the resulting salty drainage is for the most part not going out. For the valley's farmlands, the upshot is slow death. In effect, the valley's entire west side has been transformed into a flowerpot without a hole: salts are building up in the soil; crops are declining; soon they may wither and die. For the San Joaquin Valley and its 2.6 million residents, this is no trifling matter. Agriculture is the region's dominant industry, producing revenues of seven billion dollars per year and providing, directly or indirectly, more than half of the valley's payrolls. The valley is also the largest single agricultural production center in California, the nation's leader in crop value produced. From garden vegetables to raisins and nuts to cotton and dairy products, the produce of the valley's nine-month growing season is spread over dinner tables across the United States every day of the year.

Why, then, with so much at stake and with the problems and their remedies so well known ahead of time, did the state and federal governments build the San Luis Unit and the parallel State Water Project without the necessary drain? Why was Harvey Banks ignored when he warned a committee of the U.S. Senate about the disaster that would follow if the drain were not built in time? What gods did he offend, that his prophecies were ignored?

One was Senator Clinton P. Anderson, a Democrat from New Mexico and chairman of the subcommittee in that 1958 hearing. Anderson, whose passion for dams and water projects and the jobs they created knew no limits, flatly rejected Banks's recommendation to make water deliveries contingent on the drain's completion. What sense did it make, Anderson asked Banks, for the government to spend millions of dollars building the San Luis Unit only to be barred from delivering water to its service area because the drain was unfinished? That such a prohibition would have provided a powerful incentive to complete the drain on schedule struck Anderson as irrelevant. He simply could not condone even a day's delay in the delivery of water once the project's supply side was finished; to do otherwise, he believed, would be an unconscionable waste of federal pork.

A second key player was William E. Warne, water resources director under Governor Edmund G. "Pat" Brown. Warne was responsible for the first of two decisions to delay the drain's construction in order to save money, after which the project was never successfully revived. Eternally an optimist, Warne had always been casual about public money. With Brown's blessing, he ran his department like a craps player, launching grandiose projects with inadequate financing, then betting that the extra money he needed would somehow become available in time to stave off default. In 1960, Warne and Brown won voter approval for a $1.75 billion bond issue to build the State Water Project even though both knew, Brown later admitted, that the actual cost would be closer to $4 billion; as a result, large portions of the project were never completed, and the consequent lack of delivery capacity continues to haunt the state to this day. The drain was just one more casualty of Warne's habitual overreaching: in 1961, while the state and federal governments were beginning to build their twin water projects, Warne postponed the start of construction on the drain to keep from tapping out the state project's meager capital budget.

Third among the key figures in the drain's demise was Warne's successor, William R. Gianelli, water resources director under Governor Ronald Reagan. Gianelli was as different from Warne as Reagan was different from Brown, the New Deal Democrat he defeated. Reagan had made the State Water Project's financial trouble a major theme of his 1966 campaign; it typified, he said, the irresponsibility of the big-spending Brown administration. Under such political circumstances, Gianelli was obligated to err on the side of fiscal conservatism, which was his instinct anyway. On assuming office in January 1967, Gianelli took one look at the project's shaky finances and decided that the state, to avoid default, would have to concentrate its resources on finishing the project's delivery system in order to get the flow of water to its customers. The drain, which Warne had finally begun to revive the previous year—in spite of lingering uncertainty over its financing—was again postponed.

The final villain was Floyd Dominy, commissioner of the Bureau of Reclamation for most of the 1960s, who decided to start water deliveries to the federal San Luis Unit in 1967 even though there were still no firm plans to finish the drain. Dominy's bluster was the stuff of legend and his political skills were similarly prodigious; even so, he sometimes overestimated them, as in his long and ultimately losing campaign to bracket the Grand Canyon with two major dams. When John McPhee of the *New Yorker* challenged him to float down the canyon on a raft with his archnemesis, David Brower of the Sierra Club, Dominy practically jumped across the table to accept, saying "Hell yes, hell yes." Asked twenty years later why he took the writer's dare, he said, "I thought I could persuade McPhee as to the error of the conservationist viewpoint." Dominy was convinced of his success: "I think my friends think he favored me and Dave's friends think he favored him." But the dams were never built. Dominy elected to start water deliveries in the San Luis Unit, he said in the same interview, because he believed that he would somehow overcome all of the financial and political roadblocks that were impeding the drain's construction.

These four men came from differing political parties and philosophies, and some of them scarcely knew one another, but in the end, all were responding to the same imperative—to finish building the projects and get the flow of new irrigation water started as quickly as possible, regardless of whether the drainage works were ready. To delay deliveries for even a day struck them as heresy. They were on a holy mission to make the desert bloom, and they would not be stayed by some Cassandra's pessimistic carping. On that point, they got little argument from the project's beneficiaries, the farmers and would-be farmers who were awaiting their first deliveries of water. The threat of poor drainage was not an immediate one; it would take a few years, or maybe decades, before the problem grew serious enough to greatly affect their yields. "Farmers generally are much more interested in the short-term aspects of these things, and the benefits begin to accrue when you supply the water for irrigation," Banks said. "So their short-term view is, 'Let's get the water. We'll worry about drainage later.'"

The story of this flowerpot without a hole begins, like most adventures in politics, at the local level. The San Luis Unit—designed mainly to rescue a few dozen pioneer west side farmers whose wells were running dry—had been conceived by the Bureau of Reclamation, promoted by a west side grower named Jack O'Neill, and shepherded through Congress by an amiable Fresno tire salesman and Dust Bowl refugee named Bernice Frederick Sisk. Sisk's livelihood in the early 1950s depended in large part on big purchases of big tires by big farmers. Those farmers told Sisk about their longing for a new canal to supplement their wells, and about their annoyance that the local congressman, a Republican lawyer named Oakley Hunter, wasn't doing much about getting a canal built. The local Democratic party hadn't been much help either: in the 1952 election, for lack of a willing candidate of their own, the Democrats had simply seconded the Republicans' nomination of Hunter.

So one day "Tex" Sisk—nicknamed for the state where he was born—bent the ear of a Democratic party activist named Wally Henderson, a fellow Kiwanis member and later mayor of Fresno. Why, Sisk asked Henderson, were the Democrats unable to muster a candidate for Hunter's seat, when the incumbent was so obviously failing to bring home the pork? It was a casual conversation, to hear Sisk tell it later, but it launched his twelve-term congressional career. Sisk would become one of the most powerful behind-the-scenes political figures on Capitol Hill in the late 1960s and early 1970s by virtue of his tenure on the House Rules Committee. That chat with Henderson led, a few days later, to a phone call, which led to a lunch with some other Democratic party leaders, which led to a proposition: how would Sisk like to run against Hunter himself?

"Well, for Pete's sake, I didn't know anything about politics . . ." Sisk said. "I was just trying to get this water project built." Nevertheless, Sisk ultimately took the bait. Rechristened "Bernie" and wholeheartedly endorsed by the party regulars, Sisk got his first big campaign contribution—a five-hundred-dollar check—from a hopeful Jack O'Neill, president of the newly formed Westlands Water District, an entity with only one purpose: to get the San Luis Unit authorized and built.

A Canadian by birth, O'Neill had arrived in the San Joaquin Valley in 1926 to try, for the second time, to make his fortune by farming the soils of California's deserts. A few years before, growing cotton and running a gin in the Imperial Valley, O'Neill had watched helplessly as the bottom fell out of the cotton market. Broke, he had gone to work for a produce company, but it too had collapsed. Then he had opened a brake shop in Los Angeles but had found that vaguely unsatisfying. He pined for open land. He found what he was looking for in the flat, scrubby wastelands around Huron, in southwestern Fresno County at the base of the brown Diablo Range. This time, his luck was better. Picking up a section or two of land at a time, O'Neill gradually built one of the western San Joaquin Valley's most prosperous farming empires—one that eventually extended to ginning, beef packing, and even a television station.

It was a profitable set of enterprises, but it was also vulnerable, and O'Neill could see that as well as anyone. The cornerstone of his businesses, the farm, was irrigated by a series of wells that were tapping the underlying aquifer at a rate fast enough to exhaust it in a few decades. By 1940, the farmers on the west side had drilled more than a thousand high-volume wells and were pumping them so furiously that the water table was dropping ten feet per year. It didn't take a genius to see the probable outcome of that: either the aquifer would run dry and the wells would start sucking air, or the water table would fall so deep that it would cost a fortune to pump. Either way, unless a new source of water were brought into the west side—in other words, unless a new canal were built—O'Neill might very well outlive his farm.

Determined not to let that happen, O'Neill banded together with some of his neighbors to promote one of the most ambitious irrigation projects ever devised by the Bureau of Reclamation, in which a canal bigger than most western rivers would be made to run uphill from the delta through a series of pumping plants to the west side's water-starved farms. From 1942, when the growers formed the Westside Landowners Association (predecessor of the Westlands Water District), until 1960, when President Eisenhower signed into law the San Luis authorization act, O'Neill was the project's loudest cheerleader, strongest arm-twister, and largest bankroller. Harvey Banks, who dealt with—and often tangled with—O'Neill for nearly a decade, says that O'Neill "had influence over a considerable number of votes" in Congress and the state legislature. "What incentives he provided was none of my business, so I didn't inquire," Banks said. "I presume he operated as most lobbyists do: he had money in his hip pocket."

O'Neill's five-hundred-dollar check to Bernie Sisk was the first major contribution in a campaign that spent a total of only twelve thousand dollars. For fourteen of the previous fifteen terms, Fresno's congressman had been a Republican, but in a 1954 mid-term election that put the Democrats back in control of the House, Sisk was swept into office by a comfortable margin of 9008 votes. Sisk and his campaign-manager-turned-administrative-assistant, Jackson Carle, a former newspaperman and Bureau of Reclamation official, spent much of the next six years greasing the San Luis project past the considerable forces lined up against it in both California and Washington.

Hunter had introduced a San Luis bill toward the end of his term in 1954, and it languished. But Sisk and Carle pleaded and cajoled to keep the project alive, fending off challenges from three directions. First was the Metropolitan Water District, southern California's powerful water wholesaler, which wanted the proposed site of the San Luis Unit's principal reservoir for itself. Second was a group of big growers in Kern County, near Bakersfield, who were lobbying for a project to be built by the state, not the federal government, so that they could remain exempt from the federal reclamation law's 160-acre limit on farm size, even though the limits were so loosely interpreted and casually enforced as to be meaningless. Ultimately, both of these groups were placated when it was decided that two parallel projects would be built—a federal project serving O'Neill's Westlands Water District, and a state project serving Kern County farmers and urban southern California—and that the two would share a dramatically enlarged version of the San Luis reservoir, which would be big enough to accommodate both sets of users. Finally, there was another group of opponents in the farmers of the Central California Irrigation District (CCID) who occupied low-lying ground northeast of the San Luis service area. They predicted (correctly, as it turned out) that bringing more water to the western valley would worsen their own preexisting drainage problems by pushing salty groundwater into the valley's trough, which the district occupied.

The CCID farmers took their concerns to the Department of

Water Resources, which Banks headed. In response, the department drew up the amendment that Banks offered to Anderson's subcommittee: no water deliveries could be made to the San Luis Unit until a drain—already part of the state's plans—was built. Judging from the hearing transcript, Anderson's reaction lay somewhere between incomprehension and outright revulsion. Was Banks suggesting, he asked, that the government spend hundreds of millions of dollars building a water project that "would just have to stand there" unless the state built a drain to serve it? "I realize that numbers grow large in both Texas and California, but not living in either of those two states, $290 million is a right smart chunk of money," Anderson said. "You would not want to put that into the ground and not be able to deliver any water from it, would you?" Quickly, Anderson came up with a substitute amendment, far more ambiguous in wording: construction of the San Luis Unit would not begin until either the state or federal government "made provision" for a drain. Nine years later, with the drain still unbuilt, millions of acre-feet of water began pouring into the western San Joaquin Valley through that loophole. The state indeed made provision for a drain, a court later ruled, simply by drawing up plans for one. But it never actually built one.

In the intervening decade, the state's Department of Water Resources performed a long and ultimately calamitous series of flip-flops under Banks's successors, Warne and Gianelli. First, when Warne replaced Banks in 1960, the state began making plans to build a master drain for both the state and federal projects. Then, in 1961, Warne shelved the drain plan so he could devote more attention—and money—to building the State Water Project's main water delivery canal, the California Aqueduct. By 1964, when Warne was ready to resume work on the drain, he unexpectedly found himself in a fight that eventually became the most persistent obstacle, other than money, to the drain's completion. Antioch and Pittsburg, two Contra Costa County cities whose drinking water intakes were downstream of the drain's proposed

Sacramento–San Joaquin delta outlet, had persuaded Congress to forbid the federal government to contribute money for any drain discharging upstream of their intakes, at least until a study could be done of the drain's effects on delta water quality. Since Warne had been counting on the federal Bureau of Reclamation to pay half the cost of the drain's first stage, the prohibition crippled his financing. Warne spent the last days of the Brown administration in a feverish attempt to get the bureau to sign a commitment to help pay for the drain anyway—this time, it would have been the bureau that was betting on the outcome, wagering that Congress would lift the discharge prohibition—and he almost succeeded. The signing was scheduled for December 27, and Warne was to leave office at midnight on December 31. Warne wrote to Sisk on January 5:

> Just before Christmas, I learned from Assistant Secretary Holum [Kenneth Holum, Interior's assistant secretary for power and the bureau's direct overseer] that, as he described it, "The White House has a hold on the drain contract." He said he had been in touch with the [Bureau of the] Budget and there was no objection there, "but I learned very late indeed that the White House has [a] hold on it and the President will not be available until New Year's Day." I explained that I would not be director after New Year's Day. Bill Gianelli was being designated as my successor about that time. He asked that I delay on the drain until after I got back to Sacramento, which was the night of December 29. We had a briefing session with all of our interested staff present for Mr. Gianelli on December 30, and he asked for a chance to review the plan for the drain. I told him that he would have this opportunity since the Interior Department had delayed the signing of the contract beyond my tour of duty.

Warne did not offer Sisk an explanation for the White House's reluctance to sign. At face value, this hesitation makes little sense, at least from a political point of view: why would Lyndon Johnson, a Democrat, want to accommodate Ronald Reagan, who was not only a Republican (as was Representative John Baldwin, leader of the delta-based opposition to the drain in Congress) but a key supporter of Johnson's 1964 election opponent, Arizona Senator Barry Goldwater? But accommodate he did. "Bernie," Warne ended, "I regret that I did not get this done, for I am completely convinced of the urgent need of the drain and we had a fine plan thoroughly worked out after much laborious effort. But there it is." The drain was mortally wounded; within a few days, it was altogether dead.

Reagan and Gianelli came into office on January 1 with a parsimonious approach to government in general and the State Water Project in particular. The drain became their first casualty. Gianelli quickly decided that finishing the California Aqueduct was more important than building the drain because Warne had already signed contracts to deliver water, and revenues from those water sales were required to pay off the state's $1.75 billion general obligation bond debt.

Gianelli then took things one step further: whereas Warne had been prepared to build the drain first and figure out later how to pay for it, Gianelli decided that he wouldn't build the drain at all unless the valley's irrigation districts agreed in advance to pay for it in full. They refused, and in March 1967 Gianelli wrote the bureau that the state would not build the drain after all. What Gianelli did still galls Warne, who claims that *he* would have gotten the drain built one way or another: "I thought we would pay for it the same way we were paying for the project . . . through revenue bonds." As Warne saw it, the drain was like any other public utility, such as cable television: people might say they didn't want it and wouldn't pay for it, but once it was made available, they would change their minds and subscribe in sufficient numbers to repay the construction costs. But Gianelli defends his action: "Bill [Warne], I think, always felt that he could go ahead and do something, and somehow or other it would be covered financially. If he got in over his ears, then the legislature would bail him out. I came from a different philosophy. I felt that it was terribly important to be fiscally responsible."

In any case, Gianelli's action left the bureau in a bind. There it was, only six months before it was scheduled to deliver water to the San Luis lands, and not only was there no drain but there were no firm plans for one. Dominy, the bureau's commissioner, had two choices: either hold off on delivering the water or come up with another drainage plan. He chose the latter. The alternate plan was this: build a drain to serve just the San Luis Unit lands, and build it backward, starting not at the delta but in the Westlands Water District, where most of the San Luis water would be delivered. Dominy assumed the dispute over the drain's outlet location would be settled by the time Westlands needed drainage, but in case it wasn't, he approved another contingency plan: dump the drainage temporarily into a series of shallow ponds near Los Banos and let it evaporate.

It was a plan borne of desperation—and of a fear of public embarrassment. The CCID farmers, who occupied the vulnerable land downslope from the Westlands district, were threatening a lawsuit to block water deliveries unless construction began on a drain. In handwritten notes on the subject, Tony Coelho, later House majority whip but then a rookie aide to Sisk, whom he succeeded in Congress, appraised the district's chances of success in gaining an injunction as "probably 50-50." There was also, Coelho wrote, a fear of bad press: "Political viewpoint—federal government . . . spent $1/2 billion on project that can't be completed; *Reader's Digest* would exploit," he scribbled.

The plan was put into effect. Eighty-five miles of drain were built, and in 1978, when some Westlands farmers began producing drainage, the saline wastewater was shipped to the Los Banos ponds, which by that time had been rechristened the Kesterson refuge. The ponds quickly turned into verdant death traps for migratory birds. Dominy later said that it had never occurred to him that the "interim" solution would be as far as the bureau would get with its drain construction; but it was, because as years passed, the Contra Costa County opposition grew more intense. "At the time we thought that we could make sense out of it and overcome the opposition," Dominy said. ". . . And I still think that our plan would have worked, and been successful. It just didn't get done." Said Harvey Banks, "They didn't really anticipate the virulence of Contra Costa County's opposition—and its effectiveness."

Dominy retired from the bureau in 1970, still believing that opposition to the drain could be overcome, sooner or later, by sheer force of reason. "It's just like Glen Canyon Dam," he said. "California fought it like a tiger, but now that it's built, you don't hear of any problems." In truth, environmentalists still mourn the loss of Glen Canyon, which was flooded by the dam that the bureau built across the Colorado River from 1957 to 1964. They complain that the dam has robbed the river of its reddish silt and turned it a sickly green as it passes through the Grand Canyon. They complain that the bureau has used the dam to generate hydroelectric power at the expense of downstream flows, causing sharp daily fluctuations that erode downstream beaches and destroy vegetation. In essence, they say the bureau is turning the Colorado on and off in response to variations in the demand for electricity. But Dominy, like most of his contemporaries in the twentieth-century hydraulic brotherhood, is blind to the environmental damage his projects have caused. All he sees when he looks at a dam or canal is a magnificent piece of engineering; he can't understand why others would quibble over the loss of a canyon a mile deep. In the Dominy view, the dam had far greater intrinsic worth than the canyon, and if polluting downstream drinking water sources was the price of building a drain for the San Joaquin Valley's vast agricultural areas, then so be it. Irrigating a desert was too noble a goal to be abandoned.

The bureau compounded its errors in the San Joaquin Valley by failing to anticipate how bad the Westlands drainage problem would become, and how soon. Two things happened, both unexpected, though they might have been predicted if the bureau had studied the local geology more thoroughly beforehand: first, the drainage from Westlands turned out to have high concentrations of selenium; second, the San Luis area produced far more drainage water than had been predicted. The primary reason, it turned out, was a 1962 expansion of the service area, scarcely noticed at the time, that added nearly a hundred thousand acres of highly saline, poorly drained lands to the area eligible for water. The added lands lay in the lowest part of the valley, between the major alluvial fans that make up most of the west side. When the bureau drew up its feasibility study for the San Luis Unit in 1955, it declared those lands to be "class 5"—unfit for irrigation. But in 1962, it did a soil survey that moved most of the lands from class 5 to class 4, making them eligible—barely—for San Luis service.

In a memo to Dominy, the bureau's chief engineer, Grant Bloodgood, described the newly labeled class 4 San Luis lands as having "excessive deficiencies. The soils are slowly permeable, have high salt concentrations, and require artificial subsurface drainage." But the bureau's analysis also showed that the class 4 lands *could* be farmed given enough attention, so at the insistence of Westlands, they were added to the project area. The action came back to haunt the bureau—adding the "interfan" areas increased the drainage flow from the San Luis area by a considerable amount. By the bureau's own reckoning, it nearly tripled the area that needed drainage. Years later, reports by the Geological Survey showed that the interfan areas were also producing drainage with the highest concentrations of selenium. Had the drain been built, drainage from the interfan areas might now be creating catastrophic environmental problems in the delta.

But, of course, the drain was not built—at least, not beyond Kesterson. And for the foreseeable future, it appears to be dead; almost everyone involved agrees on that. The San Joaquin Valley Drainage Program—that fifty million dollar study of the peril facing the west side's farmlands—ruled out the drain at the very beginning of its five years of work as politically impossible, according to the study's director, Edgar A. Imhoff, a Geological Survey scientist. That leaves the San Joaquin Valley facing the same bleak future that Harvey Banks foresaw in 1958, only with an extra million acres of new irrigated farmland thrown into the stakes. Imhoff's study predicted that, if no comprehensive steps were taken to deal with the valley's drainage problems, at least 84,000 acres of irrigated land would become salted out by the year 2000 and 460,000 acres by 2040, a half century after the study's completion.

To head off that possibility, the drainage program is advocating a mix of measures. Some would reduce the amount of water that percolates past the roots of crops and into the groundwater; others would take some of the salty groundwater and irrigate salt-tolerant crops. The cost is high—an estimated $48 million per year over the next fifty years—and who would pay is unclear. But the program's report also cites the economic costs of doing nothing other than letting all that land be slowly destroyed by water and salt—$450 million per year in crops, $127 million per year in personal income, $64 million in retail sales, and 9500 jobs.

So the aging proponents of the San Luis Unit, who thought they had made certain that someone would "make provision" for a drain when the project was built, can only wish they had done their jobs a little better. "We didn't tie it down tight enough. No question about it. And we can see that now," said Bernie Sisk. "We were trying to tie them down as tight as we could, but at the same time we had to get the project going. We had to get water. And in desperation we yielded here and there where we shouldn't have."

On the whole, of course, California may be better off without the drain. Had it been built, it would probably have become an environmental nightmare by now, discharging millions of gallons of nutrient-rich, saline, selenium-laden drainage into the largest and most biologically productive estuary on the west coast. And cleaning up such a mess after the fact would be difficult. Though a canal is not as permanent a feature of the landscape as, say, a dam, placing a plug in it would nevertheless be more challenging politically than simply putting up with the status quo, and purging the receiving waters of contamination would take years. Still, the drain's story clearly demonstrates the sort of short-run thinking that threatens to cripple the twentieth-century's experiment in irrigation, just as it crippled the Sumerians when they tried it. There's only one difference—the Sumerians didn't have a Cassandra. California had Harvey Banks.

CHAPTER SIX

Dueling Nature
in the Lake Bed

IT WAS A LATE MAY afternoon in 1989 and the temperature was toying with triple digits near the Interstate 5 crossroads of Lost Hills, California, a ganglion of burger joints and filling stations amid the endless cotton fields of the southern San Joaquin Valley. As the sun scorched the dull gray ground, Dr. Joseph Skorupa, a biologist with the Fish and Wildlife Service's Patuxent Wildlife Research Center, walked a low earthen levee between two vast pools of shallow water. He was hunting for bird's eggs, which he would take back to his lab and dissect. Skorupa wore light-colored clothing, dark sunglasses, and a broad-brimmed hat—desert gear appropriate to the region around Lost Hills, where the mind-numbing heat can evaporate a year's worth of rainfall in a couple of weeks. But if Skorupa was in a desert, then why was he surrounded by more than a solid square mile of water? Why, on the level plains beyond the pools, were there manicured squares of green and gold crops instead of the usual desert hues of brown, gray, and rust?

The answer, of course, lay in the one thing that makes the western United States the relative Eden it is today instead of the stark brown moonscape it used to be—its plumbing. In Lost Hills and elsewhere throughout California and the West, hundreds of reservoirs, thousands of miles of canals and pipelines, and countless pumps are all delicately choreographed to move water from where God in his wisdom put it to where man, in his wisdom, thinks God ought to have put it. Now biologist Joe Skorupa, by doing nothing more dramatic than picking up eggs and taking them apart to see what was inside, was threatening to bring down that whole technological house of cards.

If Kesterson was the opening act in the selenium tragedy, then act two was what happened over the next few years in the Tulare basin, the region encompassing Lost Hills. In both cases, the plot consisted of recklessly importing water into an alien arid environment to generate new wealth for a handful of well-connected landowners.

The water nourishing the farms around Lost Hills fell to earth not in the southern San Joaquin Valley but four hundred miles away, in the Feather River basin of the northern Sierra Nevada. It was shipped south via the concrete-lined aqueducts of the State Water Project, the ill-conceived sister of the Central Valley Project's San Luis Unit, site of the Kesterson disaster. Though mostly a product of Governor Brown's grandiose vision and southern California's unending thirst for water to fuel its runaway urban growth, the State Water Project was also a desert farmer's answered prayer. It was the deal of a lifetime: the Metropolitan Water District of Southern California, which sold water wholesale to cities from San Diego to San Bernardino and west to the Pacific Ocean, would pay most of the project's costs through its water sales revenues—or, as a last resort, by levying property taxes—but Met wouldn't actually need most of the project's water until twenty years or so after the project's scheduled early-1970s completion. So with Met's blessing, Brown's riverboat gambler of a water resources director, Bill Warne, decided to allow farmers in a then-barren swath of land north and west of Bakersfield to "borrow" Met's share for a couple of decades, paying only the cost of pumping.

Since Met was already paying for the more expensive part—amortization on the infrastructure of canals, pumping plants, and dams—the farmers were getting a cut-rate price. Met's board of directors took its time reviewing the deal, but it was eventually approved. It was rumored, though never proved, that some of the directors took advantage of the delay to invest in valley farmland, which might explain both the delay and the final outcome. Whatever the case, after the deal was done, that portion of the valley that hadn't already come under the plow began to bloom with cotton and vegetable fields, vineyards, and orchards. Whether Warne gave much thought to what would happen to those farms—especially the vineyards and orchards—when Met finally claimed its water is a mystery. Most likely, he was betting on the outcome again, as he had done with the San Joaquin Valley master drain, gambling that a future generation of Californians would be willing to underwrite one more water project bailout to save valley farmers from a disaster he had helped to create.

In any event, Warne certainly didn't count on Joe Skorupa, who came to Lost Hills in 1987 to study what was happening to the multitudes of birds that swarmed around the vast evaporation ponds. And in his first summer of study, Skorupa quickly proved that whatever their value to crops, the ponds were also death traps for migrating birds—luring them with the promise of calm water, plentiful food, and safe nesting sites, then maiming their progeny with a strong dose of natural substances—mainly selenium.

As the Bureau of Reclamation had already found out at Kesterson, unless you're hunting in accordance with the game laws, killing migratory birds is illegal, so the districts and farmers that operated the Tulare basin ponds soon faced possible prosecution under the Migratory Bird Treaty Act. Unlike the federal government at Kesterson, though, the growers didn't capitulate and close their ponds. In public forums around the state, their hired experts vilified Skorupa, attacking his competence, questioning his conclusions, and accusing him of conducting bad science. Even the brass in his own branch, the Fish and Wildlife Service's Patuxent center, started to gang up on him. An outside review board commented in 1991 that Patuxent's managers seemed overly concerned with "not making waves" and viewed biologists like Skorupa as "crusaders" or "zealots." The panel added a scold: "Individual researchers should never be placed in a position of feeling that their careers are compromised because they have elected to work on a hot issue." But that's exactly how Skorupa felt. Sometimes when he spoke about his research in a public forum—even when it was a regulatory hearing to which he had been summoned to testify—Skorupa was reprimanded. His research papers had to go through several layers of review before being published, and when they finally were published, they frequently had been sanitized. He could write up his technical data, but he couldn't provide the necessary context. He could report his raw results, but if his readers were going to figure out what all the numbers meant, they would have to do so on their own. In May 1989, Skorupa had just written a report of his most recent data on birds in the evaporation ponds only to have a Patuxent deputy director cross out his conclusion, which said quite reasonably that Skorupa's mass of scientific data indicated that stricter contaminant standards were needed to prevent further damage to birds nesting on the ponds.

"The final paragraph was basically the 'so what?' paragraph. It was the whole point to the document," Skorupa said. "I began with the Fish and Wildlife Service because I wanted to work for the Fish and Wildlife Service. But what I'm working for is the Timber, Minerals and Agribusiness Service. At least that's the way it's been operating."

On that blazing May afternoon in 1989, as on most other summer weekdays between 1987 and 1989, Skorupa was out on the ponds collecting eggs. On that particular day, he was looking for the mottled brown eggs of two species of shorebirds—American avocets and black-necked stilts—which teeter through the shallows on clownishly long legs, pecking at brine shrimp and brine fly larvae. Hundreds of these birds, maybe thousands, flew away as Skorupa approached their nests, which really amounted to nothing more than shallow dents in the ground where the birds had laid their eggs.

The terrain that Skorupa crossed looks vastly different today from how it looked a half century ago. Topographically, the Tulare basin is a landlocked, low-lying depression of a type customarily found in the ultramontane states of Nevada and Utah, not California. Even in its natural state, water rarely flowed out of the basin; instead, snowmelt from the Sierra Nevada's four southernmost watersheds—the Kings, Kaweah, Tule, and Kern rivers—coursed through the foothills and came to a halt in the basin's low spots, the Buena Vista, Goose, and Tulare lake beds. Of these, Tulare was the largest by far. After particularly snowy winters, it was the second or third largest freshwater lake lying wholly within the forty-eight states, behind only Michigan and sometimes Okeechobee.

And what a lake it was. Lieutenant George H. Derby of the Army's topographical corps set out from San Luis Obispo in April 1850 to explore the southern San Joaquin Valley and find suitable sites for military posts. He took the pass that Highway 46 traverses today and found a shallow inland sea, twenty miles long and ringed by stands of tules a quarter-mile wide. To the south, he found high sand dunes and mounds of dead tules, evidence that the lake had been much higher in the recent past. On the north was a vast boggy area, where the landlocked basin evidently overflowed on occasion into the adjacent San Joaquin River drainage. All around the lake, Indians in *rancherias* feasted on fish from the lake and reptiles from the dry western highlands. Derby's party gave the Indians bread and sugar as a goodwill gesture; in return, they received dried fish, for which they offered effusive thanks, and which they later discreetly dumped.

Today's Tulare basin bears no resemblance to that early tableau. Where vast marshes once ringed a shallow lake, today the lake has been replaced by a checkerboard of cotton and other crops. A hundred years after Derby's expedition, the U.S. Army Corps of Engineers returned to the Tulare basin and began erecting federal flood-control dams on the Sierran rivers. First, in the early 1950s, it built Pine Flat Dam on the Kings River and Isabella Dam on the Kern. A few years later, it erected Success Dam on the Tule and Terminus on the Kaweah. Growers had already been nibbling at the edges of the lake bed; with the four new dams stopping the annual flood in its tracks—and at the same time making long-term water storage feasible—they quickly colonized the lake bed itself. As an added bonus, since the dams were built by the Corps of Engineers rather than the Bureau of Reclamation, the growers didn't even have to abide by the bureau's onerous farm-size limits to take advantage of the stored water. But it wasn't more than a year or two before they discovered, to their dismay, that long-term farming in the landlocked desert basin would mean draining and disposing of salty, mineral-rich groundwater.

Skorupa had been sent to the Tulare basin two summers earlier by his boss, Harry Ohlendorf, the Patuxent biologist who had first documented bird deaths and deformities at Kesterson. In the aftermath of that disaster, another Fish and Wildlife Service biologist, Fred Paveglio, had found potentially lethal selenium loads in birds and eggs from the Grassland Water District, a fifty-two-thousand-acre agglomeration of privately owned duck marshes that abutted Kesterson on two sides. The next obvious place to look was the Tulare basin, which was dotted with evaporation ponds that concentrated drainage from soils similar to those that had caused the problems at Kesterson. Initial tests of water from the Tulare ponds had already shown it to be a soup of dangerous elements—not just selenium but also arsenic, molybdenum, uranium, and a dozen or so others. And even a casual visitor could see that birds were gorging themselves on the tiny crustaceans and other food sources that

bloomed in the ponds, whose salt content was so high that fish—
the birds' primary competitors for waterborne food—couldn't survive.

The growers who controlled the ponds were some of the largest
and richest in the world. The J. G. Boswell Company, which
drained its fields into five square miles of ponds operated by the
Tulare Lake Drainage District, had long claimed the title of world's
largest cotton producer. From the forty-sixth floor of an office
tower in downtown Los Angeles, the secretive Boswell family controlled hundreds of thousands of acres in California, Arizona, Oregon, Colorado, and Australia, producing more than twenty
million dollars per year in profits on sales of more than a hundred
million dollars per year of cotton, wheat, and beef. The family also
dabbled in real estate. Arizona's sprawling Sun City, outside Phoenix, was built on Boswell land in a joint venture with the Del Webb
Corporation. In the 1980s, the Boswells were simultaneously
building an industrial park in Colorado, a housing tract in San
Diego, and condos in Walnut Creek, California.

Elsewhere in the Tulare basin, the Salyer family controlled more
than thirty thousand acres of cotton, lettuce, and almonds from its
base in Corcoran. Near Stratford, the Howe family's Westlake
Farms was growing almost fifty thousand acres of cotton. A few
miles to the northwest, the Stone family, whose patriarch, Jack,
was president of the Westlands Water District for more than a decade, farmed eighty-six hundred acres. The heirs of Westlands pioneer Russell Giffen had a thousand acres at the Sumner-Peck
Ranch near Tranquility. Some of the landowners weren't families
at all: insurance companies, oil companies, and railroads all had
vast holdings. Down near Lost Hills was a spread owned by the
Church of Jesus Christ of Latter-Day Saints with its own evaporation pond. In all, by 1989 these and other Tulare basin landowners had built almost eleven square miles—more than seven
thousand acres—of ponds and had made plans to build almost
twice as many acres more. Some of them even applied for low-

interest loans from the state to build new ponds, and until Joe Skorupa came on the scene, the state was approving those applications
just as quickly as they could be sent in.

In 1987, when Skorupa began his study of the Lost Hills ponds
and fourteen other pond systems, he found three hundred nests of
shorebirds on 398 acres of ponds at Lost Hills. After that, the growers who operated the Lost Hills ponds expanded them to 680 acres;
as more and more of their fields required drainage, the growers
needed ever-larger ponds to dispose of the resulting wastewater.
In 1988, Skorupa found six hundred nests on the Lost Hills ponds;
in 1989, as he walked those long, gray earthen levees, he was ex-
pecting to find even more. "It's not out of the question that we
could have more than a thousand pairs of shorebirds nesting there
this year," Skorupa said that hot May afternoon. "In the three years
that we've been working there, and after we reported that there was
a problem, the system's expanded and it's exposing three times the
number of birds to contaminants as it was when we reported there
was a problem." In private, Skorupa was critical of the failure of
state and federal government agencies—including his own—to
protect the birds from the contaminated ponds. But on that afternoon, he believed that things were changing—that the Department of the Interior soon would have no choice but to invoke the
Migratory Bird Treaty Act, just as it did at Kesterson, and shut
down the Tulare basin ponds. "The evaporation pond game is almost over," he said, "and the growers had better start thinking of
somewhere else to put this water."

He was wrong. The basin growers—aided by sympathizers in
Washington and Sacramento—soon started a rearguard action
that has carried the debate into the mid-1990s with no clear signs
of an imminent resolution. In their efforts, they have had ample
help from the state agency that was supposed to be regulating
them, the Central Valley Regional Water Quality Control Board. It
was no wonder—one long-time board member, W. Steve Tomp-
kins, not only worked for Salyer but also served for a time on the

board of the largest pond operator, the Tulare Lake Drainage District. In spite of that, two California governors—George Deukmejian and Pete Wilson—appointed him time and again to regulate those same entities.

The board took up the evaporation pond issue in June 1989, under intense prodding from the state Department of Fish and Game, whose own biologists were increasingly alarmed by Skorupa's research results. By law, the board was required to defer to Fish and Game on biological questions, so after a day-long hearing it ordered the pond operators to do a report assessing the ponds' environmental effects or risk having their operating permits revoked. But in the meantime, the ponds could remain in operation. And although the board set a ten-month deadline for the report's completion, the operators managed to drag out the process until the summer of 1993—four years after the initial hearing. Then, after standing by idly while the pond operators stalled, the board suddenly and inexplicably floored the pedal: after waiting the four years for the four thousand pages of reports to be finished, the board announced that it would allow only four weeks for the public to review them,

Even the Fish and Wildlife Service brass didn't hide its displeasure. At a subsequent hearing, a service biologist, Steven Schwarzbach, reading official testimony, ridiculed the board's schedule: "One would have had to read over one hundred pages an hour simply to read all of the information by the deadline for submission of comments," he said. "In our brief review so far, we have found a number of errors in responses to technical comments. We have not had time to compile a response to these errors or even catalog them. The opportunity to correct errors in these responses has been absurdly inadequate." Not that it would have mattered. At the end of its hurry-up hearing, the board simply ratified a plan that the pond operators themselves had developed. In return for having their operating permits renewed, the pond owners would have to do almost nothing. They would have to rebuild the sides of the ponds to make them deeper and therefore less attractive to shorebirds. They would have to do a few things to drive the birds away from the ponds, such as hazing them with cannonlike noisemakers and blank shotgun shells, a practice that had proved utterly ineffective at Kesterson almost a decade earlier.

And they would have to provide enough land and fresh water to create 1 acre of clean "alternate" bird habitat for every 10 acres of poisoned ponds. Though this was a step in the right direction, and might help to compensate for some of the harm that the ponds were doing, it was clearly less than was needed. One study after another, most notably the fifty-million-dollar San Joaquin Valley Drainage Project that was conducted in the aftermath of Kesterson, had concluded that to offset the ill effects of the selenium-tainted ponds would require alternate habitat on a one-to-one ratio; yet in the Tulare basin, the board voted to require only one-to-ten. A few weeks later, the Fish and Wildlife Service filed an appeal of the board's decision. The board's decision, the service said, rested on "the assumption that the wildlife currently supported by 6,000 acres of wastewater ponds could be accommodated by 600 acres of alternative habitat. If we were to accept this reasoning, we might also happily conclude that 40 slices of bread can be made to fit in a 4-slice toaster."

The service wasn't the only party to appeal the board's decision. A coalition of environmental groups led by the Natural Resources Defense Council filed its own appeal, as did Patrick Porgans, a water consultant, and Lloyd Carter, a law student and former wire service and newspaper reporter who had covered Kesterson. But the appeals seemed to fall on deaf ears. The state Water Resources Control Board, which had moved so quickly on Jim Claus's appeal of the Central Valley board's Kesterson nondecision, didn't even take up the Tulare basin appeals until more than a year after the regional board's action, and, true to form, the pond operators tried to turn the appeal to their advantage: until the appeal was resolved, they argued, they ought to be allowed to ignore the deadlines in the Central Valley board's order. Their punishment for this breach was underwhelming. In April 1994, that board decided to fine seven pond operators for their noncompliance; the biggest fine went to the Boswells' and Salyers' Tulare Lake Drainage District, which was assessed ten thousand dollars—a little less than a nickel for each of the district's 204,100 irrigable acres.

Wherever one looked, government agencies were reluctant to take on the mighty pond operators. On the one hand, the Fish and Wildlife Service grew more outspoken on the Tulare ponds after the Democrats reoccupied the White House in 1993, in sharp contrast to its earlier reticence. This benefited Joe Skorupa greatly; after spending more than five years as a pariah with dim career prospects—at one point, Patuxent's plan for dealing with its problems in the Tulare basin was to transfer Skorupa to Tennessee and be done with him—he suddenly found himself held in high regard. He still got transferred, but this shift was one he eagerly sought, leaving paralyzed Patuxent for the service's western regional office, which had direct authority to enforce the environmental laws that the Tulare basin pond owners had spent the past half decade mocking.

Yet for all the changes, the federal government still balked at playing its strongest card—criminal penalties under the Migratory Bird Treaty Act, the same law that the government had invoked against itself at Kesterson. There were plenty of grounds for filing such charges against the pond owners. In the past, oil companies had been prosecuted for maintaining ponds that trapped birds in oily wastes; and gold ore processors, who used cyanide solutions to extract the precious metal from crushed rock, had faced Migratory Bird Treaty Act charges when birds waded into their toxic ponds. On the face of it, there seemed to be no difference between those cases and what was happening in the Tulare basin. Skorupa and other biologists had found more than twenty species of birds nesting on the evaporation ponds. They found deformities in nine of those species—mallard, gadwall, pintail, and redhead ducks; black-necked stilts; American avocets; eared grebes; snowy plovers; and killdeer. The numbers of birds and species dwarfed anything that had been found at Kesterson. Selenium levels in eggs taken from the Tulare basin were higher, in many cases, than selenium levels in eggs at Kesterson. And the Tulare ponds covered almost six times the area of the 1280 acres of the Kesterson ponds.

The first person to suggest invoking the Migratory Bird Treaty Act in the Tulare basin was a Fish and Wildlife Service regional official named Steve Moore. In July 1988, during Skorupa's second summer on the ponds and a few weeks after laboratory tests on the first summer's eggs had confirmed that the deformities were caused by selenium, Moore—who at that time was the service's drainwater studies coordinator—sent a memo to his superiors asking whether the Migratory Bird Treaty Act might not also apply in the Tulare basin, as it had at Kesterson. Three months later, after the question had been bounced to the office of Interior's chief lawyer in Washington, Moore got a reply—of sorts. The reply consisted of a copy of the department's legal opinion on the act's applicability to Kesterson—thirteen pages of legal citations with no answer to Moore's central question: whether farmers, as opposed to the government officials who had run Kesterson, could be prosecuted for unintentionally killing birds during the course of their business. Although the law had been applied to oil refineries, mines, and other industries for doing exactly that, it had never been applied to agriculture. Moore saw his department's response as an attempt to duck the issue. "All they said was, 'Just read the act,'" he said. "'You guys read the act and figure out whether it applies yourself.'"

That reply came in late 1988. More than a year later, in March 1990, Roger Gephart, a law enforcement agent from the Fish and Wildlife Service's office in Fresno, finally met with Skorupa to look over his data. Moore attributed the long delay to the low priority that he says the service's top brass assigned to the Tulare basin situation. "Somebody just made that judgment call—that this wasn't as high a priority as some other things," he said. Gephart said there was another factor as well: because the Tulare basin ponds were run by nongovernmental entities, the service needed to pin down the evidence much better than it had at Kesterson. "The burden of proof placed on me and my agency is 'beyond a reasonable doubt,' and that's pretty strong," he said. "We have to be almost 100 percent certain that there's not something else causing the deaths or deformities."

Marvin Plenert, the service's regional director, angrily denounced suggestions that his office was dragging its heels. "We haven't delayed anything," he said. "What we're doing is getting the best information possible to do our jobs. I wouldn't call it a delay." And, in fact, a few months later, in early 1991, Gephart forwarded his case file to Plenert's office in Portland, where it was quickly approved and sent over to the Justice Department for prosecution. It sat there for almost two years, until finally, in October 1992, even Plenert was fed up. "There appears to be some politics with the whole thing," he told *Sacramento Bee* reporter Tom Harris, with more than a little understatement. "They [Justice] have declined to take it, for whatever reason. I can't force them to take action and I am not getting any flak from above to tell me to lay off. . . . It is very frustrating. We have been trying to do something there for years. . . . We have to do something. The death and deformity just goes on and on." The primary obstacle, Plenert indicated, was the incumbent U.S. attorney in the eastern district of California, George O'Connell, a political appointee of the Bush administration. O'Connell said he was holding up the criminal case because he believed that a civil case, seeking cash damages and deadlines for cleaning up the ponds, would have been more appropriate. Of course, the Migratory Bird Treaty Act had no provisions for civil penalties, but that didn't sway the prosecutor. "It is totally inappropriate, as a starting point, to go directly to criminal prosecution. I must tell you candidly that we are not sure this can or should be solved through the court system," he added—as though other solutions had not already been tried and found wanting.

A few months later, after Bush lost his reelection bid, O'Connell left office; it took the Clinton administration almost a year to name his replacement. Plenert retired, leaving the mess in the Tulare basin to a successor. The Regional Water Quality Control Board continued to accommodate the growers; the Water Resources Control Board refused to stop them; the Justice Department still declined to prosecute; and thousands of birds continued flocking to the Tulare basin's selenium-poisoned evaporation ponds.

And yet, amid all of the destruction was a glimmer of hope from a most unlikely source—the Howe family of Westlake Farms. Westlake's manager, Ceil Howe, Jr., is a muscular carrot-top with a perpetual sunburn, the legacy of too many mornings spent on too many blazing ditch banks. His fifty-thousand-acre ranch, which spread like syrup down the western edge of the dried-up Tulare lake bed, was founded by Howe's father and uncle in 1929, before the Sierra rivers were dammed to stop the lake bed's annual floods. Howe was no environmentalist, notwithstanding the penchant of some farmers for calling themselves "the only true environmentalists." Throughout the early stages of the evaporation ponds controversy, Howe was the leader of the dig-in-and-fight-them crowd. When pond owners formed an association to do the reports that the Regional Water Quality Control Board had ordered in 1989, Howe was elected chairman. And he was the group's public face during the seemingly endless delays that occurred over the next four years, while the reports were being done.

Throughout that time, though, Howe was experimenting. He planted eucalyptus trees and put some drainage on them, to learn whether he could use them to dispose of the salty wastewater. He planted other crops, notably bushes from the salt-loving genus *Atriplex,* to see if they could play a role. Then, about the time that the reports were being finished, Howe boldly broke ranks with his fellow pond operators. By that time, it was clear that to keep their ponds open the growers would have to create some clean compensatory marshes. But while the other growers cut deals with the board to require only one acre of clean marsh for every ten acres of poisoned ponds, Howe swallowed hard and set aside enough land to allow for a one-to-one ratio of clean habitat to evaporation pond area, in line with what Skorupa and other Fish and Wildlife Service biologists were saying would be necessary.

In June 1994, while the other pond operators were still fighting with the wildlife regulators, Howe was leading them on a tour of his new marshes and basking in their praise. "I've really been impressed with what I've seen today," said George Nokes, Fish and Game's regional manager. "You've really set a target for a lot of people to reach for." What Howe had done was set aside 770 acres in two well-separated parcels and hire a consultant with expertise in avian biology to turn those two chunks of land into freshwater marshes specially designed to attract—and nourish—stilts, avocets, and other shorebirds. The consultant had drawn up plans to dot the new marshes with small islands for nesting and with deep moats around the perimeter to keep egg-devouring coyotes away. Howe then sent in the earthmoving equipment and pumped water into the freshly sculpted basins. Soon, thin tule reeds began to sprout from seeds that had been dormant since the old Tulare Lake dried up. Birds quickly began to congregate. Meanwhile, Howe had begun to rebuild his evaporation ponds, steepening the banks and laying thick sheets of black polyethylene around the edges. Birds avoided the rebuilt ponds, whose shores were too deep for convenient feeding.

"We feel that what we're doing—and it's costly—is the only way we can survive economically and ecologically," Howe said. The ranch's low-lying fields were particularly susceptible to salt buildup, he said, and installing drainage lines had proved to be the only way to alleviate the problem. Cotton production on fields with two-inch drain lines installed about five feet below the surface was running two to five times higher than production on un-drained fields, even with the same amount of water applied. And water, because it was scarce, was the major limiting factor for farming in the Tulare basin, Howe said. "In these days of tight water supplies, [installing drain lines] means that we can grow two, three, or four times as much on the same water," he said. "It allows us to generate the income we need to pay our bills." But installing drainage, of course, meant finding a way to dispose of the resulting wastewater, and none of the other techniques Howe had tried, including eucalyptus and saltbush, had appeared viable. That left him with no alternative, in the short term, but to use evaporation ponds and, rather than continuing his fight with the wildlife regulators and environmentalists, Howe opted to do whatever they deemed necessary to mitigate the ill effects of his ponds.

There were still some problems. With water scarce to start with, finding enough water to keep the new marshes wet remained a challenge. Howe was using his own water on 130 acres and had secured enough water from the state Department of Water Resources to take care of the remaining 640 acres by restyling that area as a "demonstration" project. But that grant of water would be good for only five years, and Howe wasn't at all sure where he would turn after that. And there was at least a remote chance that birds were nesting in the new marshes but still feeding on the poisoned evaporation ponds, in which case the selenium levels in their eggs could still be high enough to kill or deform their chicks. Whether that was happening or not wouldn't be known until several seasons of sampling and laboratory testing had been completed. Nevertheless, in the bleak physical and psychological terrain of the Tulare basin, the Howe family's experiment stood out as a shining beacon, one that only a few other western irrigators had found the courage—or the desperation—to imitate.

CHAPTER SEVEN

The Once Mighty Colorado

ITS SPANISH NAME means "reddish." Back when the Colorado River bore a vast natural burden of rust-colored silt, the name was apt, but today the slender ribbon that threads its way through the canyonlands of the southwestern United States is more green than red, its silt trapped behind a seemingly endless series of dams. What was once the nation's siltiest major river is now its saltiest—the bitter legacy of a hundred-year binge of desert agricultural development.

After rising as a torrent of pristine snowmelt in the Rocky Mountains, the Colorado now suffers fourteen hundred miles of dammings, diversions, and drainage inflows before dribbling to a halt in Mexico. Each insult increases the river's salinity, either by dissolving salt from the local soils and depositing it in the river or by taking water out of the river, leaving less to dilute salt downstream. By the time it reaches the international border, the river that carved the Grand Canyon is shrunken to a small creek, its water so full of salt that the Mexican farmers who use it for irrigation live in perpetual fear of seeing their crops poisoned. Now, the U.S. government, which spent a mere forty-nine million dollars building Hoover Dam to tame the Colorado's floods in an earlier era, is spending more than one billion dollars trying to tame the

Colorado's salinity—not to make the river any less salty, but simply to keep it from growing saltier still.

Here is what a billion dollars of federal money is buying on the Colorado. First, there's the world's largest reverse-osmosis desalting plant, a $226 million behemoth designed to squeeze salt from an Arizona irrigation project's drainage before it reaches the river at Yuma. The plant, finished in 1992 after fourteen years of delays, was predicted to gobble as much as $34 million per year, mostly in electricity, while producing, at an average of $290 per acre-foot, some of the world's most expensive fresh water. Operations and maintenance were expected to cost another six hundred million dollars over the next fifteen years. Aghast, government auditors have repeatedly suggested that the plant be permanently mothballed; their pleas are routinely ignored.

Second on the list is an assortment of projects near Yuma—concrete canal linings, wells, improved equipment, and training for irrigators—totaling $170 million. Like the desalting plant, the projects are designed to help the United States meet its treaty obligation to leave Mexico 1.5 million acre-feet of usable water in the river each year. In one project, costing $48 million, 132,000 acre-feet per year were salvaged when the Coachella Canal was lined with concrete to stop water from seeping through the canal bottom into the saline soils of the below-sea-level Imperial Valley. In another, more than $30 million has been spent to drill and pump a row of wells along the border near San Luis Río Colorado; their sole purpose is to enable the U.S. government to deprive Mexico of groundwater that would otherwise flow unseen across the border.

Third on the list is a $398 million grab bag of upstream construction projects on tributaries as far north as Wyoming's Big Sandy River. These projects are designed to reduce the amount of salt entering the Colorado and thus protect downstream users—such as southern California's Metropolitan Water District and Imperial Irrigation District—from the rise in salinity that would result from building still more water-robbing irrigation projects upstream in the future. In a northwestern Colorado geological formation called the Meeker Dome, for example, Reclamation engineers put concrete plugs in eight abandoned oil and gas exploration wells that were spewing subterranean salt water into one Colorado tributary, the White River.

Finally, there is a $219 million effort to improve irrigation practices of farmers on the same upstream tributaries, thereby lessening the amount of salt-laden drainage they put back into the river system and, again, indirectly clearing the way for future upstream development. On the Big Sandy, federal Soil Conservation Service scientists are helping farmers to install—at government expense—sprinklers and other improved irrigation systems on 15,700 acres that overlie saline shales. The goal is to reduce flows from nearby salt seeps into the river.

To date, there's not much to show for all of this spending. The $226 million desalting plant stands mute at the river's edge in Yuma, an expensive warehouse full of high-tech plumbing. Heavy flooding in the winter of 1993–94 washed out its feeder canals, but even if that hadn't happened, the plant would still be idle; it is simply far too expensive to be operated. The upstream salinity control projects have fared little better. Beset by glitches that caused two to be abandoned, the upstream projects on the whole have had no real effect on the river's salt content. In one sense, virtually the entire billion-dollar package has been wasted: according to Bureau of Reclamation records, a fortuitous series of wet years in the early 1980s cleaned far more salt out of the river than all of the salinity control projects combined. Nevertheless, when this first billion dollars in projects is completed, the bureau has plans to plunge ahead with similar projects totaling at least five hundred million dollars more.

Why is this happening? The explanation is simple. To the seven states that line the Colorado, money—at least federal money—has never been as precious a commodity as water. Herbert Brownell, the retired attorney general who negotiated the agreement with Mexico that led to the desalting plant's construction, recalls that his toughest bargaining was not with the Mexican government but with the seven basin states—Wyoming, Colorado, Utah, Nevada, New Mexico, Arizona, and California—which, he said, "had a stranglehold on all the water legislation" in Congress. "They wanted the unlimited right to continue with as much irrigation from the Colorado River as they wanted," Brownell said in an interview. "I couldn't figure out any other solution that would give them what they wanted—except for building this desalting plant."

As rivers go, the Colorado is less imposing than its reputation would suggest. Sure, it once chewed its way through a mile of solid rock just north of Flagstaff, Arizona, but today, by the time it crosses the border at Yuma, the legendary wild river that nearly killed John Wesley Powell is diminished to a pathetic pea-green trickle narrow enough to heave a brick across. In less than a century, the Colorado has been transformed from one of the world's most terrifying rivers into a compliant chain of glassy pools that rise in the Colorado and Wyoming mountains and end in a dried-up delta in Mexico. In all, six major dams, more than 150 smaller dams and diversion weirs, and roughly 2200 miles of canals and ditches now harness the Colorado for irrigation, urban water use, and hydroelectric power. The first major diversion, the Grand Ditch, was built in 1892 to move water across the Continental Divide to farms near Fort Collins, Colorado. The most recent, the Central Arizona Project, started pumping almost a twentieth of the river's water from Lake Havasu uphill to Phoenix and Tucson in 1992.

This overuse of the Southwest's only major river is the principal reason why the Colorado is now being soured by salt. From giant reservoirs like lakes Mead and Powell, the desert sun bleeds off more than an inch per week of pure water and leaves all the salt behind. Natural salt springs and other geological sources eject five million tons of salt per year into the Colorado. Irrigation contributes three million tons, much of it leached from soils that grow low-value crops such as alfalfa, sugar beets, and Bermuda grass. And with its floods now captured and stored behind dams, the river is unable to flush all that salt into the ocean. The losers are the end-of-the-line water users: city dwellers in southern California and central Arizona; farmers in the Imperial Valley and the Yuma area; and, most of all, Mexico, which uses the dregs of the river to water 500,000 acres of farmland and to supply drinking water for more than two million people in Baja California and Sonora. By the time the Colorado's water reaches these last diverters, it has so much salt that drinking it can be unhealthy; it causes whitish scales to form on everything from steam irons to industrial boilers; it drives farmers crazy by ruining their soil and poisoning their crops. The costs are tremendous: for three states alone—California, Arizona, and Nevada—the Bureau of Reclamation estimates the annual damage at $311 million.

But the Colorado is not the only U.S. river choking on salt, though it is the biggest. The Rio Grande is similarly dammed and diverted in Colorado and New Mexico until, below El Paso, it absorbs an even more saline tributary, the Pecos. Farmers in southern Texas put the resulting salty mix on their cotton, citrus, and vegetables. Likewise, to the detriment of downstream users, portions of countless other rivers—the Carson, the Arkansas, the Red, the Brazos, the Gila, the San Joaquin—have been polluted by the saline effluent of desert agriculture. Whether the other rivers will get the same billion-dollar treatment as the Colorado depends in part on how well the Colorado cleanup goes. But if history is a reliable guide, the answer may also depend on the peculiar politics of water in the West.

Two presidents set the course of irrigation development in the western United States, and both were named Roosevelt. Theodore, in office from 1901 to 1909, favored creation of a federal reclamation program when he came into office and adroitly maneuvered Congress into going along. Irrigated farming, he believed, would help to populate the West and thereby secure its defense. At the same time, it would also provide a much-needed relief valve for the impoverished masses of the eastern cities.

That vision was not shared by his distant cousin, Franklin Delano. If FDR had any interest in agriculture at all, he kept it well hidden. But when he looked at the irrigation bureaucracy that his predecessor had set in place—the Bureau of Reclamation—FDR saw perhaps the most powerful machine ever created for building public works, and that was something that clearly did interest him. His subsequent embrace of this job-generating engine was borne solely of his need to lift the nation out of the Great Depression, but it forever changed the face of the West.

Largely as a result of FDR's public works pump-priming, the bureau has now spent more than thirteen billion dollars to erect 493 dams in seventeen western states. It has turned ten million acres of desert scrub and arid grasslands into farms, but for the most part, farms weren't really the point. Whatever agricultural income a project yielded on completion was far less lucrative than the public works payroll generated by its construction. At its peak in July 1934, the construction of Hoover Dam employed 5251 workers who withstood 117-degree heat to earn $5.60 per day or less at the height of the Great Depression. Three decades later and a few miles upstream, more than 2000 workers collected from $3.59 to $5.40 per hour building Glen Canyon.

No river system has paid a greater price than the Colorado. Starting in 1931 with the 158-foot-tall earthfill Echo Dam above Ogden, Utah, the federal government built six major dams and more than 150 smaller ones on a river system that carries, on average, less water than the Illinois. But in the process, it also managed to make an error that a bright second-grader could have caught. The Colorado's average annual flow is about 15 million acre-feet at most, a fact that was well established by the early

1930s. But through a series of interstate compacts and international treaties signed between 1922 and 1944, the government ended up committing 7.5 million acre-feet to Wyoming, Utah, Colorado, and New Mexico; 7.5 million acre-feet to Nevada, California, and Arizona; and 1.5 million acre-feet to Mexico—a total of 16.5 million acre-feet, or 110 percent of the river's average flow.

As usual, politics—especially the politics of the U.S. Senate—was to blame. Ever since Charles Rockwood's temporary headworks to the Imperial Valley were washed out by the floods of 1905–7, Californians had longed for an upstream dam to control the Colorado's capricious floods. As a bonus, such a dam would make it possible for California to divert water on a regular schedule year-round. Some of that water would be used in the Imperial Valley; some would go farther west. By the early 1920s, local governments on the southern California coastal plain were already making plans to build a canal across the low deserts to the fast-growing sprawl around Los Angeles. But before the canal could be built, the river's floods would have to be brought under control by a dam, and a dam would require congressional appropriation. By that time, the six other states in the river's basin—Arizona, New Mexico, Nevada, Utah, Colorado, and Wyoming, whose twelve senators could effectively veto any dam authorization—were becoming increasingly alarmed by California's growing appetite for Colorado River water.

That is why in early November 1922, delegates from each of the seven Colorado basin states convened at a hunting lodge outside Santa Fe and spent fifteen days dividing the river among themselves. Working from sketchy streamflow records, the delegates labored under the misimpression that the river carried almost 18 million acre-feet of water in an average year. Then they struck what must have seemed a quite reasonable deal, apportioning 7.5 million acre-feet to the upper basin and a like amount to the lower basin. Not until a decade later did it become clear that the river actually carried about one-sixth less than they had thought.

In any case, because it set aside a fixed amount of water for the upper basin states, the agreement was enough to win their support for the Boulder Canyon Project Act, which authorized Hoover Dam and a new canal for the Imperial Valley. Later compacts and court decisions—the final one not coming until 1963—divided the upper basin and lower basin shares among the states within each basin. In 1944, eager to shore up its ties with its southern neighbor at the height of World War II, the United States signed a treaty giving Mexico its share of 1.5 million acre-feet. In the end, there were apportioned 4,400,000 acre-feet for California, 3,855,375 for Colorado, 2,850,000 for Arizona, 1,713,500 for Utah, 1,500,000 for Mexico, 1,043,000 for Wyoming, 838,125 for New Mexico, and 300,000 for Nevada—a total of 16.5 million acre-feet on a river that carried an average of 15.

Not all of those shares were put to use right away, but by the early 1960s, the inevitable crunch had begun to develop. First, the river's flow was suddenly, sharply diminished when the river's last major dam, Glen Canyon, began storing water. Under the terms of the 1922 compact and the 1956 law authorizing the new dam, all of that stored water was the property of the upper basin. Filling the immense reservoir—big enough to hold the river's entire average flow for sixteen months—would end up taking until 1983; during the interim, there would be no excess flows to flush salt from the river's lower reaches. At the same time, growing numbers of farmers, plowing fields newly watered by the Colorado diversions, were using the 1450-mile river as a sewer for wastewater from their fields—water that contained millions of tons of salts dissolved from the soil. In 1961, with record amounts of salty wastewater entering the river, and with freshwater flows downstream of Glen Canyon having reached their lowest point ever, the Colorado's salinity at the international border soared from about eight hundred parts per million to a crop-killing fifteen hundred parts per million.

Naturally, Mexico cried foul. At first, Bureau of Reclamation Commissioner Floyd Dominy shrugged and said that Mexico was just plain out of luck—that the United States, if it wanted to, could fulfill its treaty obligations by sending the Mexican farmers 1.5 million acre-feet of sewage. For the next decade, as Mexico's farmers watched their crops die, discussions between the two countries remained on this bizarre rhetorical cul-de-sac. But by 1972, domestic politics in both countries were roiling. Mexico had been shaken by violent student protests starting in 1968; in reaction, its new president, Luis Echeverria, had campaigned on a platform invoking his long-ruling party's nationalistic—and at times anti-American— past. Meanwhile, in the United States, the Nixon administration needed Mexico's help on a whole range of issues—from illegal immigration to drug trafficking—and was acutely worried that Echeverria's efforts to distance his country from the United States might lead Mexico to cozy up to the Soviet Union. So in June 1972, after Echeverria came to Washington on a state visit and made a direct appeal to Congress for resolution of the Colorado River salinity problem, the Nixon administration agreed to work out a solution.

The man chosen for this task was Herbert Brownell, who had been attorney general in President Eisenhower's first term. A Nebraska-born New York lawyer who served on the law review at Yale, Brownell was a major behind-the-scenes figure in the Republican party's post–New Deal resurgence. Through the Lawyer's Club of New York, he linked up with another up-and-coming young Republican attorney, Thomas E. Dewey, in the late 1920s. Together, they wrested control of the local and state parties from a group of old-timers whose major activity was pining for the glory days of the Taft presidency. Running against Tammany Hall for a supposedly unwinnable state assembly seat in 1932—the year of the first Roosevelt landslide—Brownell squeaked to victory by 307 votes. He ran both Dewey campaigns for the White House, including the famous come-from-ahead loss to Truman in 1948. Gossip columnists reported that the distraught candidate broke a lamp—or maybe a chair—over his manager's head during that long evening, a story that was roundly denied by all concerned. Three years later, Brownell was a leader in the public effort to draft the reluctant war hero Eisenhower as the Republican presidential candidate. And when Nixon was selected to join Ike on the ticket, it was Brownell who phoned the ambitious young Californian with the news.

As attorney general, Brownell was Eisenhower's confidant and conscience, a man of whom the general later wrote, "I so respected him as a man and a lawyer that I did not seriously consider anyone else for the post." In 1954, the Supreme Court invited the Justice Department to file a brief in a pending school segregation case, *Brown v. Board of Education.* Afraid of offending the southern Democrats who had supported him in 1952, Ike initially wanted to send the court a mere recitation of the historical record on Fourteenth Amendment cases, but Brownell argued that the administration should throw its full weight behind a frontal attack on the "separate-but-equal" doctrine. He must have been extremely persuasive because, in the end, Eisenhower helped Brownell write the administration's brief.

After the 1956 election, and another fierce tangle with segregationists at the Little Rock schoolhouse, Brownell left government and returned to his New York law firm, the venerable Lord, Day and Lord. But he continued to advise Republican political figures, and from time to time his name cropped up in connection with a vacancy for one important job or another. In 1969, Nixon considered sending Brownell's name to the Senate to replace Earl Warren as chief justice, but decided not to for fear of inflaming the anger of southern Democrats, who were still smarting over *Brown* and Little Rock.

When Nixon took office, the internationalist wing of his party, which Brownell and Dewey personified, was still in a tug-of-war against the conservative lineage of Robert Taft and Barry Goldwater. Nixon artfully straddled the fence; still, the Dewey wing eventually was eclipsed by Ronald Reagan's ascendance. But Brownell's defining traits were less political than managerial. He was considered an organizational genius. His chief virtues were seen as honesty and a commitment to good government; his guiding principle was not ideology but a polite yet steely pragmatism. When he recommended building a desalting plant, Brownell knew exactly what he was doing—he was buying his way out of a sticky domestic political conflict that had international repercussions. "It looked as though any solution we could come to would have to go through the Congress," Brownell said in a 1989 interview, "and [the Colorado basin states] had a stranglehold on all the water legislation." Building a desalting plant was the course of least resistance, Brownell reasoned, although it was a solution whose cost, as he told a press conference at the time, was "based on dollars and not water."

He wasn't kidding. Even then, with double-digit inflation still several years away, it was estimated that the desalting plant would cost forty-two million dollars to build. Operations and maintenance costs alone would have made the fresh water the plant produced considerably more expensive than the Colorado River water for which irrigators on the nearby lettuce fields of the Yuma Valley were paying. Moreover, building the Yuma plant would be a daunting technological challenge: it would be a hundred times as large as any reverse-osmosis desalting plant then in existence.

Almost from the start, the plant's critics spared few adjectives in denouncing it. Even before Brownell delivered his report to Nixon, he got a memo from three White House offices—the Office of Management and Budget (OMB), the Council on Environmental Quality, and the president's science adviser—which called desalting "the most expensive, in terms of cost effectiveness, of the permanent measures under discussion" for settling the salinity dispute. A few years later, Guy Martin, who was an assistant Interior secretary in the Carter administration—technically, he oversaw the Bureau of Reclamation, but like many of his predecessors he frequently found himself at a loss to control it—called the desalting plant "an expensive, out-of-control project for which the technology was, let's just say, uncertain."

In the two decades since Brownell proposed it, the plant has withstood at least eight public attempts to consign it to oblivion. The OMB has tried three times. Interior has tried twice, both times over the bureau's objections. The Department of Agriculture gave it two tries, once with the help of a southern California congressman. The General Accounting Office unloaded a volley in 1979; Interior's inspector general did the same in 1989. Each effort failed. Instead, over the years, Brownell and his successors—mainly in the bureau, but also in the State Department—clung to their cash-burning beast like a hungry coyote guarding its supper. That's not an easy thing to do. To defend the desalting plant, you have to ignore overwhelming evidence that a different solution—pretty much any other solution—would be both cheaper and more effective. Why, then, has the plant survived? Perhaps it's because when big government combines with expensive technology, nothing can be harder to kill than a terrible idea.

Next to "Star Wars," Reagan's failed Strategic Defense Initiative, water desalination may be the most oversold and underdelivered technology of the twentieth century. The problem is cost. It is fairly simple to desalt water; you can do it on your stove. You just turn the water into steam and then condense it back again. The catch is that converting water from the liquid phase to the gaseous phase takes a tremendous amount of energy for the little bit of fresh water the process yields. Water can also be desalted by freezing it, changing its phase from liquid to solid, but the cost of refrigeration is not much cheaper. There's one other option, reverse osmosis, a desalting process developed in the 1950s by a now-defunct Interior agency called the Office of Saline Water. Reverse osmosis doesn't require a phase change; instead, it strains salt out of water by squeezing it, under high pressure, through a gelatinous membrane that lets water molecules pass but blocks salt molecules, which are bigger. The equipment is tremendously expensive and the membranes are susceptible to fouling by bacteria, but the energy costs are about half as much as they would be with other processes.

Yet, even with reverse osmosis, desalting isn't cheap. If distilling salt water costs $2000 per acre-foot, reverse osmosis might average $1000, including capital costs. For the Yuma plant, operating costs alone are estimated to be $290 per acre-foot at full capacity, mostly for electricity. Add $10.6 million per year in overhead costs such as personnel, and the price rises to $429 per acre-foot. Next, suppose the local utility charges $1.40 per 1000 gallons of tap water, which is the national average. Since there are roughly 326,000 gallons in an acre-foot, that works out to about $450 per acre-foot of drinkable water, piped to homes under pressure. As a rule, for irrigation, it is uneconomical to pay even $200 per acre-foot. Most farmers pay less. Most farmers in the Colorado basin pay a lot less. Even in the best light, desalting is at least five times too expensive for agriculture.

Stewart Udall, who was Interior secretary in the 1960s and seems determined to spend his remaining years apologizing for it, was a desalting advocate. Now, he calls the Office of Saline Water "a wonderful example of the technological optimism" of that era. "This was the one program that Kennedy and Johnson both got kind of rhapsodic about," Udall said, "that we could make a technological breakthrough and this would enable the world to irrigate the desert. There was a lot of optimism. We got much larger appropriations, but the program just subsided and largely collapsed in the 1970s."

Desalting wasn't the only example of the technological optimism of that era, and the Colorado River was the intended beneficiary of more than its share of misbegotten schemes. From the 1940s to the 1970s, government engineers and their peers in the private sector came up with one plan after another to augment the river's flow. There were plans to slake the Colorado with water diverted

from the Columbia, the Klamath, the Eel, the Fraser, the Macken-
zie, the Yukon, or any other river that managed to reach the sea
before it ran dry. Most audacious of all was a plan called the North
American Water and Power Alliance (NAWAPA). Among its features were a five-hundred-mile-long reservoir in the Rocky Mountain Trench of British Columbia; a canal to carry water across the
Canadian prairies and dump it into the upper Mississippi and the
Great Lakes; and a string of hydroelectric power plants along the
southern fringes of Hudson Bay. (That last feature was eventually
built by the Quebec government to produce power for sale to the
urban Northeast.) Slightly more modest, though no less imprac-
tical, was a decade-long cloud-seeding effort by the Bureau of Reclamation that spent up to five million dollars a year and produced
few verifiable results other than to raise the wrath of mountain residents who felt they were shoveling enough snow as it was.

But above all, there was desalting, which soaked up thirty million dollars a year at its peak. Interior set up the Office of Saline
Water in 1955 with visions of crisscrossing the western states with
pipelines of desalted seawater. In 1961, the program's budget
swelled when Kennedy and Udall took office; plans were made for
a nuclear-powered desalting plant off Huntington Beach, south of
Los Angeles. Then, in 1968, the Bureau of Reclamation plunged
into desalting with the boldest proposal yet: to build a nuclear-
powered desalting plant at Camp Pendleton, north of San Diego,
and to pump 2 million acre-feet a year of desalted seawater uphill
across 280 miles of desert to Lake Mead. The estimated cost: less
than ten cents per thousand gallons, or about thirty-five dollars an
acre-foot—cheaper than many canal water sources. The explanation for the low cost: cheap electrical power, supplied by a new
"breeder" reactor that magically produced more nuclear fuel than
it consumed.

This plan was more "technological optimism," Udall now says.
The breeder reactor was stillborn, and plans for the big desalting
plants died with it, as did the Office of Saline Water. The desalting

program did have some accomplishments to its credit—notably, it developed the reverse-osmosis process almost from scratch. Today, dozens of water-short U.S. coastal communities are using the technique to desalt slightly salty, or "brackish," groundwater for use in their tap water systems. But it failed miserably at its grandest ambition: desalting seawater at a cost low enough for irrigation.

By 1972, with the handwriting on the wall, the OMB had proposed abolishing the Office of Saline Water. Nixon agreed. Interior considered, then rejected, a proposal to build a larger prototype desalting plant that would have served no purpose except to prop up the dying program. In the end, there were but two desalting supporters in the entire federal government. One was Henry Kissinger, then Nixon's national security adviser, who saw a desalting plant as an easy, visible solution to the ten-year-old salinity dispute. (Mexico's foreign minister, Oscar Rabasa, was a close friend who allowed Kissinger to vacation at his Acapulco hideaway.)

The other desalting advocate was the Bureau of Reclamation. Out of step as usual with the rest of Interior and the administration, the bureau was working behind the scenes to take over the dying federal desalting program. Its motive was pure self-preservation. By the early 1970s, after erecting hundreds of dams in hundreds of places over seven decades and turning ten million acres of desert scrub and arid grasslands into farms, the bureau had begun working itself out of a job. Its last large ongoing irrigation project, the Central Arizona Project, had been authorized in 1968, and its workforce was shrinking along with its workload, dropping from a peak of more than nineteen thousand in 1950 to about nine thousand in 1972. Unless it wanted to fade away, as the Office of Saline Water was about to do, the bureau needed new challenges in new engineering-related fields. Desalting, like snowmaking, seemed a logical fit, despite its technical problems. So, in May 1972, three months before Brownell got his assignment, the bureau issued a report proposing a desalting plant to be built—of all places—on the Colorado River at Yuma.

With Kissinger's backing and the bureau's advance work, it's not surprising that a reverse-osmosis plant, despite the technology's obvious flaws, was at the top of Brownell's list when he got his assignment in August 1972. What is surprising is that Brownell weighed a half dozen other solutions—any one of which would have been more economical than the world's biggest reverse-osmosis desalting plant—then rejected them all and swallowed the bureau's plan whole.

Most alternative solutions would have involved an attack on the river's most obvious salt source—the sixty-five-thousand-acre Wellton-Mohawk Irrigation and Drainage District near Yuma. This narrow desert valley was not the sole cause of the Colorado's salinity—every water user from Green River, Wyoming, to El Centro, California, could share credit for that—but it was highly visible, especially to Mexico. Part of the problem was poor timing. The Wellton-Mohawk Valley's drainage just happened to start flowing into the river about the same time that the big floodgates closed upstream at Glen Canyon Dam. The drainage inflow on top of the reduced freshwater flows below Glen Canyon delivered a sucker punch to the Mexicali Valley's farmers, whose fields quickly began developing spots where nothing would grow but a crust of whitish salt. That salty groundwater from the Wellton-Mohawk Valley was what the bureau was proposing to purify in its desalting plant.

First, however, Brownell considered three other solutions that would have addressed the problem in less costly ways, two of which would have attacked the problem at its source. For $266 million, the government could have bought every acre of irrigated land in the valley and let it revert to desert. Amortized on the same terms as the desalting plant, the cost would have been $16 million per year, one-third less than the current estimated operating cost of the desalting plant. Or, for a one-time outlay of $13 million, Brownell could have adopted a proposal by a group of U.S. Department of Agriculture (USDA) scientists who wanted to reduce the wastewater flow by improving the valley's irrigation efficiency. By lining canals with concrete and upgrading irrigation gear, the USDA scientists estimated they could lessen seepage to groundwater—and therefore reduce the need for pumping—by more than 80 percent, enough to lower the Colorado's salinity to a level acceptable to Mexico. Both ideas involved risks. In the first case, there was the likelihood that Arizona would rebel over losing sixty-five thousand acres of farmland. In the second, there were questions about whether the USDA methods would succeed on such a large scale—but there were identical questions about the desalting plant.

A third option would have cost nothing at all. Upstream, stored mostly behind Glen Canyon Dam, was more than 20 million acre-feet of water that could have been used to dilute downstream flows and reduce their salinity. Legally, that water belonged to the upper basin states—it consisted of unused portions of their annual share of 7.5 million acre-feet from prior years—but they couldn't use it until they or the bureau built the necessary canals, weirs, and pumping plants. In other words, the river's low flows were mainly artificial: year after year, the upper basin was hoarding much of its share of the river for future irrigation projects, most of them on high-altitude plateaus with short growing seasons and low prospective crop values, and for other potential water-intensive enterprises, such as oil shale development and coal-slurry pipelines. Placing a moratorium on further upstream projects would have instantly freed enough water to solve the salinity problem forever.

Naturally, though, this idea never stood a chance—the Colorado basin states might well have gone to war with Washington before agreeing to give up as much as a drop of their hoarded water, or their right to use it in the future, regardless of the cost to the public treasury. Brownell concluded that the other two options had insurmountable problems as well. Arizona became enraged at the first mention of land retirement, and the Wellton-Mohawk irrigators were reluctant to expend much effort improving their efficiency, even if paid to do so. So though Brownell hedged by proposing that the competing options be given further study, what he finally recommended as the centerpiece of his solution to the conflict with Mexico was a desalting plant, the only solution that wouldn't require anybody to give up water.

That wasn't the end of it. Having already gotten pretty much everything they wanted from Brownell, the basin states then decided to press their advantage in Congress. They maneuvered to have Brownell's desalting plant folded into a bill authorizing construction of four unrelated upstream salinity control projects, even though the projects were still under study by the Department of the Interior, which hadn't yet ruled on their feasibility. The upstream projects had only one purpose: to stop salt from getting into the river and thereby protect downstream users from another threat that loomed on the horizon—the chance that the Environmental Protection Agency might impose Clean Water Act sanctions that would force the basin states to give up some of their water to control the river's salinity. None of the projects seemed likely to survive an objective review of costs versus benefits, but if they won congressional approval, the federal treasury would pay most of the costs anyway, while the states and their citizens would reap most of the benefits in the form of future water projects. So in June 1974, when the bill reached his desk, Nixon was forced to choose between offending Mexico and caving in to the basin states. He grumbled in a prepared statement about the "premature" authorization of the upstream projects and then signed the bill.

Two of the four upstream projects turned out to be utter failures. One, a plan to collect and evaporate salt water that was spewing like a geyser from an abandoned oil test well in Utah, was ruled technically infeasible. Another, which would have rerouted a small stream of Las Vegas sewage effluent to keep it from picking up salts from the Nevada desert soil on its way to Lake Mead, was only partly finished when it was shelved because of the damage that the rerouting would have done to wildlife that had been congregating along the stream. The two remaining projects, both in Colorado, are under construction. The first, near Grand Junction, involves lining canals with concrete to stop water from seeping into the ground and pushing salts from the subsoil into the river. The other, in Paradox Valley about sixty miles to the south, entails pumping groundwater out of a buried salt layer before it reaches the river.

In 1984 Congress authorized the Bureau of Reclamation to start work on two more projects, and a dozen others have been studied. At the same time, the Department of Agriculture has been offering to pay farmers in the upper basin 70 percent of what it costs to improve their irrigation methods in hopes of reducing the amount of salty drainage they put into the river. Together, the two agencies have already eaten $266 million in government money, but they have barely made a dent in the Colorado's salinity problem. The projects built so far are removing only 230,000 tons of salt per year from the river. A task force estimates that more than 1.2 million tons more must be removed to keep the downstream salinity from exceeding its benchmark early-1970s level.

Meanwhile, the desalting plant's construction costs rose from an estimated $42 million in 1972, when Brownell proposed it, to $62 million in 1973, to $130 million in 1975, to $178 million in 1980, and to $226 million when it was finally finished in 1992— and that was for a scaled-back version of the original design. Estimated annual operating costs, at full production, rose from $6 million in 1972 to $34 million in 1993. Delays piled on top of delays. Brownell had predicted that the plant would be ready in 1978, but the final startup didn't actually come until 1992. The reasons for the delays ranged from unexpected technical challenges to a lawsuit by desalting equipment manufacturers. But even when it was finished, the plant was almost immediately placed on standby status. Its operating costs were so high that the bureau decided that it would use the plant only as a last resort, mainly during extended droughts when there was no other way to avoid violating the Mexican salinity agreement. As of late 1994, that had not happened, so aside from occasional testing, the plant has stood idle at a cost of $10.6 million per year.

Every auditor who has taken a look at the Yuma desalting plant has come to the same conclusion—that the most sensible thing to do would be to abandon it, and the sooner the better. In 1979, the General Accounting Office said the plant's costs "have risen to the point where alternatives should be considered." In 1989, Interior's inspector general said basically the same thing, though more obtusely: "In our opinion, the questions raised about the ultimate effectiveness and economic desirability of the desalting program are serious enough to indicate that there is a potential need for a congressional reassessment of the program as currently formulated." Even some top Interior officials, such as Guy Martin, have thrown a few brickbats over the years. "I thought the Yuma desalting plant was just a travesty," Martin said. "It was too expensive, and too big, and it wasn't going to work very well."

But while the desalting plant's high operating cost is its greatest failing, its may also be its saving grace. The plant's economics are so appalling that the Bureau of Reclamation could turn out the lights, lock the doors, and implement instead the USDA conservation plan that Brownell rejected—and justify the action purely because of its cost-to-benefit ratio. Even if the plant's construction cost were written off as a total loss, its operating costs would still exceed the total costs of the conservation alternative. Moreover, there is no longer any doubt that the USDA's methods work. They've been demonstrated since the early 1970s on projects all over the West—including the Wellton-Mohawk Valley. When Brownell hedged his "permanent, definitive, and just" solution by proposing that a task force study the USDA's ideas, he opened the door to an aggressive cadre of forward-thinking soil scientists who eventually persuaded Congress to authorize a cost-sharing program that reduced the valley's wastewater flow by almost half, from 220,000 to 119,000 acre-feet per year. That investment paid dividends in 1979, when the bureau asked Congress for an extra $116 million to continue work on the desalting plant. One of the USDA scientists persuaded his neighbor, California Congressman George Brown, to oppose the appropriation in the House, and the resulting compromise shaved 25 percent off the plant's capacity and saved forty-eight million dollars. In later years, after the USDA program ended and Gila River floods recharged the valley's groundwater, some of the gains in efficiency began to slip away. But the USDA team's head, Jan van Schilfgaarde, says he believes the plant could have been eliminated altogether if the government had cajoled the Wellton-Mohawk farmers to tighten up their irrigation efficiency just a bit more and then stayed on the scene to prevent backsliding.

In fact, it may not even be necessary to do anything at all. The final option for controlling the Colorado's salinity—reducing its salt burden by scaling back upstream irrigation projects—is more viable than ever. In 1972, the upper basin states were waiting for appropriations to build new projects. In 1995, they are still waiting. Nowadays, owing in large part to the environmental movement, the pork barrel yields space stations, not dams. So what seemed in 1972 to be an imminent crunch for Colorado River water never materialized. Total consumption in 1987 was 11.5 million acre-feet, including Mexico's share. Average annual flows are 15 million acre-feet. Since the system's big dams—Hoover, Glen Canyon, Flaming Gorge—can store more than 50 million acre-feet, the equivalent of five years' consumption, there ought to be plenty of leftover water to dilute the salt even in drought years.

If a crunch did develop during an extended drought—perhaps if the Central Arizona Project, the last big project to be authorized, ever gets fully cranked up and starts diverting its full capacity of 1.5 million acre-feet per year—operating the desalting plant still wouldn't make sense. For the twenty-three million dollars a year it would cost to power the plant at full capacity, the bureau could buy 230,000 acre-feet of water from upstream farmers at a hundred dollars an acre-foot, a princely price that most would jump to take. The farmers would have to fallow their land for a year, but they would make a nice profit because they would be selling water they bought for as little as two and three dollars an acre-foot. The bureau, in return, could then let the purchased water run downstream to Mexico and dump the Wellton-Mohawk wastewater into the Gulf of California—diluted as needed to prevent ecological damage—instead of running it through the desalting plant.

Still, the plant survives. Why? One reason is the State Department, which has an irrational fear of Mexico's reaction to the plant's closure, as was typified by what happened when Martin proposed to testify in opposition to the plant before Congress: "The State Department just got catatonic. They called and said, 'You won't testify to this.' They won that debate easily, because it was international relations. I actually had to testify in support of the Yuma project, even though I wanted to oppose it." What's odd about this fear is that Mexico doesn't actually seem to care one way or the other about the plant. The international salinity agreement says nothing about a desalting plant but merely promises Mexico water of a certain quality. Ever since the agreement went into effect in 1973, the bureau has complied not by desalting the Wellton-Mohawk wastewater but by dumping it and sending Mexico water salvaged from California as a result of lining the leaky Coachella Canal with concrete. In fourteen years of delays in the desalting plant's completion, Mexico hasn't complained once, yet the State Department continues to act as though it has.

As does the Bureau of Reclamation. In 1989, when Interior's inspector general said that the desalting plant "may no longer be the most economically desirable way" to fulfill the agreement with Mexico, the bureau replied haughtily that "economic justification . . . was not a primary factor or objective of the program." It also accused the auditors of trying to renegotiate the agreement with Mexico—ignoring, as the plant's supporters customarily do, the fact that the agreement says nothing about a desalting plant. The desalting plant, the bureau said,

was an overall settlement made to avoid further conflict with Mexico
and to avoid the possibility of a solution being imposed by a third party
such as the World Court. The settlement achieved a solution that was
based on social and political factors and supported by Mexico and the
seven Colorado River basin states. By questioning the economic justification of this settlement, the inspector general is in effect calling for
a re-evaluation of the merits of an international settlement.

This attitude persists. In a 1990 interview, David Gudgel, then the
desalting plant's manager, denied that State Department pressure
was responsible for keeping the plant alive, but he also said the
bureau wouldn't dare abandon the plant without having "some
discussions with the State Department to see what kind of reaction
we'd get from them."

Not that the bureau is tempted to try. Indeed, another reason
for the desalting plant's charmed life is the bureau's support for it
as a matter of institutional survival. Abandoning the desalting
plant would deprive the bureau of one of its few remaining high-
profile projects and force it to furlough several dozen of its remaining employees. With the stakes that high, common sense is
simply not a factor.

Cloaked in this Alice-in-Wonderland reasoning, the desalting
plant may be immune to any sort of hardheaded reevaluation. Certainly Congress, in spite of its changed attitudes toward the bureau's work, has shown no interest in the plant since its 1979
review. And if it did, one can only imagine the apple-pie rhetoric
that would be employed by the bureau and other desalting advocates to explain why the federal government ought to spend hundreds of millions of dollars to protect upstream farmers who
contribute, at most, only a few million to the nation's economy—
and who, in many cases, have to work full-time jobs off the farm
just to make a living.

By draping themselves in Jeffersonian imagery, the Bureau of
Reclamation and its congressional patrons have siphoned more

than thirteen billion dollars from the federal treasury since 1902. Today, using similar language, they deride critics of the desalting plant and speak of the nation's duty to its yeomen and to Mexico. But that stance is a smokescreen. The plant's true rationale lies not in the myth of the family farmer but in another rural American shibboleth—the notion that because the West is arid, the rules of ordinary economics do not apply.

From the ultramodern desalting plant in Yuma to Pedro Niebla's ramshackle farm in the Mexicali Valley is a distance of no more than a few dozen miles, but few places pose a sharper contrast, either culturally or economically. While Americans north of the border squander a billion dollars to protect the interests of would-be oil shale moguls a thousand miles upstream, Mexican farmers like Niebla struggle, mostly without success, to hold onto their tiny slivers of prosperity.

In May 1990, when I visited Niebla's fifty-acre farm at Ejido Nuevo Leon about twenty miles south of the border, the late afternoon sun was broiling but the ground was covered in white. As Niebla hiked across a field, his feet made loud crackling noises, breaking a thin crust that looked a little like frost on the dark ground. For a half century, using irrigation water from the Colorado River, Niebla had grown cotton, barley, and wheat on this small square of land. But over time, naturally occurring salts had accumulated in the field, sterilizing the soil and taking the bloom off this man-made oasis.

Niebla's story was rags to riches. He began as an itinerant picker, living in Mexicali and harvesting crops all over the Colorado River delta, mostly on 800,000 acres of land owned by the Colorado River Land Company, a California syndicate led by *Los Angeles Times* publisher Harry Chandler. Then in 1937, political change swept the region, and Niebla unexpectedly got an opportunity that most *campesinos* only dream about. Pumped up by official pledges of land reform from faraway Mexico City, groups of Mexicali Valley peasants marched into the delta's foreign-owned fields, planted the Mexican flag, sat down, and refused to leave. Soon the government began buying out the Chandler holdings. More than five thousand families, including Niebla's, were settled on the expropriated land. Within a few years, networks of new canals were built to carry water from the Colorado to the farms, covering the desert valley with a blanket of green. Niebla prospered and built his family a house; later he built another house for his mother, right behind his own. There were *muy bellas cosechas*, he said: beautiful harvests. The Mexicali Valley became Mexico's largest wheat-producing region.

Over time, though, the imported Colorado River water grew salty and scarce. Salt shrank the usable part of Niebla's field to where it was no longer profitable for him to farm it. The problem had crept up on him: in the early years, the United States had let plenty of water run down the Colorado into Mexico, and farmers could use the excess water to flush away the salt before it could build up in their fields. But later, after Glen Canyon, water was scarce and salt was everywhere, and the farmers were helpless to stop the damage. "When there is a lot of water," Niebla said in a whisper of Spanish, "then there is something you can do about the salt. But when there is not much water there is nothing you can do."

Niebla decided he'd had enough about 1980, after salt had soured so much of the ground that he could no longer make a decent profit on what was left. He'd never been wealthy anyway. As a small *ejido* farmer—that is, one living in a settlement where the land legally remains in government ownership no matter how long he farms it—Niebla was unable to get credit to buy machinery and had to rent it instead. After he gave up farming, he began renting both the land and the water to a larger, more prosperous farmer who had his own equipment and could therefore survive on a smaller margin. Technically, it's illegal for an *ejidatário* to rent his farm to someone else, but as a practical matter, it's easier for the government to wink at the violation than to rescue the insolvent violator.

Mexico's National Water Commission now estimates that yields on 44 percent of the valley's 500,000 acres of farmland are being reduced or wiped out by poor drainage and salt, and the percentage is creeping upward every year. Mexico's agricultural and water engineers are trying an assortment of techniques to save the land they have left. They are rebuilding canals to stop excess water from seeping out and pushing salt to the surface; they are making loans to farmers so they can level their fields and thereby water them more evenly, reducing wasted water; and they are raising the price of water to twelve times its previous cost to encourage conservation.

But all of that comes too late to help Niebla and others like him. In the late spring of 1990, ripe wheat stood on the fringes of the field behind Niebla's house, but a vast area in the center was barren and coated with chemical salts, primarily gypsum. Seeds refused to germinate in that poisoned soil; only a few weeds and Niebla's footprints broke the monotony of white. Below the crust was a dark, pliable mud. It looked as if the field had just been watered, but Niebla said it had been two months since the last irrigation. The surface had been sealed by salt, so the moisture could not evaporate.

His handshake was still bone-crushing, but Niebla was in his eighties. Stopping in the middle of the field to pick at the ground, he looked back toward his homestead. A few hundred yards away, his mother's house stood abandoned and falling down. His own family's more substantial but still tiny brick home was shaded by salt cedars—a species whose presence betrays shallow, saline groundwater. The surrounding dirt yard was littered with disassembled bits of farm machinery and the other flotsam of rural poverty.

It must make him angry to walk across this field and think about what he has lost, I suggested. No, Niebla said, it didn't. His wife was upset, he admitted, but personally he accepted his condition. "It's the Lord above who decides these things," he said. "I just go along."

CHAPTER EIGHT

A Flood Down Under

WHEN THE AUSTRALIAN spring came to the Riverine Plain of northern Victoria in September 1989, Peter Avram's peach orchard near Shepparton slowly awakened and burst into leaf, as it always had before. Avram expected a good crop, one that might bring forty thousand dollars in sales once the fruit was picked and packed. But two months later he had nothing but a forest of dead wood. More than two thousand trees, most of them in the prime of their productive lives, had acquired a fatal case of root rot. They were killed by a flood from below, drowned in an unseen tide of rising groundwater caused by 150 years of over-irrigation and deforestation.

For a century and a half, as Americans settled the empty West and the British subdued the Punjab of India, Australians like Avram have farmed the low inland plains along the river Murray. First they cut down forests of eucalyptus trees to bring in the sun, then they laced the vacant countryside with canals to bring in the water. In doing so, they were following a trail blazed by their Anglo and U.S. cousins, and they helped to pave the way for the twentieth century's worldwide irrigation boom. But they also wrought huge changes in the natural cycles of rainfall and runoff by removing the land's protective natural sponges, its trees, and by pouring unprecedented amounts of water on the denuded soil. For a long time they got away with it, but now, like their counterparts in irrigated regions around the world, they are learning there is a price to be paid for trying to improve on nature.

Aborigines had been living in Australia for forty thousand years when the first European settlers arrived in the Riverine Plain in the early nineteenth century. They were living there when the last of the Neanderthals perished in Europe. They had lived there for thirty-five millennia when civilization, or at least the Western version of it, dawned in the ancient valleys of the Nile, Euphrates, and Indus rivers. Yet when Major Thomas Mitchell, the Australian explorer, crossed western Victoria in 1836, he found a landscape that was only slightly changed from what the first aboriginal Australians must have seen. Thick forests of eucalyptus, the predominant tree of Australia, crowded the low hills along the continent's eastern and southern coasts. Below them, to the north, sparsely wooded savannahs gave way to a vast, open grassland on the west. The largest river on the continent, the Murray, snaked across these lonely plains before making a sharp left to empty into the Antarctic Ocean near present-day Adelaide.

It took Major Mitchell's successors only a few years to make their mark on this wilderness. In the 1840s Merino sheep were first imported from Spain, and soon wool barons were running their herds on spreads of 300,000 acres or more, usually without bothering to attain title to the land. Then gold was discovered at Bendigo in 1851, and hordes of miners set out for Victoria. In a single decade, the state's population soared from 77,000 to 540,000. But the gold rush fizzled out as quickly as it had begun, and the government was faced with the problem of what to do with a lot of restless, immigrant ex-miners.

In the United States, the frontier traditionally had functioned as a safety valve for the crowded cities of the East. Australia's frontier soon served the same purpose. Confronted with every government's worst nightmare, unhappy subjects with a lot of time on their hands, Australia looked to the land for relief. Over the next twenty years, the Crown reclaimed more than 20 million acres of the public domain from the squatting sheep barons and doled it out to landless Australians. The new settlers got parcels of 320 to 640 acres each, and grew wheat instead of wool, but drought and rabbits soon bankrupted many. By the early 1880s, desperate Victorian politicians were more than ready to listen to any new idea. And the new idea that happened to be sweeping the world at that moment was irrigation.

Leading Australia's irrigation lobby was Alfred Deakin, the commonwealth's second prime minister. Born in Melbourne in 1856, Deakin was the closest thing Australia had to Thomas Jefferson—the intellectual and political leader of a native-born generation that was stitching a set of disparate British colonies into an independent nation. Deakin was a bundle of contradictions. An eloquent and hypnotic speaker, he wrote reams of bad poetry in his spare time. Strictly moral and even pious, he also dabbled in the occult: for a while, he believed he was a medium for John Bunyan, the seventeenth-century author of *Pilgrim's Progress*. Like Jefferson, he was also precocious: in his early twenties, he practiced both law and journalism, and by the time he was thirty, he had become the coleader of a coalition government in Victoria, his native state. Also like Jefferson, he had a soft spot for the yeoman farmer, which explains why, as a twenty-six-year-old minister in the Victorian parliament, Deakin took his wife, an engineer, and two journalists to California to make a landmark report, "Irrigation in Western America."

Deakin and his group spent three months touring California and four other western states and came to a conclusion that would have pleased William Gilpin, the Coloradan who persuaded thousands of naïve Americans to homestead the arid West. Settling the arid plains of rural Victoria was not just a good idea, Deakin said, it was a societal obligation whose cost was not really relevant: "If

Victoria is to continue to progress in the settlement of her people upon the lands and the multiplication of her resources . . . it must be by means of irrigation. No price, it may be said, is too high for such a promise of progress." It was manifest destiny, slightly modified for a new continent. Australians must stop clinging to the humid coasts, Deakin argued, and set themselves to work subduing the wild, dry interior.

Deakin wasn't alone in this enthusiasm. In the late nineteenth century, it seemed as though every nation in the English-speaking world was getting into irrigation in a big way. The British were attempting to end the scourge of famine in India by diverting the Indus onto the arid plains of the Punjab. In the United States, a generation of westerners was trying to imitate the Mormons of Utah by making the desert bloom. Australia climbed on board in 1886 with the Waterworks Construction Encouragement Act, which permitted private construction of irrigation systems at a time when such ventures in America were failing with stunning regularity. Australia proved no different, and some entrepreneurs even managed to fail on both continents: George Chaffey, a Canadian, left a pair of fledgling irrigation colonies in southern California in 1886 to set up a 250,000-acre scheme near Mildura, an old cattle station in southwestern New South Wales; the venture went belly-up seven years later. When he returned to California, Chaffey joined Charles Rockwood in his scheme to divert the Colorado River into the Imperial Valley, which ultimately resulted in the Salton Sea, one of the nation's costliest man-made disasters. Even then, Chaffey was considered one of the most competent irrigation engineers of his day—the industry's lesser lights merely failed on a smaller scale.

In the end, both Australia and the United States finally resigned themselves to government-sponsored irrigation schemes, the kind the British were creating in the canal colonies of the Punjab. The two nations have continued to follow parallel courses to this day. Both Australia and the United States built powerful irrigation bureaucracies within their governments, and in the mid-twentieth century, both plunged into dam-building with the zeal of the newly proselytized. While the United States was building Hoover and Glen Canyon, Australia was building its own monuments: Hume, Dartmouth, Eildon, and Burrinjuck. The two nations even joined forces in the 1960s to turn the rivers of the Snowy Mountains, on Australia's southeast corner, out of their coastal drainages and into the Murray basin.

So it's not surprising that the Australian and U.S. irrigation juggernauts both broke down at about the same time. In the United States, the causes were varied—the escalating costs of water projects; a massive shift of population from farms to cities (and therefore a shift of political support away from irrigation); a controversial plan to build two high dams in the neighborhood of the Grand Canyon. In Australia, there was only one cause—a head-on collision with a monumental drainage problem.

There is no little irony in this. Australia is the driest by far of the world's inhabited continents. It gets a third less rain, on average, than North America, Europe, Africa, or Asia, and not even a quarter of what South America gets. Yet its biggest environmental problem is one of too much water.

For thousands of years before the Europeans arrived, the hydrological cycle in northern Victoria was exquisitely balanced by nature. Rain fell on the uplands, as it does now, but the vast eucalyptus forests, their leaves transpiring prodigious amounts of moisture, put most of the water right back into the atmosphere. Of course, the English settlers couldn't see that happening. What they saw when they looked at the great stands of eucalyptus was a source of firewood and an obstacle to be done away with in the interest of better pastures. For years, starting in the 1860s, the Crown actually required settlers to clear the trees from their land before gaining title to it. And as late as 1983, the Australian government offered tax incentives for land clearing—in other words, a bounty on trees. In the 1880s, half a million tons of timber were shipped by rail to Melbourne every year, mainly for firewood. To-day, millions of sheep graze where forests once stood.

Deforestation was the first of two deadly changes that the set-tlers made in Australia's ecology; the second was the introduction of irrigation. First, the immigrants removed the forests that had sopped up nature's excess rainfall, then they imported still more water to grow crops on the newly cleared land. In planting pad-docks of wheat or maize and pastures of clover, the settlers were also planting, unwittingly, the seeds of their own destruction. It took a while for the damage to become apparent. In most places, the water table was deep at first, a hundred feet or more. Through-out much of the Murray basin, it took almost a century for the ground to fill up. But when it did, the earth was filled down to the bedrock—filled with excess rainfall from the old forests and ex-cess irrigation water from the new farms, filled until it could finally take no more. From that day on, when the winter rains came it was like pouring water on an already sodden sponge. The precipitation couldn't soak in, and because the land was nearly flat it couldn't run off either. It just sat there, pooling atop the water that was al-ready in the ground.

Virtually every irrigated nation in the world fights a constant war against the desert's steady effort to reclaim what was taken from it. But few of those countries have struggled with the drainage nem-esis for as long as Australia has. In the low-lying region around Kerang, where irrigation began in the 1880s, pioneer farmers were abandoning their land after just a decade because of soil salting caused by poor drainage.

Peter Avram's farm lies a hundred miles southeast of Kerang. Irrigation began later in his area, and the water tables were lower to start with, so it took a lot longer for drainage to become a prob-lem. The first sign of trouble came in 1956, during one of the wet-test winters in Australia's history. Heavy rains fell all across Victoria, and with the soil already wet from irrigation, the rainwater had nowhere to go but straight down to the water table. Dozens of orchardists in the area around Shepparton watched their trees drown in the resulting underground flood.

The same thing happened in 1974, another wet winter, and farmers began to drill wells so that they could periodically pump out the high groundwater. But in each of the wet winters, the Avram orchard was untouched. Maybe it sat slightly higher than its neighbors, or maybe the subsoil was more porous, so that water drained away rapidly. Whatever the reason, it seemed to be charmed. Avram and his father, who started the farm, felt certain that they were immune from water table problems.

"Never in our minds did we think we would lose our trees here, because we never lost them before," Avram said. "Fifty-six was the wettest year, and this place was the only place that survived, so. . . ." He shrugged. The winters of 1988 and 1989 were extremely wet, but when spring came in 1989, Avram was as confident as always. He shouldn't have been; a large part of his orchard was about to die, and it happened quickly. "Everything started to leaf out, and then the blossoms came, and that was it," he said. "The blossoms came, and before the petal fall the trees just died." Why? "It was the stress. The trees were starting to take from the roots, and the roots said, 'No more.'"

In November 1989, while orchards all around him were setting a heavy crop of fruit, Avram stood amid dead and dying trees. Here and there a few pathetic leaves clung to the ends of twigs, and green fruit the size of marbles hung like Christmas ornaments from the gray branches. Avram reached up, pulled a branch toward him, broke off the end, and put the splintered wood to his nose. "Dead wood," he said, making a face. "You break a stick, and it just smells an off smell, like there's dead fruit lying around. The roots just go black, they rot. And when they go black, that's it."

Avram's family emigrated to Australia from Greece in 1960, when he was only a few months old. His father worked in a relative's orchard until the mid-1970s, when he bought the twenty-two acres that are the nucleus of the family's present orchards. They grow apples, pears, apricots, nectarines, and, until the spring of 1989, peaches. But the only peach trees they had after their losses that spring were the very young and the very old. "The trees that we lost were the ones that were productive for us," Avram said. "They were the ones that were making the money for us. They were from five to twelve years old, and they were in full production."

After the trees died, Avram began to wish he had invested in wells to lower the water table or in water-conserving irrigation gear such as sprinklers. If he had, the soil might not have been so waterlogged. It might have been able to absorb the winter rains better, and his trees might not have drowned so quickly. "We know now," he said. "We have to put the pumps in, we have to hill up the trees, put sprinklers in. And that's going to cost a lot of money."

Nineteen sixty-seven was a year of drought, one of the severest Australia had ever seen. The river Murray nearly ran dry, something that hadn't happened since the government started building dams in the early twentieth century to regulate its formerly erratic flow. For most of the summer and fall of that year, the preponderance of water in the river's lower reaches, in the state of South Australia, came not from the upstream catchments but from the downstream irrigation areas. It was used water—groundwater, for the most part—some of which made its way to the river through a network of drainage ditches that farmers had dug to lower the water tables on their land, and some of which simply seeped into the river when the saline water table rose so high that it intersected the riverbed. In one place near Mildura, salty groundwater spilled out of the face of a cliff and into the river, pushed out by the pressure of water seeping into the highlands above. Whatever its source, the quality of the seepage was generally terrible. Groundwater draining into Barr Creek, a once-dry streambed that empties into the Murray near Kerang, was saltier than seawater. As a result, the little dribble of water in the lower end of the Murray gradually got saltier and saltier, to the point that it was downright unpleasant to drink. Which might not have mattered, except that sitting at the mouth of the Murray was the capital of South Australia, Adelaide, a city of a million people whose drinking water was drawn from what was left of the river.

People in parts of southern California, which gets a large share of its water from the Colorado River, know what it's like to drink salty water. Maybe that's why more bottled water is sold there than anywhere else in the United States—and why the area's restaurants routinely drop a twist of lemon into a glass of ice water. In any case, the sharp rise in salinity in Adelaide's drinking water set off a furor among its politicians. About the same time, citrus farmers in the Sunraysia region near Mildura noticed that their trees were losing their leaves. The problem was quickly traced to high salinity in the irrigation water that the farmers were spraying on their groves—water drawn from the beleaguered Murray. Angrily, both groups started pointing their fingers upstream toward the irrigated farmlands of Victoria and New South Wales.

The rains returned in 1968 and took the edge off the crisis by diluting the river's salt content, but the issue continued to simmer for almost two more decades. The River Murray Commission, an interstate agency whose job it was to control the river's flows—so that upstream irrigators wouldn't divert every drop of water—ordered a study on the problem and identified a long list of major salt sources, including some in the irrigation areas of South Australia itself. That state immediately started spending millions of dollars on evaporation ponds even though the two upstream states continued to blithely poison the Murray with their own salt-laden drainage. Unfortunately, the southerners' cures only made the problem worse, partly because the region's geology was not well understood.

"They built evaporation basins in absolutely the most inappropriate places you could put them," said Don Blackmore, deputy executive director of the River Murray Commission's successor, the

Murray-Darling Basin Commission. "They put them on the flood plains, on alluvial material. They displaced far more salt than they actually stopped from getting into the river. People thought they were doing the right thing, but it was a disaster." The evaporation ponds were built on land that lay slightly higher than the river. When drainage water was dumped into them, it seeped into the underlying soil, pushing displaced groundwater into the river. While the drainage water was about one-tenth as salty as seawater, the groundwater it displaced was about equal to seawater in its salinity. For every pound of salt that the ponds kept out of the river, another ten pounds were forced into the river by the hydraulic pressure of the ponds on the underlying groundwater. A report in 1978 by South Australia's Engineering and Water Supply Development Department estimated that the evaporation ponds, rather than lessening the river's salt burden, were actually adding 100,000 tons of salt a year. In the end, the state had to spend another ten million dollars piping the salty water across the river to a new basin constructed in a natural depression twelve miles away, where it wouldn't pollute the river.

But at least South Australia was trying to fix the problem. New South Wales, which controlled most of the northern bank of the river Murray, spent most of the 1970s trying to deny that a problem existed—or at least that its own farmers had anything to do with it. And Victoria, though it could scarcely evade the problem as long as white crusts of salt were forming on its own pastures, was in no mood to pay for expensive salt-interception schemes that would mainly benefit its downstream neighbor. South Australia threatened to sue the other two states and thereby block any new irrigation projects from being built. But that in itself didn't make the river any less salty.

Another reason the upstream states balked was that there was no real way to tell how much of the problem each state was actually responsible for. Sorting out the individual salt contributions from dozens, even hundreds of irrigation and drainage systems over a river basin the size of California and Texas combined proved nearly impossible, as the commission proved in 1982, when it tried to create a mathematical model of the river's flows and salt levels. The model proved that salinity was a problem—it was costing Adelaide twenty-eight million dollars a year just to repair salt-corroded plumbing—but it also proved that it was pretty much impossible to tell how much each state was contributing to the problem.

A new council of government ministers from the three states and the federal commonwealth—which had just been established to oversee the River Murray Commission—then proposed a compromise. "The states were always fighting," Blackmore said. "And we said, 'Oh, come on now, this is bloody ridiculous.' So the governments finally agreed that as of the first of January 1988, we were all the same." Instead of continuing to argue over who was responsible for past pollution, Blackmore said, the states would call it a draw. Moreover, he said, "Each state would then be responsible for any further effect on river salinity. If they built another dam which affected river salinity, they would be responsible for that. If they put in more drainage which affected river salinity, they'd be responsible for that."

Fortunately, the model was slightly better at predicting the effects of new projects than it was at sorting out which existing projects were to blame for the river's existing salinity. It didn't work perfectly—being mere approximations of reality, models never do—but it worked well enough to make the compromise an effective one. Henceforth, if any of the three states proposed to do something that would put more salt into the river, it would have to pay for another project that would be expected to take out at least an equal amount of salt. Beyond that, the three states also agreed to pay three hundred million dollars up front for five salt-interception schemes in the river's lower stretches. In return for its investment, South Australia got slightly better water to drink. Meanwhile, the two upstream states, New South Wales and Victoria, were issued "salt credits"—licenses to add salt back to the river in the future as they tried to fix their own drainage problems. The salt that the credits would add to the river amounted to only one-fifth of what the interception schemes would take out; the net result would be an average of sixty parts per million less salt in the river at Adelaide's intake.

But exactly how the states would divide up their salt credits was a question that seemed likely to be kicked around for years. And even if the salt credits were somehow divided up to everyone's satisfaction, there was still a chance that the model would be wrong—that the Murray's salinity would rise anyway. A hundred years of rainwater had already seeped into the once-forested slopes that line the basin's southern and eastern fringes. Slowly, that water was making its way to the basin's lowest point, the Murray's bed. Skeptics pointed out that with a century's head start, most of that giant mass of groundwater was probably going to reach the river, bringing countless tons of salt with it. When that happened, three hundred million dollars in salt-interception schemes might well come to nothing.

When he crossed Victoria in 1836, Major Mitchell made a stop in the Tragowel Plains near the present site of Kerang. He climbed Pyramid Hill, an eight-hundred-foot mound of decomposing granite in the center of a broad, grassy plain, and looking out over the shallow creeks, the gentle slope of the land, and the fine clayey soil, proclaimed the region ideal for irrigation. He was wrong.

Late in 1989, Ken McDougall, a struggling farmer, stood atop the same hill and gazed into the distance toward the dying town of Pyramid Hill, population 540, a quarter of that population older than sixty. Most towns in rural Victoria are well swept and prosperous looking, but Pyramid Hill is an eyesore of peeling paint, potholed streets, and lawns of bare earth. The surrounding countryside isn't much better. Bullock Creek snakes past at the foot of the hill, separating it from the town. Its banks are lined with the black skeletons of dead eucalyptus trees, killed when groundwater seeped upward into their root zones, wicking toward the surface as a droplet of water wicks into the corner of a paper towel. Eucalyptus trees ordinarily don't mind a high water table, but because the Tragowel Plains have gotten so little cleansing rain over the eons, the subsoil still contains a lot of salt, which the groundwater dissolved, carried to the surface, then left behind through the process of evaporation, killing the trees.

Beyond the creek lie vast pastures in a checkerboard of brown and green. The brown ones are obviously dying, and the green ones, which look healthy, are salt-affected as well, said McDougall. Instead of clover and other good forage, the green pastures are sprouting salt-tolerant plants that sheep shun. A good pasture can graze six sheep per acre; these, he said, can graze fewer than three.

The Tragowel Plains contain 520 struggling farmers and their families, many of whom, including McDougall, have been forced to take jobs off the farm because their soil has gone bad. "I used to drive a milk truck around at night to make ends meet," McDougall said. "Now I'm working on salinity for the Rural Water Commission. I'd like to think I'm working part-time and farming full-time, but I'm not quite there yet." But McDougall's moonlighting has given him an impressive degree of knowledge about Tragowel's drainage problems. Besides his Rural Water Commission job, McDougall is also chairman of a community group that the state government has set up to work on the drainage problem—part of Victoria's effort to allocate its Murray salt credits equitably. The government gave the group money to hire consultants, put its own staff at the group's disposal, and told the group to come up with a solution it could live with. It did, and as McDougall stood atop Pyramid Hill, the plan was under review in the capital of Melbourne, as were similar plans for three other regions.

Graham Hunter, manager of the Salinity Bureau in the state's Department of the Premier and Cabinet, described the community-group approach as having been borne of desperation. In the past, Hunter said, the government's experts had regularly come up with plans for solving an area's drainage problems, and the plans were just as regularly rejected. Either the farmers thought the solution too costly, or they objected to being told they would have to shift away from sensitive clovers to salt-tolerant crops. Finally, after a leftist Labour party government took over the parliament in 1983, the farmers were given the power and resources to decide for themselves. "I think you'd say we're empowering the community to make its own decisions," Hunter said.

The community groups spent two years studying the technical data, debating the options, and writing their plans to send to Melbourne. The results, Hunter said, were "very interesting. We now have farmers on these groups who are as conversant with the issues as most of the technical experts." Still, some of the plans sent to Melbourne had what apppeared to be fatal flaws. In Shepparton, for example, the group said it wanted to dump water with 178,000 tons of salt into the river Murray every year, which would have consumed all of the state's salt credits—and then some—to benefit one small region. In another area, near Rochester, the community group came up with a plan that was acceptable to everybody in the group, but farmers outside of the group rejected it by a four-to-one margin.

Neither of those areas is quite like the Tragowel Plains; for one thing, they are still fairly prosperous. Farmers in the Tragowel Plains and other areas near Kerang, in contrast, are on the ropes—and that fact, McDougall said, may account for their support of his working group's plan. Stunningly simple, it called for farmers to give up part of their land to salt-tolerant plants and to concentrate their irrigation on the less-affected pastures. A careful farmer might still coax the salt-affected areas to grow something that sheep will eat, but mostly he will just try to keep his good pastures from going bad by letting the salty areas serve as relief valves, places where rising groundwater can come to the surface and evaporate, sparing the good pastures. In short, the farmers of the Tragowel Plains are cutting off their right hands to save their left; that they are willing to do so is a sign of how desperate they have become. "Everybody's on their last legs here," McDougall said. "People start to pull together in a crisis, and we've got a crisis on our hands."

In the Tragowel Plains and elsewhere, Australia is encountering a fundamental law of irrigation that might be stated as a corollary to the law of gravity: what goes into the land must sooner or later come out. Putting trillions of gallons of water onto land that has never had to deal with so much water before is asking for trouble, unless a way for the water to escape is also provided. Usually that means installing drains, whether tile drains, wells, or merely shallow ditches that intersect the groundwater. The only real alternative is to use irrigation water sparingly, as though it were liquid money (which it is), and thereby delay the onset of drainage problems for decades if not centuries. But like so many other irrigated nations, Australia has chosen to irrigate with the mentality of a child on a candy binge: if a little bit is good, then a whole lot must be even better. It thus accelerated its drainage problem even while it was putting off doing anything about it. Even now, as Victoria struggles to keep its hundred-year-old irrigated farms from drowning in their own effluent, a new irrigation project is being built in Queensland, on the northeast edge of the Murray-Darling basin—without drainage.

"It's an old story; they spend the money putting the water on, but they never spend the money putting the water off," said Mark Gardiner, an agricultural extension officer in Echuca, near Kerang. Gardiner has the unenviable task of assisting the Tragowel Plains working group and defending its proposal for land retirement, which amounts to original sin in the world of irrigation. If the group's plan is put into effect without major changes, a third of the region's irrigated land, or fifty-seven thousand acres, will no longer be irrigated. That such a solution is even being considered is a reflection of how bad Australia's drainage problems are.

But the truth is, Australia probably wouldn't even miss the food it lost by taking that land out of production. The country's population is only sixteen million, and as a result Australian farmers have a hard time finding markets for their products. What's more, in recent years their biggest traditional market, Great Britain, has begun to close as the European community has turned inward and erected external trade barriers. Tens of thousands of fruit trees that once provided food for British stomachs have been pulled up and the land replanted in annual crops or pastures. Australia's leaders speak wistfully of the huge Asian markets to the north of them, especially in China. They suggest that, with a little effort, Australian produce could find a home there, but they overlook the fact that China has built a huge irrigation infrastructure of its own and is on its way to becoming a net exporter of food and cotton at least for the near future. All of these market forces are conspiring to make Australian agriculture far less lucrative than it used to be. As a result, Australian farmers ultimately may come to grips with drainage problems on their farms simply by walking away from them.

Meanwhile, though, other solutions are being considered for Australia's drainage woes: planting thousands of eucalyptus trees to soak up groundwater or grading fields with laser-guided leveling devices to guard against uneven watering, a prime cause of over-irrigation. And then there's the ultimate solution, the one that even its backers admit would be an economic disaster: the Pipeline to the Sea, a closed conduit to carry salty drainage water to the sea, a San Luis drain to the Antarctic Ocean. One such proposal, written in 1984, called for a steel tube three feet in diameter to carry pressurized drainage water 270 miles from the Kerang area to Port Phillip Bay west of Melbourne. Even if the pipeline ran along railroad tracks for most of its route, thus eliminating the cost of buying an easement, the project would have carried a price tag of $149 million, and it would have cost another three million dollars a year to pump the salty effluent over the eighteen-hundred-foot Great Dividing Range to get it to the coast. The pipeline's cost would have been seven times what the state of Victoria spends annually on salinity control, and it would have benefited only one small part of the state. Other experts have pointed out that the pipeline probably wouldn't be allowed to discharge into Port Phillip Bay because it would add to the nitrate pollution that already is choking the bay with seaweed. Extending the pipeline beyond the bay would cost another twenty-five million dollars; total costs have been estimated to be as high as $240 million. "Paying for a pipeline to the sea would be very difficult," Blackmore said. "It may not be out of the question, but it comes down to a question of sustainability, and at what price?"

At what price? Australia's century-long rampage of irrigation and deforestation has already exacted a frightening price on its natural environment, as it has in the United States. Even the koala, Australia's somnolent national mascot, is being threatened with extinction, as its habitat—the once vast forests of a dozen species of eucalyptus—is wiped out by the timber and grazing industries, and its numbers in the small pockets where it remains are reduced by disease. The Australian farmer may not be far behind. Victoria's salinity bureau estimates that the state is losing 7 percent of its agricultural production at present, and the figure could treble in the next thirty years.

McDougall once farmed 807 acres of land in the Tragowel Plains, near Macorna. He put a lot of money into the land in hopes of making it more productive. He experimented with crops; he was the first farmer in the area to grow sunflowers, for example. But all the time, the salty water was creeping up beneath his feet. His yields were low; his pastures poor. All the money he was spending only made matters worse, adding to his debt without increasing his production. Three years ago, things got so bad that McDougall had to sell most of his land. He was left with 375 acres that he is trying to turn into something resembling a farm.

He is thinking about growing saltbush, the shrubby plant that farmers in the western United States know as *Atriplex*. Sheep can graze it, at least for part of the year, he reasons, and it actually likes the salty soil. Besides, maybe he can sell the seed. "There are getting to be a lot of salinity problems in China and Thailand, so there will probably be a market for it there."

CHAPTER NINE

The Gift of the Indus

I F ANY ONE PLACE deserves to be called the birthplace of modern irrigation, that place is the Punjab, a sandy triangle of pancake-flat alluvium where India's British rulers built the first of their "canal colonies" in 1849. The first colony consisted of only a few thousand Sikh soldiers dispossessed by the British invaders. But today, half a century after India's four western provinces—including most of the Punjab—were transformed into what is now Pakistan, a hundred million people are coaxing sustenance out of the irrigated soils of the Indus basin.

No other nation has so many people who are so utterly dependent on artificial rain; four-fifths of Pakistan's food comes from the irrigated Indus plains. No other nation has more to lose if its farms are poisoned by the inevitable buildup of natural salts from irrigation, and no other nation is trying harder to avoid that fate. Heroic drainage projects are a tradition in Pakistan, and since the early 1950s, a dozen developed nations have sent planeloads of cash and advisers to lend a hand. But the technological fixes that work in places like California aren't working in the Punjab. The foreign experts know perfectly well how to do battle with the forces of nature, but in Pakistan, the enemy is more likely to be culture, politics, poverty, language, ignorance, or fear.

Pakistan is a Babel of a nation; its hundred million inhabitants speak at least two dozen languages, and the simplest of communications can be a nightmare. The two official languages are Urdu and English, but neither one is native. English is a relic of British occupation; for lack of a better alternative it still functions as the language of government, business, and academia. Urdu is an import from the pre-partition Muslim communities of north-central India; it seems to have been chosen as an "official" language mainly to avoid the outcry that would have resulted if one of the major indigenous languages—say, Punjabi or Pashto—had been favored over another.

Few of the country's peasants speak either of the "official" languages, so it was a surprise when another American and I heard a shouted "Hello! Hello" as we walked toward a Punjabi farmer outside a little mud-brick village near Jaranwala, southeast of Faisalabad in the central Punjab. The gregarious farmer was sitting under a tree; he had been taking turns with his brother plowing a half acre of brown-gray earth. As we approached he leapt to his feet and ran toward us, grinning broadly, his clothes flapping in the breeze.

"I am farmer; this is my land!" the sinewy peasant shouted, punctuating his speech with a proprietary sweep of his arm toward the tiny field. "I am farmer" wore the national costume of Pakistan, the *shalwar kameez*—a pair of light, baggy cotton trousers topped by a knee-length shirt. He had sandals on his feet. When he shook his visitors' hands, the calluses were thick and hard as tree bark.

One glance at the plow the brothers were using made clear the reason for the calluses. To call it a "plow" is to use the word recklessly; it was really just a few thick timbers lashed together and pulled by a pair of scrawny bullocks. Where that crude apparatus met the ground there was a heavy, pointed piece of steel—not a blade, but a point. That plow, the state of agricultural art in the rural Punjab, was not capable of turning over the earth like a conventional moldboard plow; it merely gouged it and broke it up.

Before sowing their seeds, the brothers would spend days following their team back and forth across the field, wrestling that medieval tool into the ground until either they or the underfed animals dropped from exhaustion. Then, after they had turned the ground into a minefield of clods the size of basketballs, they would hitch their beasts to a huge, flattened timber and start dragging it around to pulverize the clods. Only after several days of this brutal labor were the brothers ready to broadcast their wheat seeds and start irrigating.

The language barrier being what it was, it was impossible to say for certain what the personal circumstances of "I am farmer" might have been. But if he were typical of Pakistani farmers, he owned ten acres at most, and probably a lot less. Islamic laws of inheritance say that each son inherits an equal share of his father's estate, so Pakistan's farms tend to get chopped up into smaller and smaller portions with each generation. Three-quarters of Pakistan's hundred million people live in the countryside, and most of them are either small landholders or sharecroppers on one of about two dozen vast feudal estates controlled by the country's elite families. Much of the food these farmers produce feeds their own families, who live six or more to a room in forty-five thousand tiny villages scattered across the plains. Some crops go to market, especially sugarcane and basmati rice, but half the resulting income goes only for more food. A little extra cash is sent home by young Pakistani men who go to work for a few years in the cash-rich but labor-poor nations of the Middle East. They come home not just with cash but with luxuries like air conditioners and video cassette recorders, happily paying duties that amount to two or three times the purchase price simply to own appliances that are mostly unavailable in Pakistan. Often the cherished prizes sit in boxes for years, their owners waiting patiently for the day when the slow-moving government electrification program finally reaches their village.

It is jarring, to say the least, to see television aerials sprouting from the roofs of the mud-colored hovels of a rural Punjabi village.

But it is no less jarring to see the farmers of Pakistan working their fields with their Iron Age tools, because if nothing else their nation still has one of the most technologically advanced systems ever devised for delivering water to the land. It is as though America's interstate highways carried nothing more sophisticated than mule trains, except that in Pakistan nobody seems to think twice about the contrast.

When the British brought irrigation to the Punjab in the mid-nineteenth century, they built the world's first modern irrigation system on what had been a bleakly arid plain overrun by bandits. With a huge infusion of foreign aid after independence, Pakistan expanded the British system. Today the nation owns two of the largest earthen dams ever built—Tarbela and Mangla—and its canals and diversion weirs are technological marvels. But the system is far from perfect. For one thing, it is chronically short of water. Bountiful as it is, the Indus River system simply doesn't carry enough water to irrigate all of the land served by the system's canals, so it's not unusual for a farmer to find that his canal has run dry just as his crops have started to wilt in the 115-degree summer heat.

But to make matters worse, the system is also schizophrenic. Once the water reaches the *mogha*—the local term for a canal turnout that serves a cluster of small farms called a *chak*—the irrigation system changes abruptly from modern to primitive. The government steps aside, the farmers take over, and often they end up not underwatering but overwatering. They know that the canal may be dry the next time they need water, so when water is available, they give their crops far more water than is needed, even though the excess seeps downward past the roots and is lost to the water table. Most of the world's irrigated farmland is either underwatered or overwatered; Pakistan's unfortunate distinction is that it manages both at the same time.

The rudimentary tools the farmers use only aggravate the problem. As water leaves the *mogha,* the farmers steer it into a shallow, weedy, leaky hand-dug ditch called a watercourse, and 22 percent of the water, on average, immediately seeps into the ground. Then, the farmers irrigate their fields in the most wasteful manner of all; they simply let the water flood over the land until everything is soaked. Since they don't have real plows, they can't create furrows, and since they don't have any kind of grading equipment, they can't level their fields either. The high spots may be four or five inches higher than the low spots, so to make sure the high spots get enough water, the farmers must give the low spots far more water than they need.

Certainly, Pakistan isn't alone in practicing Iron Age agriculture, but it is one of the few countries in which such an ancient system of farming is served by such a modern system of water delivery. Pakistan's rivers have impressive gated weirs called barrages, automated concrete-and-steel structures a half mile in length, but Pakistan's farmers have nothing but old, beat-up spades and hoes. While the government engineers work on computers in air-conditioned offices, the peasants work their fields with bullocks or water buffalo and haul their produce to town on donkey carts. They are not ignorant, but they are by and large illiterate, and their own government speaks to them indifferently in a language that most of them cannot understand. They have too little water to start with, but for lack of better equipment and training, they waste much of what they have. Salt builds up in the soil where they are underwatering, and it builds up in the groundwater where they are overwatering until eventually the water table reaches the surface and brings the salt back up. So beneath the feet of the peasants, the fertile ground of the Indus basin is slowly becoming a desert once again.

If Egypt is the gift of the Nile, then Pakistan ought to be called the gift of the Indus. One of the largest rivers in the Muslim world, the Indus carries almost twice the water of the Nile, and three times as much as the Tigris and Euphrates combined. Like the others, the Indus was a cradle of ancient civilization. It gave its name to a race of people, the Hindu; their language, Hindi, and their subcontinent, India. It was enough of a river to persuade Alexander the Great to change course in 326 B.C. He had conquered the Middle East and kept on going, but when he came to the Indus, he was faced with the biggest river he had ever seen. Rather than cross, he gave up marching eastward and built a fleet to sail downstream to the Arabian Sea and back toward Persia.

The mountains this river drains, the Himalayas, are the highest on the planet, so it is fitting that the Indus has laid down one of the biggest alluvial plains in the world. Sediment more than a mile deep, washed out of the highlands by sixty million years of monsoons, now fills what geologists call the former Himalayan Sea. Today, the northern half of that vast alluvial plain is the Punjab— "Land of Five Rivers" in the language of the Persian conquerors who overran it late in the second millennium B.C. The western edge of the Punjab is delineated by the Indus, and five major tributaries—the Jhelum, the Chenab, the Ravi, the Beas, and the Sutlej—are draped across it to the east, like a hand with an extra finger, spread along the base of the Himalayas. The mother Indus originates deep in the Tibetan plateau, then sweeps west in a looping curve around the west end of the Himalayas before turning south to cross the Punjab. The five tributaries drain the southern face of the mountain range and gradually merge with each other as they cross the Punjab, until finally the last two, the Chenab and the Sutlej, join to empty into the Indus for the last leg of a 1790-mile journey to the Arabian Sea.

The plain that this web of rivers created is like a giant sponge of soil, almost perfectly flat, with a gradient of less than a foot per mile from the mountains to the sea. Lahore, the historical capital of the Punjab, lies roughly eight hundred miles inland and eight hundred feet above sea level. Water moves across the surface of this plain and through the soil at a pace that is downright glacial. Where man has built structures that interrupt the natural lines of drainage—roads, canals, levees—the water reluctantly pools up behind them, sometimes on the surface and sometimes underground. Farmers add to the problem by giving their crops more water than they can use. On top of everything else, even the major canals leak like sieves—40 percent of the system's water disappears upstream of the *moghas*. It's no surprise, then, that the Indus basin is not only the largest expanse of irrigated farmland in the world but is also widely considered to be the most endangered.

While the Nile has supported a huge irrigated civilization since antiquity, irrigation on the Indus is much more a modern phenomenon. There were ancient hydraulic civilizations centered on the Indus at Mohenjo-Daro and Harappa, but at most they watered a few narrow strips along the river and its tributaries. Only in 1849, when westward-moving British colonialists routed the Sikh armies and took control of the Punjab, did the Indus basin begin to assume its present form. The British spent a century turning the rivers of the Punjab out of their banks, and in the process they did more than just build canals; they established the first modern, mechanical irrigated civilization.

With so much water and so much dry yet arable land, it is safe to say that the Punjab eventually would have been irrigated by somebody, sometime. But the British? Of all the peoples of the world, the British might have been the least likely to develop an interest in irrigation. They had scarcely heard of it at home; it certainly wasn't practiced in Scotland or Wales, and though a few British generals had seen irrigation in Egypt, what was happening there was suited only to a river basin that had a regular, reliable flood—an attribute unique to the Nile. But the British had a compelling motive in those restless Sikhs; to keep them from taking up arms again, they decided to turn them into farmers, which meant creating farms in a province where, except along the rivers, there was little but dry brush. A century later, U.S. reclamationists would adopt the cause of soldier settlement to justify their dam-building projects not once but twice, after each of the world wars.

They might have been only slightly aware that they were following a tradition started in the mid–nineteenth century by nervous British colonialists.

Farming must have seemed like a natural outlet for all that Sikh military energy, but farming in the Punjab figured to be a losing proposition unless a way could be devised to bring water to the land in quantities that were virtually without precedent in human history. But the British had one advantage: they had the best civil engineers in the world. Their engineers had spent the early decades of the nineteenth century lacing their home islands with railways and barge canals, and they were eager to have a go at this exciting new project in a distant colony. Still, without a model to follow— without any real idea of how difficult a job they were tackling— they were bound to fail.

The first canal they built was on the Ravi, and it was a disaster. First the headworks silted up and got clogged with timber during the flood season. Then during the dry season, the river level dropped until it was lower than the intake for the canal, and the canal ran dry. It turned out the British engineers had been in such a hurry to get started that they badly overestimated the Ravi's minimum flows. To make matters worse, they built the canal with a drop of four feet per mile, which turned out to be far too steep. The water ran so fast that it scoured out big holes in the canal's bed and banks. The canal was originally supposed to run 247 miles, but when the British finally gave up on it, they were still a hundred miles short of the goal.

The second canal was built on the Sutlej. Determined not to repeat their mistake from the Ravi, the British went careening to the other extreme and built their new canal with a slope that was two-thirds less. The water consequently moved so slowly that it dropped most of its silt in the canal, steadily clogging it up. And so went the irrigation program for more than four decades. The engineers built their canals, turned the water into them, and then waited to see what would go wrong. They patched them up as well as they could and went on to the next project. By the end of the nineteenth century, the British had built seven major canal systems in the Punjab and had jerry-rigged all of them until they worked in spite of horribly flawed designs. But the British also learned from their mistakes. By trial and error, they eventually developed a formula, based on the depth and width of a canal and the type of earth in its bed, which told them exactly the right gradient to use so that their canals would neither silt up nor scour. With minor refinements, that formula is still in use today, and probably more than anything else, that tidy little snippet of civil engineering is what gave birth to the modern age of irrigation.

At the same time, though, almost from the instant they started turning the Punjab's rivers out of their beds, the British noticed that the land was becoming waterlogged. One traditional trouble spot was in the Rechna Doab east of Faisalabad, where "I am farmer" and his brother were cultivating their wheat. (Doab is the term for the flat land between two rivers; Rechna is a contraction of the names of the rivers that bound that doab, the Ravi and the Chenab.) A few years ago, much of the land in that area was not even farmable. It was full of salt, left there when moisture evaporated from the soggy ground, only to be replaced by more moisture drawn upward by capillary action from the shallow water table. Even though the local groundwater is classified as fresh, or "sweet," it still contains enough natural salts to sterilize the soil after just a few years of this relentless cycle of wetting and drying. Many of the farmers in the area had tried in vain to solve the problem by scraping up the top few inches of the soil, piling it up in long, narrow mounds called bunds, and thereby exposing the slightly less salty soil below. It worked for a few seasons, after which the soil just salted up again.

The government finally called for outside help, and it came in the form of money and technical aid for a network of buried, perforated pipelines, or "tiles," to drain off excess groundwater and lower the water table. While the brothers worked their field, a short distance away dozens of Pakistani laborers were scurrying around a huge Dutch tile-laying machine, which in one smooth operation dug a trench for the pipeline, installed the line in a bed of gravel, and then filled in the trench, moving at a rate of ninety feet per minute. The perforated lines, about eight inches in diameter and made of blue corrugated polyvinyl chloride, joined each other at a brick-lined sump about twenty feet deep. Eventually, a pump would be installed to lift the salty subsurface drainage water out of the sump and eject it into a surface ditch emptying into the Ravi. The idea was to remove enough water from the ground to lower the water table, stop the salt from rising to the surface, and let the farmers try to revive their salted-out fields. The brothers' field had been given the treatment just two months earlier.

The $230 million project was funded by the World Bank, designed by the Bureau of Reclamation, and supervised by a U.S. contractor, and it relied on Dutch machinery. A thoroughly international effort, but not without its detractors. Willem F. Vlotman, a Dutch scientist working for the national Water and Power Development Authority (WAPDA) in Lahore, raised a fuss when he predicted that the drainage lines would dry out the subsoil so much that they might increase the salting problem by causing, in effect, under-irrigation. The Bureau of Reclamation's resident expert responded by saying that Vlotman didn't know what he was talking about. Other critics pointed out that dumping salty drainage water into the Indus system was bound to create problems for downstream irrigators, who were taking water out of the river to grow their own crops. But if this infusion of capital and technology ultimately ended up causing more problems than it corrected, it wouldn't be the first time that had happened.

Starting in the late 1950s, Pakistan took the Western world's advice and spent $650 million to drill more than twelve thousand deep wells—called tubewells to distinguish them from open, hand-dug wells—and fit them with pumps to draw down the

water table and reuse the groundwater for irrigation. Today, only
a few of the original wells are working; the rest are clogged or broken or pumping water that is too salty to use. Even when they
work, the wells are pumped for only a couple of hours per day
because of the high cost of electricity or diesel fuel. Still, in some
areas, the wells actually led to a higher water table by encouraging
over-irrigation. It wasn't difficult to figure out why: water-starved
farmers figured out how to turn on the pumps themselves, or
bribed the attendants to get the wells turned on whenever they
wanted.

Meanwhile, Pakistan's problems—as opposed to mere symp-
toms such as the high water tables—are still largely unaddressed.
Its farmers are a disorganized lot. They have no way of sharing the
limited amount of water they've been given; while some of them
watch their fields turn to salt dust for lack of water, others still
flood their fields, watering as much as they can whenever water is
available from whatever source. And for reasons having a lot to do
with the British colonial legacy, the nation still has no effective way
of teaching them to do otherwise.

The British didn't exactly withdraw from India in 1947 so much
as they ran for their lives, abandoning their once treasured colony
almost a year ahead of their own schedule. Friction between the
Hindu majority and the Muslim minority over whether the independent India would be one nation or two—one Hindu and one
Muslim—was beginning to degenerate into rioting. After resisting
the idea at first, Gandhi reconciled himself to a partitioned India,
perhaps recognizing that a united and independent India would
explode into civil war and the nation would split apart anyway, and
probably into four or five pieces instead of two. So with their colony crumbling around them—and knowing that they needed to
devote their energy to rebuilding their war-wrecked homeland
anyway—the British hastily divided India into two nations: an independent, Hindu-dominated India in the center and an indepen-

dent, Muslim Pakistan on either end. Like most simple solutions, this one concealed a reality that was devilishly complex. To start with, Muslims were scattered throughout India, not just in the parts that were to become Pakistan; and Hindus and Sikhs—the latter a religious minority consigned to India—lived in parts of Pakistan, especially in the Punjab. Members of each group had to fight their way through murderous mobs of the others to get to their new homelands; half a million people were slaughtered amid cries of "Death to Muslims" and "Death to Hindus." The tensions have never eased completely; India and Pakistan have fought three wars since independence, two over the disputed northern state of Kashmir, and one over East Pakistan, which metamorphosed with the Indian army's help into Bangladesh in 1972.

Dividing the Punjab posed the thorniest problem of all for the British administration because Hindus, Sikhs, and Muslims lived there in roughly equal proportions. Both of the new nations coveted the Punjab's farmland and its irrigation network, which had made the state the breadbasket of British India. In their haste to get out, though, the British drew an essentially arbitrary line that assigned the eastern end of the Punjab to India and the rest to Pakistan. India got Amritsar, the Sikh holy city; Pakistan got Lahore, the Punjab's traditional capital. The Punjab irrigation network, which had been built as a unified system, suddenly was split between two none-too-friendly nations. There were canals, for example, which began in India and ended in Pakistan; and the headwaters of the three easternmost rivers—the Ravi, the Beas, and the Sutlej—were indisputably in Indian territory. Recognizing the perils of such an arrangement, the British pressed the leaders of the new nations to agree to continue to operate the system as one until March 31, 1948, about seven and a half months after partition. On the morning of April 1, India shut off the canals that ran from its territory into Pakistan.

It took twelve years and the intervention of the World Bank to resolve the resulting dispute, and the resolution was mostly on India's terms. The Indus Waters Treaty of 1960 gave India the entire flows of the three eastern rivers in perpetuity; if it wanted to, India could dry them up altogether, which it promptly did. Pakistan got the flows of the Indus, Jhelum, and Chenab, none of which India could really put to use anyway, at least not as long as Kashmir remained in dispute. Probably the only reason Pakistan went along with the deal was what amounted to an $895 million bribe from the World Bank. The money was used to build two large storage reservoirs—Mangla on the Jhelum and Tarbela on the Indus—and a series of eight new "link" canals to divert water from the three western rivers into the three bled dry by India.

Foreign aid quickly became an ever-present feature of Pakistan's irrigation system; the next thing it brought was tubewells. The British had come up with the idea of using tubewells to ease the waterlogging problem in the Punjab as early as 1911, but the wells they drilled were too few and too scattered to have any real effect on the water table. After independence, Pakistan asked the United Nations' Food and Agriculture Organization for help with the perennial waterlogging problems in Rechna Doab, and the FAO experts set up a series of modest tubewell projects. Then in the late 1950s, West Pakistan set up WAPDA, which immediately set to work on what it called Salinity Control and Reclamation Project No. 1, or SCARP I. Over the next few years WAPDA crews drilled two thousand tubewells reaching more than three hundred feet deep in the most waterlogged parts of Rechna Doab.

It was a start, but the Pakistanis must have wanted the foreign experts to reassure them that they were on the right track, because in 1961, President Mohammad Ayub Kahn visited Washington and asked President Kennedy for help. Kennedy, whose staff had already been discussing the problem informally with some Pakistani officials, promptly named a commission with a University of California oceanographer, Roger Revelle, as its chairman. Revelle was science adviser to Stewart Udall, Kennedy's Interior secretary, and though he took the assignment intending to work on Pakistan's waterlogging problem, he quickly steered the panel toward a much broader mission.

"Actually, I thought the problem of waterlogging and salinity was a nonproblem," Revelle said in an interview almost thirty years later. "The real problem was poor agricultural technology. They weren't using enough water, among other things." Simple arithmetic told Revelle all he felt he needed to know about Pakistan's water use: divide the amount of land Pakistan was irrigating (twenty-three million acres at that time) into the amount of water it could divert from the Indus rivers in a year (about forty million acre-feet) and the result was an average of less than two feet of water spread across the land, about half of what a crop typically needs in that climate. Though it was true that some of Pakistan's land was waterlogged, the waterlogged land represented only about 18 percent of the nation's farmland, and the amount of waterlogged land was increasing by less than 1 percent a year. In the long run, Revelle reasoned, Pakistan would be better off letting that land stay waterlogged and concentrating its energy on bringing more water to its remaining good farmland. And what better way to do that, Revelle concluded, than by drilling more tubewells and using the pumped water to supplement the canal water?

With that, Pakistan started four new SCARP programs and began drilling tubewells everywhere, a total of twelve thousand of them in the next twenty years. Everywhere the wells were built, farmers put the extra water to use, either by farming more land or watering their existing land more heavily. They also increased their use of fertilizers and pesticides, as Revelle suggested—part of his plan to upgrade Pakistan's agricultural technology—and they planted new, more productive strains of wheat. Yields shot up as a result, but the boom was temporary. In the decades that followed, the tubewells clogged; their capacity dropped until they were pumping no more than a trickle; their motors broke and stood idle for long periods until crews and parts could reach the field to fix them; and even when they were running, the cost of electricity to run them was eating into the nation's treasury, especially after the oil shortages of the 1970s doubled and tripled the price of power. Worst of all, many of the wells started to pump water that was too salty to use for irrigation: the wells had been drilled too deep, and when pumped too heavily had begun to tap a deep pool of old seawater that had been trapped when the basin first filled with sediment.

By 1988, Pakistan's National Commission on Agriculture was forced to admit that the "SCARPs have not met with much success." It discretely blamed the Revelle committee, saying that the SCARP program's "initial purpose of saline water reduction was negated over time by its subversion into a program for sweet groundwater recovery." Pakistan had asked for help with its waterlogging problem; what it got was a lecture on its failure to farm the way Americans do. It had followed most of the experts' advice and yields had risen, but not as fast as in other Third World nations where the new Green Revolution seeds were put in use about the same time—even next door, in the Indian Punjab, much to Pakistan's embarrassment.

Now, almost thirty years later, Pakistan has a generation of farmers who are accustomed to having not one but two sources of water—the canals and the tubewells. Once the SCARP wells went into operation, it didn't take long for the farmers—at least the prosperous ones—to catch onto the idea of supplementing their unreliable canal water with tubewell water; in fact, they liked the idea so much that they started scraping together the money to put in little tubewells of their own. By 1987, there were a quarter million privately owned tubewells in Pakistan, and though the capacity of each was far less than the typical SCARP well, there were so many of them that they produced three times as much water as all the SCARP wells combined. Farmers drilled wells, used part of the water on their own crops, and sold the rest to their neighbors. Entrepreneurs even got into the act, drilling wells and selling the water to nearby farmers for whatever price they could get. With access to a tubewell, a farmer no longer had to worry about his crop withering in the sun; if the canal ran dry he could simply turn on the pump and water away. Some experts began to worry that chronic overwatering was forcing the basin's water tables to rise even higher. Others saw a more ominous portent in data that showed the average private tubewell was pumping saltier water than the SCARP wells had; that, they suggested, meant the private wells were simply recirculating shallow groundwater and concentrating the soil's salt content through evaporation.

But the irony of the tubewells is that even if they had been rousing technical successes, Pakistan would still be in serious trouble. After thirty years of effort, neither the public nor the private tubewell programs have done anything to solve the underlying cause of Pakistan's drainage woes—the primitive technology its farmers were using to manipulate water. While crews were drilling tubewells, building dams, dredging link canals, and installing drainage lines, the nation's farmers continued to push their water around with shovels, just as their ancestors had in the mid-nineteenth century, and just as farmers elsewhere have for seven thousand years. Their inefficiency is mind-boggling; the 1988 commission on agriculture estimated that when all the water lost to seepage was added up—the water lost from the storage reservoirs, from the government canals, from the local watercourses, and from the farmers' fields—Pakistan was losing 60 percent of the water it was diverting from the Indus rivers. For ever five gallons the country takes out of the river, in other words, only two go into producing a crop, and three go into the ground.

The conceit of engineering is that no job is impossible. Want to go to the moon? Just build a rocket powerful enough to escape the earth's gravity. Got a leaky canal? Line it with concrete. Water table too high? Drill a bunch of wells and pump it right down. But as skilled as engineers are at bending nature to their will, they have never learned how to perform the same trick on humans. Politics vex engineers; social problems mystify them. Building a drainage system is a straightforward task, but teaching illiterate farmers how to manage their water better is a task beset by confusion, argument, and unpredictability. Forty years of imported Western capital and technology have left Pakistan with much the same mess it began with, but as long as the Pakistanis were satisfied with what they were receiving, the Western banks and governments that were supplying them were not about to stop. It was far easier to send money and experts, obviously, than to retrain tens of millions of peasant farmers in the techniques of modern agriculture.

"The physical side has tended to get an increasing amount of emphasis because it's easier to do," said Edward Vander Velde, a geographer with the International Irrigation Management Institute in Lahore, a branch of the Consultative Group on International Agricultural Research, the brain stem of the Green Revolution. Structures like canals and tubewells are visible signs of achievement, Vander Velde said; a foreign aid officer can point to them and say, "We built this." Imagine the same officer taking political leaders to a meeting of Pakistani farmers who are trying to form a water users association: "They hear a discussion," Vander Velde said, "which they can't understand anyway because it's not in the language they speak. It sounds like an argument. Voices are raised; people pound the table. And you say, 'Well, we're building an institution here.' Not too many congressmen or members of parliament are going to be impressed with that; it sounds too much like Congress." But in the final accounting, the easy physical fixes have failed, and on such a scale as to finally occasion a reappraisal.

Pakistan inherited more from the British than just a common language and the custom of driving on the left. It also inherited a style of government and an attitude about the proper relationship between a government and its subjects—distant. When the British took over an Indian city, they built cantonments for their families so they wouldn't be obliged to mingle with the masses, and they ran their colonies the same way, in a detached, military style. If they wanted something done, they issued orders to their armies of native civil servants, whose loyalty was beyond question because their livelihood depended utterly on British largesse. In that sense, at least, nothing much has changed since partition. The English faces have been replaced by Muslim ones, but the imperial style remains intact. The average Punjabi farmer has about as much chance of impressing his views on the provincial assembly as he has of obtaining an audience with the pope.

"The farmer really has very little to say in our system. He's at the mercy of the people who run the system," said Mohammad Badruddin, who was chief of the section of WAPDA that oversees the SCARP wells until he went to work as senior principal irrigation engineer for the International Irrigation Management Institute in Lahore. In Badruddin's opinion, the fact that Pakistan's farmers are so divorced from their government explains a lot about the trouble Pakistan is having with its irrigation system. From the giant storage reservoirs far upstream on the Indus and Jhelum to the comparative trickles that ripple through the *moghas* and into the watercourses, Pakistani irrigation is a government operation all the way—top-heavy, centralized, bureaucratic in the extreme, and utterly unresponsive to the wishes of the peasants whose interests it is supposed to be serving. Irrigation farmers in the United States are organized into districts, which either own the water outright or sign contracts for government water and then arrange for its distribution; at their best—admittedly an infrequent state of affairs—the districts are simultaneously effective lobbyists for the farmers and effective policemen for the government. No such beast exists in Pakistan; in fact, until 1979, even the mere act of organizing an association of water users was illegal. By all accounts, the government was terrified of what would happen if the downtrodden peasants, who represent 70 percent of Pakistan's population, ever found a political voice, so it did its best to stifle them.

Still, the government's monopoly on power might not have been so bad if it had been complete. Pakistan's bureaucrats saw their job as limited to developing water and delivering it, and once they had moved the water to the *mogha*, they walked away from it. "The irrigation department has no responsibility as to what happens to the water, or what relationship it has to crop needs," Badruddin said. Meanwhile, the agriculture department, the only other government agency that most farmers ever deal with, never considered irrigation to be any of its business—after all, there was an irrigation department for that. To this day, students in Pakistan's agricultural colleges don't study irrigation, Badruddin said; that's a subject for engineering students.

In the resulting vacuum of leadership, many farmers make up their own rules. And when the government noticed that farmers were scraping together the money to drill tubewells of their own, it began to realize that it had been underestimating them. If the farmers of the Punjab were capable of organizing themselves to drill a tubewell—no simple task—then what else might they be able to accomplish? Perhaps the way to solve the twinned problems of waterlogging and salinity was not to improve the physical structures in isolation, but to improve the farmers, to help them modernize their farming practices and move from the Iron Age into the twentieth century.

Mohammad Munir Chaudry oversees a section of WAPDA that runs a pair of agricultural research stations where the government, for the first time in memory, is working directly with farmers to change the way they put water on their land. Groups of farmers are being organized to rebuild their own watercourses—filling in the old buffalo wallows and other wide spots that allow water to seep into the ground. Munir said that twelve thousand watercourses have already been rebuilt, leaving seventy-eight thousand to go. Farmers provide the labor; the government provides the materials; and once the work is finished, the government hopes that the farmers will catch on and start maintaining the watercourses themselves, just as they have built and maintained their own tubewells. "We did not particularly involve the farmer in the past," Munir said. "But now we feel this is the only way. We want to convey a sense of participation, a sense of ownership to the farmers. Once they invest in the reconstruction of the watercourses, they will maintain them better because they think they are the owners."

Even more ambitious are the government's efforts to build from scratch something that resembles a U.S.–style agricultural extension service. American farmers have long availed themselves of a far-flung system of university extension offices whose agents visit farmers in their fields, advising them on practices such as irrigation, chemical use, seed varieties, and equipment. In the United States, that sort of support is taken for granted, but in Pakistan it is practically unheard of. Only the barest bones of an extension service exist. Cost is one reason; another is a chronic shortage of qualified agents, attributable in part to a grossly inadequate university system. There is also the problem of language: to function in rural Pakistan, an extension agent would have to know at least three languages—the Urdu of his government, the English of the scientific literature, and whatever indigenous language is spoken by the local farmers. The government has vowed to overcome these obstacles, but it is not easy to imagine how that will be accomplished in a nation whose literacy rate is around 20 percent—and falling—and whose per capita annual income has stagnated at the equivalent of three hundred dollars. The 1988 commission on agriculture suggested putting the extension service on videotape, since practically every village with electricity has a video cassette player and a television; they function as illegal alternative theaters for the entertainment-starved masses. Though this suggestion may seem a poor substitute for a live extension agent, it may be all that Pakistan can afford for now.

There may not be much time left. At partition in 1947, what is now Pakistan contained some thirty million people; forty years later, the population had passed a hundred million and was growing at an annual clip of 3 percent, one of the world's fastest rates of increase. It's still a well-fed nation, thanks to the adoption of the higher-yielding wheat seeds of the Green Revolution, the development of new water supplies from the big dams and the tube-wells, and the forced jettisoning in 1972 of Bangladesh, a net importer of food. The serendipitous streak may continue, but either way a Malthusian day of reckoning looms unless Pakistan can find a way to keep its thirty-five million acres of irrigated land, which produce 80 percent of its food, productive indefinitely. Nature may never have intended for a hundred million people to live in the arid Indus basin, and unless they learn to husband the land instead of just farming it, nature may eventually drive them out.

CHAPTER TEN

Science Searches for Answers

FOR THE DESERT FARMING empires that now account for one-third of the world's agricultural production, there are two alternative futures. One version is bleak: farmers keep using big floods of water to flush salts from their fields, as most do now, but in time run out of places to dump the saline effluent. Salt and water then build up underground until crops are either drowned or poisoned, and today's desert bloom quickly withers. The other future is brighter: farmers learn to irrigate gingerly, using only enough water to keep the soil's salinity tolerable. Perhaps they capture the resulting trickle of saline drainage and reduce its volume further by reusing it to irrigate salt-tolerant crops. Then they dispose of what's left, concentrated by then into a much more easily managed fraction of the drainage they were producing before, thus keeping salinity problems at bay for decades, if not centuries.

Which of these paths the future of desert farming will follow is still uncertain. But if the future turns out to be bright, then historians may find significance in what happened in a cluster of Moorish-style buildings at the foot of Mount Rubidoux in Riverside, California, in the late 1960s and early 1970s. There, in a cerebral ferment that seems out of place in the humdrum world of irrigation, a small group of soil and plant scientists and engineers in the Department of Agriculture's U.S. Salinity Laboratory came up with a new vision of the future. First they studied the interplay of plants, soils, salt, and water and evaluated new technologies such as drip irrigation. Then they showed how farmers could save water and ease their drainage problems by striking a balance between using too much water—the traditional approach to desert agriculture—and using too little. Their techniques have the potential to revolutionize the way we grow food in arid lands. They could enable farmers to grow more and better food with less water and fewer chemicals, while spending less money and creating far smaller amounts of environmentally damaging drainage. But before that can happen, science will also have to overcome the fears of tradition-bound desert farmers—fears based on some lingering superstitions about salt.

"Salt balance" is a time-honored precept of irrigation that says, in essence, that what goes in must eventually come out: all of the dissolved salts that farmers unavoidably put on fields when they irrigate—salts that hitchhike in even the purest water supplies—must be carried away sooner or later in drainage water. For most of the twentieth century, the notion that long-term irrigation is impossible without salt balance has been an article of faith in desert agriculture. In the name of salt balance, entire rivers like the San Joaquin, the Colorado, and the Rio Grande have been polluted with the saline drainage of desert farms. Generations of farmers were afraid that if they didn't use plenty of excess water to rinse away all the salts they were importing, then their fields would be poisoned by the buildup. There was only one problem with salt balance: it was utterly unnecessary.

For most of its half century of existence, the U.S. Salinity Laboratory, housed on a parklike campus on a back street in a 1920s Riverside neighborhood, has stood in the front row of the salt balance choir. In 1954, the laboratory digested the results of its first decade and a half of research and produced a definitive text on

managing irrigation in arid regions, titled "Diagnosis and Improvement of Saline and Alkali Soils" and known in USDA shorthand as
Handbook 60, in which salt balance was the one true gospel. In
Handbook 60, a dozen of the lab's most senior and credentialed
scientists—including Charles Bower, a leading authority on soil
chemistry, and Leon Bernstein, the world's foremost expert on the
salt tolerance of plants—held forth on matters of soil, salt, water,
plants, and all of their interactions. The book's centerpiece was its
discussion of the leaching fraction, which it defined as the portion
of the irrigation water that must be trickled through the root zone
to keep soil salinity from rising above a given level. Handbook 60
boiled down the many complexities of the leaching fraction to a
simple yet elegant formula—the ratio of the salinity of the irrigation water to the maximum salinity that could be tolerated by the
crop without a yield loss. Reduce leaching fractions to less than
that, the handbook said, and salt balance would be lost. The effects
might not be noticeable at first, but over time crop yields would
decline and the soil would be rendered unproductive.

Handbook 60 became an instant classic. Its formulas and classification schemes were transplanted directly into agronomy text-
books; to this day, agriculture students sit in lecture halls and listen
to their professors recite its terse, cadenced prose, only slightly altered to disguise its true authorship. Among its virtues was its
brevity. In only 160 pages, Handbook 60 reduced the complexities
of soil and water chemistry in arid regions to a mere handful of
fundamental principles and algebraic equations. In the world of
Handbook 60, there were three types of saline or alkali soils: those
with salt, those with sodium, and those with both. There were two
factors affecting the usability of water—the salt content and the
proportion of sodium to other cations—and four classifications for
each, from low hazard to very high hazard. Seven principles
guided management of arid-region soils for salinity and alkalinity;
five categories spoke to the salt tolerance of plants.

So simple and sturdy was Handbook 60 that it was widely regarded as the final word on the subject of salinity, and for a while the salinity laboratory's work appeared to have reached its logical conclusion. "I can remember Bob Ayers, who was the extension man for salinity at the University of California in Davis, telling me that at that time he thought that salinity issues were just about dead, that there was nothing new coming out of salinity," said Glenn Hoffman, an engineer who worked at the salinity laboratory as a water management specialist from 1966 to 1984. Some knew better, including scientists whose work formed the foundation for Handbook 60. "What Handbook 60 did, for one thing, was identify some knowledge gaps that needed to be filled by new fundamental research," said Steve Rawlins, a soil physicist who joined the lab in 1964. "During the lab's initial couple of decades, prior to the publication of Handbook 60, there was a lot of argument and a lot of interaction and some real effort to integrate concepts of salinity into principles that could be applied. Then, after Handbook 60, I think that was lost a little bit. There was a frustration that they couldn't go any further because they didn't have some fundamental response functions" for things like the salt tolerance of plants and their reaction to being irrigated with waters of varying salinity in varying soil types. "There was a period of backfilling there, in the late 1950s and early 1960s, filling some of the holes that had been identified with Handbook 60," Rawlins said.

During that period, Bower, Bernstein, and the lab's other scientists went back to the lab bench. Bernstein ran hundreds of tests to determine salt-tolerance curves for all types of crops, from strawberries and beans to cotton, corn, and alfalfa. Other scientists studied the details of soil chemistry—the interplay of ions of such elements as sodium, calcium, and magnesium in solutions of soil and water. Still others looked at physical questions: How does water move through the soil after irrigation? How much of it fills the pores of the root zone and how much migrates downward past the roots to the water table? As the 1960s progressed, the older scientists were joined by younger ones eager to make names for themselves—bright, ambitious men with fresh doctorates from some of the nation's best agricultural schools: California, Purdue, North Carolina State. Rawlins arrived in 1964 with a degree in soil physics from Washington State and four years of experience at an agricultural experiment station in Connecticut. Jim Rhoades, a chemist, came the following summer, while he was finishing his doctorate at the University of California at Riverside. Another physicist, Jim Oster, came that same year with a doctorate from Purdue. Hoffman, from North Carolina State, arrived in the fall of 1966.

Of all the lab's projects during that time, Bernstein's plant work appeared to be making the most progress. Bernstein's basic mission was to reexamine the theoretical underpinnings of the most important Handbook 60 concept, the leaching fraction. It was no secret in arid regions that some kind of leaching fraction was necessary; without the cleansing rains that are typical of humid climates, the only way to flush excess salt from the soil was to apply extra water. But Handbook 60's simple formula for calculating the leaching fraction was based on experiments that Bernstein regarded as suspect. The problem lay in the way the experiments had been designed. To gauge the tolerance of plants to saline water around their roots, previous researchers had given their plants lots of water, enough to ensure that there would be no change in the salinity of water from the soil surface to the very bottom of the root zone. Each root would then be exposed to "soil-pore water" of the same salinity, no matter whether it lay near the soil surface or far below it. This approach made experiments simple to design and easy to reproduce, but it required heavy, steady irrigation, enough to maintain a constant downward flux of water through several inches or even feet of soil.

With help from agronomist Lee Francois, Bernstein tried to determine how plants would respond if their water rations were cut to less than what was needed to keep soil salinities constant. Working in a greenhouse, he used a series of devices called lysimeters to carefully control and monitor how much water each of his alfalfa test plants was given. The lysimeters—concrete pipes sixty inches long and twenty-four inches in diameter, standing on end—each held a single plant or a cluster of plants. They had collectors at the bottom for drainage water and sampling points every twelve inches along their walls, so that soil water salinities could be tested at various points in the root zone. The scientists fine-tuned their water applications until they were running a different, carefully calibrated leaching fraction in each lysimeter. In one group of lysimeters, leaching fractions were 25 percent, roughly what farmers outside the lab were using. Other lysimeters had lower leaching fractions—12.5 percent in one group, 6.2 percent in another, and 3.1 percent in a third.

According to the thinking that prevailed when Handbook 60 was written, the plants irrigated with the lower leaching fractions should have been sickly. But very quickly Bernstein found that he could cut the leaching fraction dramatically without seeing any yield reduction at all, especially with waters of low salinity. At the same time, some interesting things happened to the salinity of the soil-pore water as the leaching fraction was reduced. Instead of there being a constant level of salinity from the top to the bottom of the root zone, a gradient developed with less saline water at the top and higher salinity at the bottom. Moreover, Bernstein's plants adjusted to the salinity changes by altering how they took water from the soil. Instead of taking relatively equal amounts of water from each depth in the root zone, the plants began to show a preference for the low-salinity water at the top. Their roots absorbed large amounts of water in the first few inches of the soil and progressively less in the lower, saltier regions. In effect, as the water trickled downward, the plants concentrated the water and its salts into a smaller and smaller volume. This finding was tremendously significant. Whereas plants watered in the traditional way unleashed great floods of water at the bottoms of their root zones, Bernstein's stingily watered plants released similar amounts of salt in much smaller volumes of water. The plants, in essence, were wringing all of the utility they could from the irrigation water before letting it go. And then, instead of a torrent of hard-to-manage drainage, they released a tiny trickle.

While Bernstein studied his lysimeters, over in soil chemistry, Bower and his young assistant, Jim Rhoades, were coming up with similarly provocative results. Bernstein's findings, for all their importance, did not represent a direct indictment of salt balance. For the most part, the conventional wisdom remained intact: every molecule of salt that came in with the irrigation water would have to leave with the drainage, albeit in more concentrated form. But the soil chemistry group was onto something altogether different. Setting up their own rows of lysimeters, Rhoades and three collaborators sowed alfalfa and irrigated it with waters of eight different salt and mineral compositions, chosen to represent a cross section of irrigation waters from the western United States. For each type of water, they set up three experiments, one using a high leaching fraction, one moderate, and one low. In all, there were twenty-four experiments.

They found, as Bernstein did, that there was no obvious yield reduction at the lower leaching fractions. But they also did calculations to determine how much salt was entering the lysimeters with each irrigation and leaving in the resulting drainage, and they found, oddly enough, that less salt was leaving than had entered. Rhoades and the others surmised that some of the salts—mainly calcium-based salts—were precipitating in the subsoil as carbonate and gypsum minerals. These minerals were largely innocuous; unlike the more dangerous sodium ions, which can bind tightly with clay particles and turn soil into a tightly packed powder that repels water, the calcium and magnesium ions were harmless unless dissolved in water. And reducing leaching fractions had another beneficial effect—it slowed the natural "weathering" or breakdown of soil particles into simpler particles, many of which were salts. The implication of those two findings was simple: salt balance wasn't just unnecessary, it was harmful because it wasted water and led farmers to flush benign salts out of the soil, where they weren't hurting anything, and into the nearest river, where they could cause all kinds of problems.

While all of this was going on, the soil physics group led by Rawlins was focusing on the mechanics of irrigation—trying to find a way to moisten a patch of soil as uniformly as possible and with as little wasted water as possible. Traditional irrigation systems, little changed since their development in ancient Egypt and Sumeria, relied on gravity to move water around and get it into the soil. Rawlins was convinced that modern irrigation systems, such as sprinklers or drip irrigation, could be far more efficient. The new systems had one thing in common: they were pressurized. Instead of conveying water across the field by gravity, they used pipelines, which meant that farmers no longer needed to put extra water on the near ends of their fields to make sure enough water reached the far ends. Nor did they need to continue to apply their water all at once; instead, they could apply it slowly (or, in the case of drip irrigation, continuously), filling the soil gradually and stopping before water began trickling past the bottom of the root zone. Using pressurized systems, in short, allowed farmers to simulate in the field the conditions Bernstein created in the lab with his lysimeters—a gradient of steadily increasing salinity from the top to the bottom of the root zone.

Each cluster of scientists at the salinity lab during that time was discovering things that defied the conventional wisdom about how to irrigate a desert soil. Bernstein was demonstrating that crops would tolerate higher salinity than had been supposed; Bower and Rhoades were showing that some salts could be parked in the soil indefinitely, instead of being drained away; and Rawlins's group was proving that pressurized irrigation systems could drastically reduce wasted water. But for a long time these tantalizing pieces remained just that, pieces, and no one knew what the puzzle was supposed to look like.

One reason was the lab's peculiar culture. Under Bower, who was the lab's director throughout the 1960s, the freewheeling debates that had accompanied the development of Handbook 60 were set aside in the interest of producing publishable research. Partly, Rawlins said, this shift was attributable to Bower's personality: "His concept of doing research was, 'You run some experiments, you get some data points, you draw a line through them and you publish it.'" But Bower also seemed threatened by the younger scientists and their powerful egos. He clashed with Rawlins over an expense voucher and held the grudge for months; he fell out with another young scientist—a man who had been his protégé—when he learned that the younger man was talking to recruiters from a university agriculture department. And he grew weary of mediating intramural fights among the young scientists. Rhoades and Rawlins were barely speaking; though the disagreements were mostly scientific—Rhoades liked to base his work strictly on the results of his experiments, while Rawlins preferred to formulate sweeping theories that could be applied more widely —they were nonetheless intense. Even the more mild-mannered scientists, like Hoffman and Oster, saw themselves as rivals for funding and recognition. Bower did little to soothe these matters and retired in 1971, soon after he became eligible.

It took more than a year for the Department of Agriculture to name his replacement, and when the selection was finally made, the choice was a surprise: Jan van Schilfgaarde, a respected drainage engineer and assistant director of the soil and water division of the department's Agricultural Research Service. Until then, van Schilfgaarde had been Bower's boss, overseeing the salinity lab and several other ARS stations. But in Washington he had just led an unsuccessful middle-management revolt against a proposed agency reorganization plan, and in retaliation had been demoted and sent to Riverside, "because that was small enough that I couldn't do any damage."

His career up to that point had been exemplary. Born in the Netherlands, he came to the United States in the late 1940s and got three agricultural engineering degrees—bachelor's, master's, doctorate—from Iowa State University. He moved to North Carolina State University as a professor of agricultural engineering, then joined ARS in 1962. "He was in research for only about ten years, but he was editor of the Agronomy Society's monograph on drainage, which is a world's authority book," Hoffman said. "He had already gained the respect of everybody in the world in terms of his drainage authority." In Washington, his job had been to do the agency's dirty work; when there was a need to fire someone, he broke the news. From that experience, he learned to be simultaneously diplomatic and firm. He was also eloquent in a way that seems to come only to those who have mastered English as a second language. He had a rare ability to understand and synthesize raw research results and to sense the common threads that could be melded into new practical knowledge. And having been bounced out of the nation's agricultural research hierarchy in mid-career, he had something to prove.

Van Schilfgaarde was already familiar with the puzzle pieces of the salinity lab's recent work because he had supervised it from one step removed, but he could afford to take a broader view than the scientists themselves. Bernstein thought that his plant work opened the door to using saline waters for irrigation, and it did; Rawlins believed that his studies of irrigation technology would permit farmers to stretch scarce water supplies, and they did; Rhoades felt his soil chemistry research would help reduce salt loading into rivers like the Colorado, and it did. But until van Schilfgaarde's arrival, no one had assembled all of the pieces, and mutual animosity was getting in the way.

Van Schilfgaarde quickly sized up the situation: "They thought they were competitors, especially for money." He immediately enlisted Rhoades, Rawlins, and Bernstein to help him write a paper that would meld the lab's findings into a new ethic of water conservation for desert farmers. He also looked for money to set up demonstrations, figuring that an influx of cash would force the scientists to settle their differences. "I think most of the ideas were already there, and I don't think Jan did the integration himself; I think it was shared," Rawlins said. "But what he did do was he built a team. That's a good way to build a team—throw down a chunk of money and say, 'In order to have some of this money, you've got to work together.'"

"One thing that's unique about Jan," Oster said, "is that he can stir people up and lead them without causing internal frictions that aren't resolvable. . . . He didn't bang heads. It was question-and-answer time. It was sitting down and writing a paper." Without van Schilfgaarde's leadership, Oster said, "We would never have struck out to combine that research into a minimized leaching concept. Hoffman wasn't inclined at that stage of the game. Jim Rhoades has since developed that sort of leadership ability, but back then he was still stuck at the lysimeter stage. It was just a matter of good timing, and Jan being the kind of leader who could bring it about."

Van Schilfgaarde brought his diplomatic skills to bear outside the lab as well. At a meeting of soil scientists, Rhoades and Oster ran into Ron Reeve, a former salinity lab scientist who had moved into the ARS hierarchy and had just been appointed to a committee that was studying ways to reduce the Colorado River's salinity. President Nixon had promised Mexican President Luis Echeverria that the United States would try to resolve Mexico's longstanding grievance over the high salt levels that the river carried when it reached Mexico's diversion point at Yuma. The front-running solution was the giant desalination plant the Bureau of Reclamation wanted to build at the river's edge just north of the Mexican diversion. "Jim and I came back from that meeting," Oster said, "and mentioned to Jan that as far as we could tell nobody was going in there and talking about farm water management improvements" as a way of reducing the river's salinity. "Well, it didn't take Jan very long at all to get started on that one."

A few weeks later, van Schilfgaarde was called to meet Herbert Brownell, whom President Nixon had appointed to negotiate a settlement to the salinity problem. Van Schilfgaarde recalled:

> He said, "We have a proposal from Interior to solve the problem by having the federal government pay for it and build a desalting plant. My contacts at the Office of Management and Budget tell me that's not a good proposal. I want you to get me a counterproposal, based on agricultural insights, and I'd like to have it before you leave town." This was on a Wednesday. And I told him that he was crazy, that I wasn't about to do that. That first of all, I didn't even know where Wellton-Mohawk was. I hadn't been in the West long enough to know. I had to get out a map to find out where it was, and he thought that I, by myself, was going to write a counterproposal to an agency that spent five years learning about it?
>
> So he said, "Well, I have a car standing by. I'll send you over to OMB, and there are some EPA people over there. You can find out what kind of work they've done, and I would very much like to have your insights by Friday night." Well, I finally dickered myself into Tuesday night, which still wasn't very much time. I called the lab and told the guys more or less verbatim what I'd been told, because I didn't know enough to give them any instructions. I said, "Cancel anything you're planning this weekend. We're going to be working Saturday and Sunday to see what we can do." And that's what we did; we developed a counterproposal.

Van Schilfgaarde, Rawlins, Rhoades, Oster, and Hoffman spent the weekend around a table punching numbers into desktop calculators and writing them on chalkboards, referring to wall maps and stacks of reports from other agencies. "We had access to some worthwhile reports," van Schilfgaarde said. "The Bureau of Reclamation had gone to the Agriculture Department earlier and asked for advice when the drainage problem first started in the early 1960s. So in the files there were a number of reports that gave us areas and numbers and drainage volumes and cropping patterns."

From these data, the scientists produced a short memo that outlined how improving irrigation efficiencies in the Wellton-Mohawk Valley could accomplish the same things as a desalting plant. From 220,000 acre-feet of drainage that Wellton-Mohawk farmers produced each year, desalting would have generated some 45,000 acre-feet of salty brine, which would have been dumped into the Colorado delta below Mexico's diversion. The remaining 175,000 acre-feet, its salinity now acceptable to Mexico, would have gone into the river. Implementing the salinity laboratory's plan, farmers would have improved their efficiency by enough to reduce their diversions from the Colorado by 181,000 acre-feet per year. That water would have stayed in the river for Mexico's use, while the valley's remaining drainage, totaling only 39,000 acre-feet—essentially the same amount as the desalting plant's briny reject stream—would have been dumped into the Colorado delta just like the desalting plant's brine. "We projected into the future and showed that you could achieve essentially the same thing by management as you could by desalting," Rawlins said.

Van Schilfgaarde said Brownell was struck by the fact that the salinity laboratory's proposal would save almost the same amount of fresh water as the desalting plant at a much lower price. At the next meeting of his task force, when OMB delegates made a strong pitch for the salinity lab's plan, Brownell directed that improving the valley's irrigation efficiency be studied further, although his principal remedy remained a desalting plant. In an interview in 1989, Brownell said he was reluctant to embrace the lab's plan because it was unproven, but van Schilfgaarde said Brownell gave him another explanation:

> He called us back in December and he said, "I have made my decision. My report is handwritten so there can be no leaks, and I will present it in person to President Nixon tomorrow." But he wanted to brief us first, since we had given him input. So he talks for half an hour or so to tell us what he was going to do and why. He ignored my proposal entirely. He called me aside afterward and said, "Technically, you're

right, but politically I can't sell it." I said, "Well, you're the ambassador; I'm the engineer. That's your privilege." Obviously I was disappointed, but I had no hard feelings.

Archives from Brownell's assignment make clear that the salinity lab's plan was torpedoed by the seven Colorado River basin states, who wanted to make sure that the full burden of whatever solution was chosen would fall on the federal government. Since the lab plan required Wellton-Mohawk farmers to make wholesale changes in the way they irrigated, it would not have met that requirement, and the basin states stubbornly refused to consider it. Yet the lab's plan clearly appealed to the White House's budget watchers. The OMB protested Brownell's desalting plant recommendation even after it went to Nixon; the president's science advisor and the chairman of his Council on Environmental Quality voiced objections as well. Their joint letter prompted a testy response from the usually diplomatic Brownell: "The memorandum fails to cover the attitude of the basin states . . . [and] without their support one does not have a solution to the problem with Mexico." The OMB used its influence with White House Chief of Staff H. R. Haldeman to keep Brownell's recommendation from reaching Nixon's desk for several months, but in the end the states got their way.

Shortly after Nixon accepted Brownell's proposal, the salinity lab's plan was reborn. Without warning, the Bureau of Reclamation revised its estimate of what the desalting plant would cost from forty-two million dollars, as it had promised Brownell, to sixty-two ι.llion dollars, an increase of 48 percent in less than a year. Bureau officials blamed inflation, refinements of sketchy initial plans, and unforeseen factors such as the need to buy some of the desalting plant's power from costly private sources. But Brownell smelled a rat. "That's what happens to all big federal projects," he said. "Everybody underestimates the costs to get the thing started, then after it's started they figure they can be more realistic and get additional money so the original money won't be wasted," he said. "It's the bureaucratic attitude." Equally annoyed was Nixon's national security adviser, Henry Kissinger, who had been an early supporter of the desalting plant, which he saw as a painless solution to a nagging diplomatic problem with Mexico. "It just irritated the holy hell out of him that he had obviously been snookered," van Schilfgaarde said. "That's the way he looked at it. His letter didn't say that, but the tone was harsh and it's pretty obvious that he was pissed off as hell. And that was our entrée."

Concern over the desalting plant's escalating costs gave a boost to plans for an interagency task force that would look into the salinity lab's ideas for Wellton-Mohawk. Brownell had proposed the panel almost as an afterthought to the desalting plant, a hedge against what he saw as the remote chance that the plant's reverse-osmosis desalting technology might not work. After Kissinger's outburst, the committee suddenly had attention from the upper levels of the White House. As long as the seven basin states controlled fourteen Senate votes, including key committee assignments overseeing the Department of the Interior, the Bureau of Reclamation, and their appropriations, prospects for doing away with the desalting plant altogether remained dim. But if the task force could provide evidence that the salinity lab's methods would accomplish the same ends, then there would be at least a slim chance.

The task force was based in Washington and consisted of agency heads and other policymakers; van Schilfgaarde was appointed to a field-level technical committee that did much of the nuts-and-bolts work. By then, the minimized leaching concept was further along than it had been during that rushed weekend meeting. The lab had finished its minimized leaching paper and was working with another Department of Agriculture agency, the Soil Conservation Service, to test the minimized leaching concept in a cornfield near Grand Junction, Colorado, where over-irrigation was pushing salt out of the naturally saline soil and into the Colorado. In addition, because he was no longer operating under Brownell's rushed deadlines, van Schilfgaarde was able to build a convincing case in the committee meetings for what his scientists were proposing. Still, the desalting plant's backers in the Bureau of Reclamation clung tenaciously to their cherished blueprints.

"The Bureau of Reclamation from the beginning thought this on-farm program was foolish," van Schilfgaarde said. "It was like pulling teeth all the way through. The bureau started out with the idea that this was not possible, that obviously Wellton-Mohawk was one of the best irrigation districts in the world and therefore we couldn't possibly improve its efficiency." But van Schilfgaarde had the bureau outnumbered. He had formed an alliance with another Department of Agriculture official and with the committee's two Environmental Protection Agency delegates, whereas the bureau had only three representatives. He also worked on the consciences of the bureau officials, appealing to their sense of engineering ethics, which they like him had acquired through years of rigorous technical training:

> We insisted on good water measurement. At one stage, we had a meeting. It got a little raucous; we were arguing about whether the district's water measurements were any good. A couple of the bureau engineers insisted they were just excellent. We said we didn't think so, but I didn't have any real basis for that except hearsay. So we decided to call the water master and get in the car and go out to Wellton-Mohawk and have him show us how they measured. When we got there, the *zanjero* [ditch tender] opened a gate, then went to his pickup and got out his impellor water meter, which is a perfectly good piece of equipment if things are going right but doesn't work worth a damn if there's air coming out of the pipe with the water, and this thing was bubbling air like mad. The meter has a needle on top that goes around, and he used a wristwatch to time it, which was not very accurate. And the needle was broken off, but you could see there was a scratch on the shaft, so he was just watching the scratch go around. Then he looked at a table and converted his measurements from one-decimal-place accuracy to three-place accuracy by interpolating, essentially. Those of us who were engineers were just standing around saying, "My God.

Jesus." Then—and this was the clincher—he took the meter out and
tossed it into the bed of the pickup from about ten feet away, and it
landed on the bearing. Nobody said anything. We'd made our point.

In the end, van Schilfgaarde said, the bureau people were ready
to concede that the salinity lab's plan could work—that the
Wellton-Mohawk farmers were using so much water that a simple
conservation effort incorporating minimized leaching would be
likely to reduce drainage flows by enough to eliminate the need for
a desalting plant. But the engineers were unable to get their superiors to sign off on the idea, so a curious compromise was struck.
"We proposed to do both," van Schilfgaarde said, "to put in the
on-farm improvements, and at the same time to build the desalting
plant. It was a lousy compromise in a technical and financial sense,
but politically it was interesting." The panel concluded that it
would be cheaper to improve the efficiency of the Wellton-
Mohawk farmers than to operate the desalting plant, let alone
build it, so even if the plant were constructed, the government
could still abandon it, continue to implement the on-farm improvements, and justify the decision under a cost-benefit analysis.
Van Schilfgaarde said this odd compromise was proposed by a bureau engineer, John Maletic, the agency's water quality office chief.
"Even though he was a dyed-in-the-wool bureau man, he really
saw things our way," van Schilfgaarde said. "It was an obvious non-
sense statement, but by writing it that way he was able to get everybody to sign off on it so we could go ahead with the on-farm
program."

A few months later, in 1974, the EPA came through with a grant
for the salinity lab to do some demonstration projects in Wellton-
Mohawk. The scientists holed up in a motel in Tacna, a dusty
truck-stop crossroads at the center of the long valley. Said Hoffman, who led the field teams:

> The scientists went down [from Riverside] with the technicians for
> weeks at a time to put the experiments in. There was one motel. We

would go down on a Sunday afternoon. We would arrive late, and the motel operator would leave the back door unlocked for us. There was a big feedlot there at the time, and there were truckers hauling manure out of the feedlot, so some of our rooms smelled kind of ripe, depending on who was staying there the previous week. We probably made them smell worse after a day or two.

There were two principal growing regions in the Wellton-Mohawk Valley. Along the south edge, just north of the present route of Interstate 8, was a high, sandy mesa dotted with ten thousand acres of citrus groves. Growers in that area had fallen into the habit of giving their trees at least twice as much water as they needed. They built low dikes about every sixth row of trees and flooded the resulting basins. "There was a little bit of a slope, and the soil was very sandy." Hoffman said, "so they would have to apply ten inches in order to get the water six inches deep over the entire area." Even to the casual observer, the results were obvious. "There was water running out of the slope of that mesa, eight feet above the valley floor," recalled one Wellton-Mohawk farmer, Bob Woodhouse. Below, on the low ground Woodhouse farmed, the over-irrigation was less extreme but still notable: farmers there were giving their crops, primarily alfalfa, cotton, and melons, about one-third more water than they needed.

The scientists set up separate experiments for each area. On the sandy mesa, they installed drip irrigation in a mature grove of Valencia oranges to precisely control the amount of water that went to each tree. After calculating how much water an average tree required for evapotranspiration the scientists then applied that amount plus one of three small leaching fractions. "We put on what we thought was ET plus 5 percent, plus 10 percent, and plus 20 percent, to see how much water was really needed over the long term," Hoffman said. "And what we found was, it took five years before even the 5 percent leaching was not sufficient."

Down on the valley floor, a similar experiment was conducted. The scientists divided a twenty-acre alfalfa field into two portions.

On one, measuring five acres, they installed what they called a "traveling trickler," a giant device similar to the center-pivot sprinkler rigs that farmers on the Texas high plains use, only fitted with drippers instead of sprinklers. On the other, they created a "dead-level" system with a big gate in one corner to let the water in and a perfectly leveled field that allowed it to spread quickly. "The idea was to apply the water in a large volume, very quickly," Hoffman said, "so you could put the same amount of water on all parts of the field. We would put on fifteen cubic feet per second of water, and in less than an hour we'd have six inches of water across fifteen acres."

The twin experiments established beyond any doubt that leaching fractions in the valley—and the drainage volumes that resulted—could be cut sharply without affecting crop yields. Soon, the Soil Conservation Service was offering cost-sharing grants to farmers on 23,800 of the valley's 65,000 acres for irrigation efficiency improvements modeled on the salinity lab's methods. "We demonstrated that we could make progress," van Schilfgaarde said. "But in the process, we ran into one problem after another when the bureau realized that we were trying to crack down on the size of the desalting plant." The technical committee was still convened, and van Schilfgaarde and Rawlins attended the increasingly tense meetings. Rawlins said:

> Boy, those were some rough meetings, let me tell you. The people who were there from the bureau were just like a military organization. They had this technology that they were going to use come hell or high water. Even their own economist pointed out that there were better ways of doing it. In fact, he pointed out that the cost of the desalting plant, just to run it, was equal to the entire gross product of the Wellton-Mohawk Valley.

Meanwhile, the plant's costs continued to escalate, fueled by rampant late-1970s inflation on top of the usual bureaucratic revisions. While the bureau busied itself building a small pilot desalting plant just upstream of Yuma, costs for the full-sized plant ballooned from the forty-two million dollars that Brownell was promised in 1973 to a July 1977 estimate of $178 million—an increase of more than 300 percent. Inflation accounted for only one-third of the increase. The plant's estimated completion date also slipped: Brownell had predicted the plant would be ready by 1978, but when that date arrived, the bureau was saying that completion was still four years away. In the technical committee meetings, van Schilfgaarde goaded the bureau engineers into re-evaluating the need for the desalting plant in light of the early results from the on-farm program. As he expected, the results showed that extending the effort to the entire Wellton-Mohawk Valley would eliminate the need for the plant altogether. The committee produced a report, and in early 1979, when the bureau went to Congress to ask for still more funds for the desalting plant, the salinity lab's scientists decided to intervene.

Rawlins made an appointment with one of his neighbors, George Brown, who happened to be a member of Congress and sat on the House Interior Committee:

> In my unofficial capacity as a citizen and a taxpayer, my wife and I sat down with George Brown one day in his office and told him what was going on. And he said, "I don't like it any better than you do. I'll take this up and deal with it, and if it turns out that it's something we can win, I'll take full credit for it. If it's not, you won't hear anything about it." Of course, as a government employee I certainly didn't want my name used.

It was a high-risk strategy, but it won tacit approval from van Schilfgaarde. "It was strictly against the rules," he said. "I felt that I couldn't afford to get caught, but if he [Rawlins] wanted to, then what the hell." After the meeting, Brown began a sustained—and in the end, partially successful—attack on the desalting plant, with salinity lab scientists steadily shipping him incriminating documents. Van Schilfgaarde said:

He wrote a letter to the secretary of the Interior asking whether all alternatives had been considered and whether in fact we had to go through with the desalting plant, and the answer he got was that there were no alternatives. [Brown] then returned the letter, with a copy to the White House, saying, "You've just told me that there are no alternatives. Then how come I have in my hand a report from one of your committees that discusses half a dozen alternatives?" In other words, our report. We fed him all the stuff that he needed, but obviously not officially.

Brown bottled up Interior's appropriations request for more than a year. "That put the bureau on notice that they had better pay some attention to the on-farm program and not just give it lip service," van Schilfgaarde said. Although Brown ultimately couldn't kill the desalting plant, he was able to get its capacity downsized from ninety-six to seventy-three million gallons per day and to get the on-farm improvements expanded from 23,800 acres to 38,000 acres. The effort paid dividends: by 1981, the valley's average leaching fraction had dropped from 31 percent to less than 12 percent, and the amount of salty drainage it was dumping into the Colorado had been cut in half. But construction—as well as delays and cost escalation—continued on the desalting plant. When at last it was deemed complete in 1992, the plant had cost $226 million to build, and would cost eleven million to thirty-three million dollars per year to run, depending on how much it was used. Meanwhile, for almost exactly the same results, the federal government had spent less then thirty million dollars to improve the irrigation efficiency of the Wellton-Mohawk Valley's farmers.

As its Wellton-Mohawk project matured, the salinity lab's scientists moved on to other things. Having already demonstrated how farmers could reduce their drainage to insignificant levels by using efficient modern irrigation methods, the scientists—especially Rhoades and Rawlins—turned to a related question: what to do with the tiny fraction of salty drainage that remained after leaching fractions had been reduced as much as possible.

On the chalkboard, this problem should not have existed. Reducing leaching fractions to their minimum levels and letting crops concentrate the salts in the soil-pore water to their theoretical maximums should have wrung every last bit of utility from the applied water, leaving only unusable saline drainage to come out of the bottom of the root zone. But the reality was not that simple. "Generally, you can't concentrate the drainage enough in one cycle to take all of the crop-producing value out of it," Rawlins said. "You just can't irrigate that uniformly. There's always some water that leaks past. You always had a higher leaching fraction than the theoretical model would predict, and so you always ended up with a bit more drainage water."

So over the next few years, in the late 1970s and early 1980s, former rivals Rhoades and Rawlins joined forces to set up experiments in two of California's most important agricultural valleys—the San Joaquin and the Imperial—and to develop a scheme for reusing drainage water by alternating high-salinity drainage and low-salinity irrigations on successive crops. They began in 1976 in the Lost Hills Water District, located in the remote southwestern corner of the San Joaquin Valley along I-5 northwest of Bakersfield. At that time, the state Department of Water Resources (DWR) and the federal Bureau of Reclamation were launching another in an interminable series of studies of the valley's severe drainage problems; and as usual, their efforts seemed destined to rely on the controversial drain to the Sacramento–San Joaquin delta. Correctly sensing that the studies were being rigged, Rhoades threw down a gauntlet. "I was a voice crying in the wilderness," he said. "No one else was speaking up about the fact that part of the solution could be the reuse of these drainage waters. So I wrote a paper and went to a meeting and presented it. In a way, I did it as a challenge, to say, 'Hey, you guys really ought to be considering this.'" The paper, which Rhoades presented at a meeting of the American Society of Civil Engineers, challenged the state water planning agencies to prove him wrong in his basic contention: that moderately saline drainage waters could be used on many different crops so long as fresh water was used at the crop's most sensitive stages, especially germination, and so long as subsequent crops were watered with fresher water so that salinity didn't build up to dangerous levels in the soils over time.

Rhoades's ploy had the desired effect: four agencies—the DWR, the bureau, the Lost Hills Water District, and the Kern County Water Agency, which was the water wholesaler for that region—accepted the challenge and agreed to pay for testing Rhoades's reuse scheme on cotton fields in the Lost Hills area. The plan was to establish seedlings using low-salinity delta water from the California Aqueduct, the region's major canal, followed by higher salinity drainage water during later growth stages. An unexpected complication arose during the experiment's second season: the regional groundwater, which had been rising slowly over time, shot suddenly upward. Practically overnight, the water table rose from fifteen feet below the surface to less than three, and it became difficult to sort out the effects of the saline irrigation water from the effects of the high though somewhat less saline water table. Nonetheless, yields on the drainage-irrigated tracts were nearly identical to those watered purely with low-salinity canal water.

Rawlins left the salinity lab in 1980, moving eventually to an administrative job in the Agricultural Research Service's national office. But Rhoades worked with more junior scientists to continue the drainage reuse studies in the Imperial Valley starting in 1982. Again funded by the Department of Water Resources, Rhoades this time designed an elaborate trial involving two cropping rotations—wheat, sugar beets, and cantaloupes in one plot and cotton, wheat, and alfalfa in the other. Both ran for four years in the Imperial Valley's twelve-month growing season, producing two full rotations of each crop in the first case and two cotton crops, one wheat crop, and two full years of alfalfa harvests in the second rotation. There were two water sources: water with relatively low salinity from the Colorado River, and water from a local stream, the Alamo River, which consisted mostly of drainage from Imperial Valley farms. The Alamo water was about three times as salty as the Colorado water. Rhoades used the fresher Colorado water to establish seedlings on all rotations, but for subsequent irrigations, he substituted salty Alamo water for one-half to two-thirds of the crops' water needs. He planned the rotations to include both salt-tolerant crops like cotton and more sensitive crops like alfalfa and melons, and he set up his irrigation schedules so that, after a period of watering a salt-tolerant crop with Alamo water, he then watered a sensitive crop with Colorado water. Although soil salinity levels rose when the Alamo water was used, they dropped when the Colorado water was substituted; in the end, the soil salinity was roughly what it was in the beginning, and there was no reason why the entire cycle couldn't be repeated over and over in perpetuity. For all the crops and all of the combinations of Colorado and Alamo River water, the results were essentially the same as in Lost Hills: yields were no different from those produced by a steady diet of low-salinity water.

The results of these two experiments supplied a way to circumvent the dilemma identified by Rawlins—that no matter how efficient their irrigation methods, farmers would never be able to reach the theoretical minimum leaching fractions that could be produced in the lab's lysimeters. Reusing drainage to irrigate crops in carefully planned rotations and in alternation with fresher water supplies, Rhoades showed, could give farmers two chances to concentrate their drainage instead of just one. Each reuse reduced the volume of the drainage water a little bit further, as part of the water evaporated and part was used by the crop. In the end, Rhoades estimated that total drainage volumes could be reduced by 80 percent through a combination of minimized leaching and drainage reuse. Though the remainder still required disposal, reducing the total quantity of the drainage would make that disposal both easier and more economical, just as it had in the Wellton-Mohawk Valley's minimized leaching trials. Carried to its logical conclusion, the process could reduce drainage volumes to a mere trickle by adding a final rotation of extremely salt-tolerant plants such as eucalyptus or *Atriplex*.

And yet, on a gray winter afternoon more than five years after the Imperial Valley experiments had concluded, Rhoades sat in his office at the salinity laboratory and lamented the lack of acceptance his methods had found among desert farmers. Rhoades by that time was the lab's director. Age had softened some of the rough competitive edges that had led to his earlier battles with the other scientists, and former rivals now applauded his newfound colleagueship and leadership skill. "I couldn't be happier with what I see happening at the salinity lab right now," Rawlins said. "I think that it's never been in better shape than it is right now, and I give a lot of credit to Jim Rhoades." The lab's minimized leaching and drainage reuse concepts also began to win much wider acceptance, at least among water planners. In 1990, when five agencies including the Bureau of Reclamation and the Department of Water Resources completed a five-year, fifty-million-dollar study of the San Joaquin Valley's chronic drainage problems, they gave a vigorous endorsement of minimized leaching and drainage reuse as a key feature of their proposed cure.

Nevertheless, acceptance from desert farmers has been slow to come. For the most part, the farmers still see salt as the enemy, see salt balance as a necessity, and believe with all their hearts in a 30 percent leaching fraction. "They don't want to use saline water voluntarily," Rhoades said. "They all believe that it can only lead to trouble for them, so they want to avoid it." But he remains philosophical about the lack of progress. When farmers finally run out of places to dump their saline drainage, he reasons, then they will be ready to listen to him and change their practices. When that happens, Rhoades and the other salinity lab scientists will have the techniques the farmers need, ready and waiting for them. Rhoades said:

No farmers are going to voluntarily do this, and I never believed that, even in the very beginning when I started this work. I never felt that farmers are going to jump on the bandwagon and go rushing up and down the road congratulating me, because they all come from a different viewpoint: "Just give us more good-quality water. That's the solution." But when push comes to shove and they've finally got to start to do some things, then at least they're going to have some evidence and some understanding to base it on.

CHAPTER ELEVEN

A Vision for the Future

B URIED SOMEWHERE IN the archives of the U.S. Patent Office is an 1874 document describing the first device ever invented for drip irrigation. It was a model of simplicity, consisting of an iron pipe drilled with nearly microscopic holes to let trickles of water dribble from its slightly pressurized innards—an ingenious device, but one that was fatally flawed. For one thing, it cost too much. To irrigate a fair-sized orchard would have required many miles of pipe and a correspondingly enormous outlay of capital. Besides, it didn't work. The tiny holes clogged almost instantly; corrosion and bacteria sealed them tight in a few days if a sand grain didn't do the job first. Nor surprisingly, the device never went into commercial production.

In the decades that followed, other inventors tried to perfect similar devices. In the 1930s in the Goulburn Valley of southeastern Australia, growers punched holes in galvanized pipe to water their fruit trees, but their efforts fared no better. Throughout the first half of the twentieth century, eager inventors experimented with various iterations of perforated pipe, but none succeeded— not until 1959, when the development of cheap, durable plastics allowed the invention of a workable drip irrigation device by three men from the new and intensely arid nation of Israel. A resourceful

retired tinkerer and a pair of younger, ambitious agricultural scientists, they showed the world how the ancient Sumerian art of
irrigation could be reborn in the age of high technology.

The life story of Simha Blass has become a legend in the world of
irrigation technology, and like most legends, it now consists of
about equal portions fact and fantasy. The basic story goes something like this: in the late 1950s, Blass had just retired from Tahal,
the Israeli government's water resources agency, and was working
with his son to develop new irrigation technologies. One day, he
was transfixed by a slowly leaking sprinkler head and the green
and vigorous grass that surrounded it. Watching droplets of water
gradually swell before breaking loose and striking the ground,
Blass began to ponder drip irrigation and its problems, which by
then must have seemed insurmountable: the clogging; the cost; the
challenge of ensuring that each outlet emitted the same amount of
water despite pressure variations within the pipelines.
    Soon Blass set to work in his garage, experimenting with dif-
ferent designs and materials. When he emerged weeks later, he had
developed a new plastic dripper whose design was distinctly different from the failed earlier models. Whereas the others had consisted simply of holes drilled into pieces of pipe, Blass's new device
added a serpentine internal passage that the water had to zigzag its
way through before reaching the outlet. Forcing the water to take
such a tortuous route accomplished two things. First, it created
turbulence, which helped to keep sediment in suspension and reduced the buildup of algae and bacteria. Equally important, the
complex switchbacks sharply reduced the pressure of the water as
it passed through them. This meant that Blass could use high pressure to even out the natural pressure variations while maintaining
a slow rate of drippage. It also meant that he could make the drip
orifices themselves considerably larger than those on earlier drippers, which helped to reduce clogging. Blass's new device with its
zigzagging drippers enabled irrigators to lace their fields with high-
pressure water lines leading directly to each individual drip outlet;

then, with no moving parts, the drippers magically transformed the high-pressure water into a lazy dribble. The device was reliable and cheap, and it seemed to have strong market potential. Soon Blass had licensed its manufacture to Kibbutz Hatzerim, a small collective farm that was looking to diversify into manufacturing; thus was born Netafim, one of the world's largest producers of drip irrigation gear.

But success did not come as quickly as Blass and his partners might have expected. In initial trials in southern Israel's Negev Desert, the new drippers failed miserably. Early experimenters, hoping to use the devices to reduce evaporation to its absolute minimum, buried the drip lines in the ground, where they quickly became clogged with sediment and root growth. Digging up the lines for repairs was hugely expensive, and for a while the promise of the new technology seemed like another cruel hoax. But then in 1964, the Hebrew University opened a research station in the broiling Arava Valley of extreme southern Israel—a below-sea-level oven lying between the Dead Sea and the Red Sea. The Arava is the lowest point on earth not covered by water; a permanent low-altitude haze smothers the valley like hot fog. At the time, there was not a hint of green on its saline brown and gray soils, and there was no good water to speak of. Yet Israel, worried that its unpopulated frontier was vulnerable to then-hostile neighbors like Jordan and Egypt, was determined to promote agricultural settlement in that bleak desert basin. The station's assignment was to find a way to make that possible.

To staff its new research post, the university sent S. Dan Goldberg, a Jerusalem-born irrigation lecturer, and Menachem Shmueli, one of Goldberg's recent graduate students and an immigrant from the prewar Netherlands. During the next two years, Goldberg and Shmueli worked closely with newly established kibbutzim to create fertile farmlands from the harsh Arava plains. They sowed winter vegetables for European markets and installed elaborate drip systems, this time with the lines running over the ground instead of below it. In time, they not only proved that it was in fact possible to grow crops in the Arava with drip irrigation but also showed that simply by mixing fertilizer with the irrigation water, they could produce yields twice as large as by conventional farming methods. "The results that we received were outstanding," Goldberg said in a 1990 interview, "I have pictures, slides, where you can't see me for the tomatoes."

Goldberg and Shmueli's work in the Arava resulted in a 1970 article in *Transactions of the American Society of Agriculture Engineers*—a paper that sparked interest around the world in the new technology. Four years later, there were two world congresses on drip irrigation, and by 1982, an estimated one million acres world-wide were on drip systems. In later years, the Israelis exported their innovation everywhere, even to their erstwhile enemies: by 1990, only one nation outpaced Israel in the proportion of its farm-land watered with drip, and that was its neighbor, Jordan. Mean-while, scientists at such institutions as the Hebrew University, the Volcani Institute, and Ben-Gurion University of the Negev used drip irrigation to reassess old notions of what constituted usable water. In the Arava, Goldberg and Shmueli had tapped into brack-ish aquifers to irrigate their crops; they found that by using drip-pers to keep a constant flow of water through the root zone, they could prevent the spikes in soil-water salinity that resulted from the wetting-and-drying cycles of traditional irrigation. That, in turn, made it possible to use water of higher salinity for irrigation: as long as there was no further increase in salt concentrations as the water moved through the soil, the plants were in no osmotic danger. In succeeding years, one Negev kibbutz not far from Sde Boker successfully grew sweet corn—a notoriously salt-sensitive crop—with brackish groundwater that had a salinity content of about three thousand parts per million, about three times as salty as the Colorado River at the United States–Mexico border. Other scientists focused on breeding plants that could tolerate still higher levels of salinity. At the Ben-Gurion campus in Beersheba, Samuel

Mendlinger, a New York–born plant biologist, came up with a melon that tastes like a canteloupe, matures early enough for lucrative export markets, and thrives on water with salinity at four thousand parts per million. At the Sde Boker campus, Jiftah Ben-Asher tinkered with nutrient levels for drip-watered plants and proved that the simple expedient of adding fertilizer can help many plants adapt to water of higher salinity.

Behind all of these projects lay a peculiarly Israeli combination of meteorological realism and Zionist ideology. An emphatically dry nation, especially in its southern half where most of its arable land lies, Israel from its birth in 1948 has searched, struggled, and sometimes fought for water. Water has always been an important—though often unrecognized—factor in the conflicts between Israel and its neighbors. When in 1965, two years before the historic Six-Day War, Syria began constructing diversion works on a Jordan River tributary called the Banias, Israel attacked, stopping construction and raising tensions. In the subsequent war, Israel seized not just the nearby Golan Heights, from which ramparts Syrian soldiers had been firing on the kibbutzim below, but also the lower-lying headwaters of the Banias, which posed no military threat. Israel also has clashed with both Syria and Jordan over those nations' claims to the Yarmuk River, another Jordan tributary that joins the main stream a few miles below Yam Kinneret, the biblical Sea of Galilee. And critics have suggested that Israel overran the highlands of southern Lebanon in 1982 partly in order to divert the Litani River, which drains the Bekaa Valley before emptying into the Mediterranean just north of the Lebanese-Israeli border.

This lust for water was driven principally by a severe shortage of it at home. Israel's water resources, always few and fragile, are concentrated in the rugged Galilee region of the country's north. To move water from there to the dry but arable south, the nation began shortly after independence to construct a 108-inch pipeline called the National Water Carrier. Finished in 1964, the pipeline traverses the forty-eight miles from Yam Kinneret to Tel Aviv, picking up small amounts of spring and well water along the way to mix with an initial infusion of water pumped from the lake where Saint Peter fished. At Tel Aviv, the pipeline splits into two branches and continues another sixty miles to the northern Negev, an arid, mostly barren extension of the Sahara that occupies more than half of the nation's territory. That precious water, pumped uphill more than six hundred feet from the Kinneret and across more than a hundred miles of terrain, now supplies virtually every farm, home, and business within the pre-1967 borders of Israel. But this water is not nearly enough for a nation that, despite its aridity, yearns to be agricultural.

From the start, agriculture has been deeply engrained in the Zionist ideology that defines modern Israel. It is considered a key to the nation's military security—settled land being far easier to defend than empty land—and its economic survival, and it is pursued with a single-mindedness of purpose that borders on the messianic. The nation's first prime minister, David Ben-Gurion, exhorted his compatriots to "bloom the desolate land, and convert the spacious Negev into a source of force and power, a blessing to the state of Israel." In retirement, Ben-Gurion kept faith with his words and made his home on a Negev frontier kibbutz abutting the desolate Sde Boker campus of the university that bears his name.

"The Zionist ideology fostered a return to the land," explained Moshe Brawer, a Tel Aviv University geographer. In biblical times, when the Jews last had their own state, the principal occupation of most had been agriculture; its revival would link the new Israel with its ancient predecessor in a palpable way. But that was not the only factor; pragmatic issues of security were at least as important. With waves of immigrants arriving, Israel had severe food shortages, and surrounded as it was by hostile neighbors, self-sufficiency seemed to be an imperative. In addition, the new nation's grip on its sliver of real estate was so tenuous that land settlement was considered necessary for national defense, just as it had been on the U.S. frontier a century earlier. Finally, agriculture filled another critical need, Brawer said: "There weren't many job openings to occupy the many immigrants who came, and agriculture was one of the main possibilities for employment."

The fact that few of those immigrants had previously worked in farming actually made the transition easier, Israeli experts say. The nation quickly developed an efficient extension service, set up collectivist kibbutzim and moshavim, and began educating newly employed workers in the latest agricultural techniques. The instructors found their students eager to learn. "When we look back and try to understand why agriculture in Israel developed so quickly, and to such a high level, probably one of the reasons was that these people knew nothing about agriculture," said Yona Kahana, general director of the Israel Institute for Waterworks Appliances, which develops and promotes technologies like drip irrigation. The neophytes were blank slates, Kahana said. "They would listen to the instructor, and they were open to what they were told, whereas most established farmers have their own traditions, beliefs, and prejudices." For the same reasons, Israeli irrigation systems have always tended to be technologically advanced—sprinklers in the early years, with drip making inroads beginning in the late 1960s; systems like those cost more but were far easier for the beginners to run than the traditional ditches, siphons, and furrows of surface irrigation. "All they had to know was when to open the valve and when to close it, and where to go if something went wrong," Kahana said. "They learned by doing. We actually invested much more per unit, but our farms produced almost immediately."

Israel's experience shows what can happen when a society starts with a clean slate and builds an agricultural infrastructure using only the best, latest, and most sensible equipment and techniques. By taking advantage of drip irrigation's ability to calibrate a crop's water and fertilizer rations with great precision, the Israelis have produced harvests that outdo those produced by traditional methods. Well-managed drip systems, the Israeli experience shows, can more than pay for themselves through increased yields, especially when water is priced at market value, as it is in that country. But why, then, haven't drip irrigation and other high-tech systems made a dent among tradition-bound desert farmers elsewhere, not even in places like the United States, which could easily absorb the systems' admittedly high capital costs? The reasons may be rooted in fear—the fear of taking a risk, of deviating from past practice, of learning something now.

In the fall of 1990, Jack Stone, the crusty and outspoken septuagenarian chairman of the Westlands Water District, sat in his ranch office on a blustery morning and talked about his objections to the new technology, which had been the subject of a recent experiment by scientists from the University of California Cooperative Extension Service and the Agricultural Research Service, who installed drip lines under ten acres of cotton on Stone's eighty-six-hundred-acre ranch. "I'd be delighted if somebody would come up with a drip system that would be practical for me or anybody else to use," Stone said. "Up to this point, for field crops, I haven't seen such a system." Stone admitted that drip systems could be useful for tree and vine crops—in fact, he had just finished installing one in an almond orchard—and that fact set him apart from many of his peers in the San Joaquin Valley. "I think it's a tremendous success," he said, "although I don't think it saves much water. But it uses water efficiently so you don't have any tailwater, and you get a good crop."

Stone was less sanguine about drip's prospects for cotton, tomatoes, and garlic, the mother lodes of the western San Joaquin Valley's agricultural bounty:

> The only other experience I've had with drip was that subsurface drip on that ten acres, and that has been quite a problem for us. There's the problem of keeping the lines repaired if they break for some reason or another. There's the problem of keeping them clean—no way in the world can you clean them if they get plugged up. And there's the prob-

lem of the growth that gets in there, bacteria and so on. We have to flush that out with chemicals. All of that is very technical work. We've got ten acres, and the folks that work with that have to watch it like a hawk. If I had a large acreage of that, I'd certainly have to have a good man on it. It couldn't be just any regular irrigator. He'd have to be some kind of a technician.

As a result, even though he farms in an area that has severe drainage problems and chronic water shortages, and thus would seem ideal for drip's water-saving capabilities, Stone said he would rather continue to irrigate by gravity, just like the ancient Sumerians. Drip "looks real good, but this old ditch and a truckload of siphon pipes and a good irrigator," he laughed, "boy, that works great."

Claude Phene, research leader at the Agricultural Research Service lab in Fresno and a designer of the subsurface drip project at Stone's ranch near Lemoore, scoffs at such comments. Phene spent most of the 1980s looking for solutions to the flaws that torpedoed Israel's early subsurface drip experiments and succeeded in almost every respect. He found several ways to prevent roots from clogging the emitters; his favorite was regular injections of phosphoric acid, which deterred root growth while also giving crops needed nutrients. Chlorine controlled algal growth, and improved filtration helped keep sediment out of the system. By 1990, Phene's lab was testing subsurface drip on farms throughout the San Joaquin Valley, and it found, just as the Israelis did, that drip systems not only saved water but raised yields dramatically. "Drip irrigation requires a more intensive level of management, but it also gives you more manageability than a furrow system," Phene said. Not the least of its advantages has nothing to do with water: drip also enables farmers to deliver nutrients to their crops in the exact quantities required for each stage of growth. While conventional farmers might have to send tractors into their fields to apply extra fertilizer in midseason—assuming they don't just apply an extra heavy dose at planting—drip farmers can simply spike their systems with nutrients when needed, delivering them automatically.

That not only saves money by reducing fertilizer waste, it also ensures that plants won't be undernourished either, which helps to boost yields toward their theoretical maximums.

But where drip irrigation truly shines is in its ability to micromanage the flow of water. Phene is convinced that drip irrigation is the best way for San Joaquin Valley farmers to battle their twin menaces of poor drainage and meager water supplies:

> There's a reason for the drainage problems they're having now: they've over-irrigated for many years. Now, the water table is high and it has no place to go. And you've got two ways to address it. You can either treat the source of the problem or you can treat the results. Personally, I think you have to look at both; you have to look at applying less water more uniformly, and you have to look at disposing of some of the drainage water, because you cannot operate irrigated agriculture in a semiarid climate without drainage.

Drip can help to apply water sparingly and uniformly because of its precision, Phene said. It allows farmers to control water use down to the millimeter, which in turn allows them to reduce leaching to the absolute minimum required by the crop, soil, and water they have. "The quality of water that's coming down the California Aqueduct is excellent; all you need to leach is about 2 to 3 percent per year," he said. "Unfortunately, you cannot do that with furrow irrigation. With drip irrigation, on the other hand, you can do it." Such minimized leaching can drastically reduce the amount of drainage produced, and that may prove to be the key to making agriculture sustainable in the San Joaquin Valley. If dumping the valley's saline drainage into the Sacramento–San Joaquin delta is out of the question, as it appears to be, then farmers will have to consider more expensive options—desalting, evaporation ponds with nets to prevent bird use, or pipelines to the deep ocean, for example. Such options are obviously too expensive as long as drainage flows are in the hundreds of thousands of acre-feet per year. But if those flows could be reduced to, say, tens of thousands of acre-feet, then the alternatives may be viable.

Some valley farmers are taking Phene's work seriously. John

Harris, son of Westlands pioneer Jack Harris and a major power in the valley's agricultural establishment, is gradually converting his seventeen thousand acres of tomatoes, cotton, and vegetables to a subsurface drip system using a lightweight plastic drip "tape" buried eight inches below the surface. The tape is cheaper than heavier drip hoses, and because it's buried shallower, it's less expensive to install. On tomatoes, the system uses 40 percent less water and produces more and bigger fruit, with less rot because the tomatoes don't rest on moist soil. Not far away from Harris, another grower converted 750 acres of raisin grapes to subsurface drip and cut his water use in half. His vines are now healthier too, Phene said, because unlike surface irrigators he can continue watering them during the three-week period in late summer when growers lay paper trays of grapes on the vineyard floor for drying.

Still, most valley farmers remain wedded to the tried-and-true methods of gravity-powered irrigation, Phene said. "There is some conversion to drip irrigation, but by and large it's relatively small scale. California has close to ten million acres of irrigated agriculture and maybe one-half to three-quarters of a million acres is drip-irrigated. And the drip-irrigated acreage is mostly on trees and vines and high-priced crops like strawberries and some vegetables." Besides the up-front capital costs, Phene said, the main obstacle to greater acceptance of drip is ignorance:

> Most of the farmers, they don't know anything about it. The young guys have a tendency to go easier; it's easier for them to see the difference. But the guys who have been around for twenty or thirty years, they don't want to change. They are used to doing things one way, and they've been successful, so they figure why should they change? And they won't change until somebody pushes them enough to do it.

What ends up pushing the farmers, and the society they feed, may be simple survival. Suppose for a moment that the progress of human civilization had stopped at the hunter-gatherer stage. Suppose that the Nile tribes had never sowed seeds behind the river's annual floods; that animals had never been put to work in the fields; that the British had never diverted the Indus rivers to faraway deserts; that the Colorado River still ran red to the Sea of Cortez; that the miracle dwarf grains of the Green Revolution had never been developed, nor the chemical fertilizers and pesticides and irrigation systems required to support them. Suppose all this were true, and then imagine how sparse the world's population would have to be. At the birth of the Nile, Indus, and Mesopotamian civilizations, the entire planet held fewer than 100 million people, maybe far fewer. In the mid-nineteenth century, at the dawn of modern irrigated agriculture, it had about 1.3 billion. By the 1950s, when Asian famines prompted the research that led to the Green Revolution, there were just under 3 billion. Now, at the end of the twentieth century, with high-yielding seeds and modern, massive irrigation in use on every continent except Antarctica, the world has more than 5.3 billion people.

Yet except when food supply lines are disrupted by wars and other disasters, almost all of the world's current multitudes are fed at least enough to subsist. The proportion of people who go to bed hungry has actually declined in the past forty years, from 23 percent in the early 1950s to 9 percent in the mid-1990s. Without irrigation, this almost certainly would not be the case. Take away the extra increment of yields attributable to the use of imported water, and the food surplus that enables the world to carry its current population would quickly vanish. In this light, two disconcerting trends are worth nothing: world population continues to spiral upward, with current estimates now projecting 8.6 billion people by 2025, less than half a lifetime from now. Meanwhile, the productivity of the planet's hard-won irrigated acres, now responsible for one-third of the world's food supplies, is stagnant or in decline, with some 150 million acres—25 percent of what was brought into production over a century of feverish dam and canal construction and water diversion—now affected by salinization, waterlogging, or both.

Some experts foresee a Malthusian crisis in decades to come.

"Soil erosion, air pollution, soil compaction, aquifer depletion, the loss of soil organic matter, and the waterlogging and salting of irrigated land are all slowing the rise in food output," writes Lester R. Brown, president of the Worldwatch Institute. "At present there is nothing in sight to reverse the worldwide decline in grain output per person. The bottom line is that the world's farmers can no longer be counted on to feed the projected additions to our numbers." Malthus, of course, was wrong in his predictions of an eighteenth-century global population crash, and these latter-day experts may be proven wrong as well. But Malthus erred mainly in failing to foresee how industrialization could stretch scarce resources to accommodate a burgeoning global population. Whether agriculture in the twenty-first century will be able to perform a similar magic act—building on the technological advances of the last century and a half without losing ground to side effects like salinity—remains an open question.

Still, there is good reason to be hopeful. At present, agriculture worldwide is not even close to making full use of the technological innovations that have brought it to this point. The recent history of agriculture is characterized by a steady rise in average yields brought about through increasingly more efficient management of the inputs of production. Today, the popular image of the farmer as a barely educated bumpkin is laughably out of date, at least in the developed world. Farming these days requires degrees in agronomy, familiarity with personal computers, and a good working knowledge of chemistry, botany, and economics. Producing crops is now much like producing manufactured goods. The manager of a large farm today has more in common with a General Motors factory superintendent than with a backyard gardener. Instead of steel, rubber, and fabric, the farm's inputs are sunlight, nutrients, water, and germplasm; its machinery is the soil; and nature does much of its labor. But the process is strikingly similar. And just as the automakers have increased productivity by investing in new factories and new materials, so has agriculture increased per-acre yields by tinkering with its inputs. At first, farmers saved seeds from their best plants and set them aside for the next year's crop. Later, plant breeders began crossing strains with desirable traits to produce superplants, like the dwarf wheat and rice of the Green Revolution. Now, scientists are using the polymerase chain reaction and other genetic engineering tools to tinker with the DNA of plant cells to produce still stronger and more fruitful crops. Chemical fertilizers supplanted manures after World War II; today's high-tech organic farmers are nourishing their soil by planting leguminous cover crops in their orchards and vineyards and planning complex crop rotations that include nitrogen fixers. Water management made its first great leap forward when the British diverted the Indus rivers; then, during the twentieth century, it made another with the introduction of plastic siphon tubes and laser-guided land levelers, devices no Sumerian could have dreamed of.

Now it is time for another great leap. Drip irrigation, or something like it that is similarly stingy with water and allows farmers to micromanage their crops' water and nutrient rations, would complete the technological revolution that the British engineers began a century and a half ago, just as genetic engineering has the potential to complete what Gregor Mendel began with his pea plants in the monastery. When the British diverted the Indus rivers they transformed the ancient Sumerian art and gave the world the ability to feed its teeming populations of the twentieth century, but the transformation was left unfinished. In the Indus, where illiterate peasants today struggle with one of the world's most technologically complex irrigation networks, the introduction of Green Revolution wheat seeds by itself boosted yields by 60 percent in two years in the late 1960s. But yields there and in other developing nations from Mexico to Morocco still fall short of what they should be, mainly because farmers lack the training necessary to manage their fields to the demanding standards of the last decade of the twentieth century. Meanwhile, in developed nations like the

United States, even well-educated farmers cling to outmoded methods because they won't accept the risk that accompanies change. A 1982 study by the United Nations' Food and Agriculture Organization estimated that there is enough farmland, sunshine, and water on the planet to support not five or ten billion but thirty billion people—but only if all of that land is managed to maximize yields with technologies that are now in use. A world with thirty billion people may be frightening to contemplate, but a world with ten billion is probably a certainty within the lifetimes of today's children. Highly efficient irrigation systems, and the concomitant increases in the efficiency with which nutrients are delivered to plants, may be all that will permit agriculture to make a graceful transition into the twenty-first century, when it will have to feed twice as many people as today.

Considering the evidence to date, the transition is not at all certain to be made. The environmental side effects of modern irrigation are creating problems all over the world in places like the Kesterson National Wildlife Refuge, the Tulare basin, the Colorado River delta, the Aral Sea, the Riverine Plain, and the valleys of the Nile, Indus, and Tigris-Euphrates. In some places, as in Pakistan, the damage is already severe; in others, such as the San Joaquin Valley, the reckoning may be still a few years or decades away. But there is not much time. An expert study completed in 1990 predicted that 460,000 acres of the valley's irrigated farmland may go out of production because of drainage problems by 2040, at a cost of nine thousand jobs and $441 million in crops. Meanwhile, production on irrigated land worldwide is stagnant on average and declining in many places. And even aside from any loss of production, as world populations continue to double and redouble they may soon outstrip the gains won by decades of improved plant breeding, nutrients, and irrigation. No one knows for certain when the two curves of population and food production will meet, or where the first effects will be felt. All that can be said safely is that it is still uncertain whether this civilization of ours, on the cusp of its third millennium, will continue to prosper or collapse like its predecessors.

The climate of the valley of the Tigris and Euphrates rivers has changed little over the millennia. It is a desert today, and it was a desert at the dawn of Sumerian civilization forty-two hundred years before Christ. At least eleven empires have risen and fallen in that arid valley, but today modern Iraqis are able to produce only a little salt-tolerant barley there, even after spending vast sums of money to reclaim the salt-poisoned soil. Five thousand years ago, in contrast, the ancient Sumerians grew bountiful crops of wheat on those same lands. Their surpluses enabled them to expand their city-states from their bases in the southern end of the valley; they built fortifications, raised armies, and attacked their neighbors, just as modern civilizations are prone to do. They prospered for at least a thousand years. But today, the southern Mesopotamian plain is a lightly populated and impoverished region, insignificant in comparison with the more prosperous central and northern parts of Iraq.

What happened? What could explain the slow but calamitous decline of the world's most highly developed civilization—a society that achieved literacy three millennia before Christ? Some clues were provided by a group of anthropologists from the Oriental Institute at the University of Chicago, who deciphered cuneiforms and other records and found evidence of an ancient dispute over water that turned disastrous. Two Sumerian city-states shared a watercourse that struck out from the Euphrates into the desert. About 2400 B.C., the upstream city, Umma, decided to cut off some of the flow to its downstream neighbor and keep more of the water for itself. The downstream city, Girsu, responded by building a canal in the opposite direction that linked with the Tigris. The new canal was safe from Umma's larceny, and with its water supply secure, Girsu continued to thrive. Over the succeeding years, it gradually enlarged the Tigris canal. New lands were irrigated, and more water was made available to the surrounding plains. But with so much water at their disposal, Girsu's farmers became profligate in their water use. They over-irrigated, and with nowhere else to go, the excess water merely seeped down to the water table. Slowly, the water table rose. The groundwater, which may have been only slightly salty at the time, was wicked up toward the surface as if through a sponge. After several centuries, so much salt built up in the soil that wheat would no longer germinate.

The anthropologists counted the impressions left in pieces of carbon-dated pottery by the different types of grain and found that wheat farming had been almost completely replaced by barley in the lower Mesopotamian plain by 1700 B.C.; two thousand years earlier, the region's production had been equally divided between the two grains. Eventually, the soil grew so salty that even barley refused to germinate. When that happened, ancient Sumeria went into eclipse, and the locus of Mesopotamian civilization quickly shifted upstream toward what became Babylon. What had started as a great civilization based on a successful irrigation system ultimately was transformed, by virtue of over-irrigation, into a salt-poisoned wasteland.

At more than 3000 years, the longevity of the ancient Sumerian civilization exceeds that of any other civilization to this day. In contrast, what we have built in the world's arid regions in modern times is still in its infancy. It has been only 150 years since the British overran the valley of the Indus; less than a century since the Bureau of Reclamation was founded; not even five decades since the Central Valley Project was built. Without a sustained effort to head off the disastrous side effects of that project and others like it, future archaeologists may be left to puzzle over what became of us as well.

Bibliography

Because the predominant source for this book is the author's decade of reporting on desert agriculture in California and elsewhere, this bibliography is not intended to be exhaustive but rather a summary of major published and documentary sources for each chapter. Those who want to read more on desert agriculture and water should start with such books as Tom Harris's *Death in the Marsh* (Washington, D.C.: Island Press, 1991); Marc Reisner's *Cadillac Desert* (New York: Viking, 1986) and *Overtapped Oasis* (Island Press, 1990); Philip Fradkin's *A River No More* (Tucson: University of Arizona Press, 1984) and other titles by the same author; Donald Worster's *Rivers of Empire* (New York: Pantheon, 1985); and Norris Hundley's *Water and the West, Dividing the Waters,* and *The Great Thirst* (all from University of California Press). John McPhee's *Rising from the Plains* (New York: Farrar, Straus & Giroux, 1986) is an excellent read on selenium and its geology. The Worldwatch Institute's annual *State of the World* (New York: Norton) reports and its other publications do an outstanding job of illuminating the otherwise neglected threat of stagnant or declining agricultural yields in the face of steadily rising populations.

Chapters 1, 2, and 3

The literature of irrigation and the development of the U.S. West is a treasure trove; the titles below represent a mere sampling. The Bureau of Reclamation publications listed are the best resources for learning about the broad sweep of the bureau's works in the seventeen states that it serves. In addition to the sources listed below, many of those listed under chapters 6, 7, 8, 10, and 11 were also used in preparing these chapters.

222   *Bibliography*

Ackerly, Neal W. "False Causality in the Hohokam Collapse." *The Kiva,* 53 (4, 1988): 305–19.

Brown, Lester R., et al. *State of the World 1990.* New York: Norton, 1990.

Clark, Ira G. *Water in New Mexico: A History of Its Management and Use.* Albuquerque: University of New Mexico Press, 1987.

Clawson, Marion. *Uncle Sam's Acres.* New York: Dodd, Mead, 1951.

DeVoto, Bernard. "Geopolitics with the Dew on It." *Harper's* (March 1944): 313–23.

Gates, Paul W. *History of Public Land Law Development.* Washington, D.C.: Public Land Law Review Commission, 1968.

Glenn, Edward P. "Survey and Model of Cienega de Santa Clara Wetland." Unpublished paper, Environmental Research Laboratory, University of Arizona, Tucson, May 1, 1991.

Gressley, Gene M. *The Twentieth-Century American West: A Potpourri.* Columbia: University of Missouri Press, 1977.

Hadingham, Evan. "The Mysterious Hohokam: Masters of the Arizona Desert." *Early Man,* 4 (4, Winter 1982): 20–28.

Haury, Emil W. *The Hohokam: Desert Farmers and Craftsmen.* Tucson: University of Arizona Press, 1976.

Iakisch, J. R. *Preliminary Report of Drainage Survey, Riverton Project, Wyoming, and Heart Mountain Division, Shoshone Project, Wyoming.* Denver: U.S. Department of the Interior, Bureau of Reclamation, 1947. National Archives, Denver Branch, RG no. 115, Bureau of Reclamation E&R Center, Project Reports 1910–1955, box 733.

Karnes, Thomas L. *William Gilpin: Western Nationalist.* Austin: University of Texas Press, 1990.

Kishk, M. A. "Land Degradation in the Nile Valley." *Ambio,* 15 (4, 1986): 226–30.

Kovda, V. A. "Loss of Productive Land Due to Salinization." *Ambio,* 12 (2, 1983): 91–93.

Lee, Lawrence B. *Reclaiming the American West: An Historiography and Guide.* Santa Barbara, Calif.: ABC-Clio, 1980.

Lilley, William, III, and Lewis L. Gould. "The Western Irrigation Movement, 1878–1902: A Reappraisal." In Gene M. Gressley, ed., *The American West: A Reorientation.* Laramie: University of Wyoming, 1966.

Manning, Thomas G. *Government in Science: The U.S. Geological Survey, 1867–1894*. Lexington: University of Kentucky Press, 1967.

Masse, W. Bruce. "Prehistoric Irrigation Systems in the Salt River Valley, Arizona." *Science, 214* (23 October 1981): 408–15.

Micklin, Philip P. "Desiccation of the Aral Sea: A Water Management Disaster in the Soviet Union." *Science, 241* (1988): 1170–76.

Postel, Sandra. "Water for Agriculture: Facing the Limits." *Worldwatch Paper 93*. Washington, D.C.: Worldwatch Institute, 1989.

Powell, John Wesley. *The Exploration of the Colorado River and Its Canyons*. New York: Penguin, 1987; first published as *Exploration of the Colorado River of the West and Its Tributaries*. Washington, D.C.: U.S. Government Printing Office, 1875.

Powell, John Wesley. *Report on the Lands of the Arid Region of the United States*. Cambridge, Mass.: Harvard University Press, 1962.

"Preliminary Checklist of Project Histories, Feature Histories and Reports of Reclamation Bureau Projects, 1902–1919." National Archives, Washington, D.C., RG no. 115, Records of the Bureau of Reclamation.

"Requiem for the Aral Sea." *Ambio, 20* (3–4, 1991): 109–14.

Roberts, B. H. *A Comprehensive History of the Church of Jesus Christ of Latter Day Saints*. Salt Lake City, Utah: Deseret News Press, 1930.

Robinson, Michael C. *Water for the West: The Bureau of Reclamation, 1902–1977*. Chicago: Public Works Historical Society, 1979.

Sibley, George. "The Desert Empire." *Harper's* (October 1977): 49–68.

Smith, Henry Nash. "Rain Follows the Plow: The Notion of Increased Rainfall for the Great Plains, 1844–1880." *Huntington Library Quarterly, 10* (2, February 1947): 169–93.

Smith, Henry Nash. *Virgin Land: The American West as Symbol and Myth*. Cambridge, Mass.: Harvard University Press, 1950.

Stegner, Wallace. *Beyond the Hundredth Meridian*. Boston: Houghton Mifflin, 1953.

Sterling, Everett W. "The Powell Irrigation Survey, 1888–1893." *Mississippi Valley Historical Review, 27* (December 1940): 421–34.

Swain, Donald C. *Federal Conservation Policy 1921–1933*. Berkeley: University of California Press, 1963.

U.S. Bureau of Reclamation. *Kendrick Project, Wyoming, Status Report.*

April 1955. National Archives, Denver Branch, RG no. 115, Bureau of Reclamation E&R Center, Project Reports 1910–1955, box 357.

U.S. Bureau of Reclamation. *1984 Summary Statistics. Vol. 2, Finances and Physical Features.* Washington, D.C.: U.S. Department of the Interior, 1984.

U.S. Bureau of Reclamation. *1984 Summary Statistics. Vol. 3, Project Data.* Washington, D.C.: U.S. Department of the Interior, 1984.

U.S. Bureau of Reclamation. *1987 Summary Statistics. Vol. 1, Water, Land and Related Data.* Washington, D.C.: U.S. Department of the Interior, 1987.

U.S. Bureau of Reclamation. *Statistical Compilation of Engineering Features on Bureau of Reclamation Projects.* Washington, D.C.: U.S. Department of the Interior, 1986.

U.S. Congress, Senate. *Federal Reclamation by Irrigation.* S. Doc. 92, 68th Cong., 1st sess., 1924.

U.S. Fish and Wildlife Service. *Draft Environment Assessment, Acquisition of Water Rights for Stillwater Wildlife Management Area, Churchill County, Nev.* March 1989.

U.S. Water and Power Resources Service (Bureau of Reclamation). *Project Data: A Water Resources Technical Publication.* Washington, D.C.: U.S. Department of the Interior, 1981.

"Water of Life." *Reno Gazette-Journal,* August 21–26, 1988.

White, Gilbert F. "The Environmental Effects of the High Dam at Aswan." *Environment,* 30 (7, September 1988): 3–11ff.

Woodbury, Richard B. "A Reappraisal of Hohokam Irrigation." *American Anthropologist,* 63 (1961): 550–60.

Chapter 4

Much of the history of the Kesterson tragedy was pieced together with the help of an investigatory report obtained under the Freedom of Information Act from the U.S. Department of the Interior's Office of the Inspector General. The congressional hearing transcripts listed below also helped to fill some gaps. Much of the information on agricultural drainage at other sites in the western United States comes from a series of irrigation drainage "reconnaissance investigations" and "detailed studies" issued by

Interior's National Irrigation Water Quality Program since 1987. Each of these investigations has been published by the U.S. Geological Survey as part of its Water Resources Investigations series.

Coggins, George Cameron, and Sebastian T. Patii. "The Resurrection and Expansion of the Migratory Bird Treaty Act." *University of Colorado Law Review, 50* (Winter 1979): 165–206.

Howard, Alice Q., ed. *Selenium and Agricultural Drainage*. 4 vols. Sausalito, Calif.: Bay Institute of San Francisco, 1985–89.

Lemly, A. Dennis, and Gregory J. Smith. "Aquatic Cycling of Selenium: Implications for Fish and Wildlife." Washington, D.C.: U.S. Fish and Wildlife Service, Leaflet 12, 1987.

Norris, Robert M., and Robert W. Webb. *Geology of California*. New York: Wiley, 1976.

Ohlendorf, Harry M. "Bioaccumulation and Effects of Selenium in Wildlife." *Selenium in Agriculture and the Environment*. Special publication 23, Soil Science Society of America, 1989.

Ohlendorf, Harry M., and Joseph P. Skorupa. "Selenium in Relation to Wildlife and Agricultural Drainage Water." Proceedings of the Fourth International Symposium on Uses of Selenium and Tellurium, Banff, Alberta, Canada, May 7–10, 1989.

Patuxent Wildlife Research Center. *Effects of Irrigation Drainwater Contaminants on Wildlife*. Laurel, Md.: U.S. Fish and Wildlife Service, 1990.

Presser, Theresa S., and Nigel T. W. Quinn. "The Identification and Management of Irrigation-Induced Selenium Contamination Problems in the Western United States." Paper presented at meeting of the American Association for the Advancement of Science, San Francisco, February 1994.

Smith, Felix E. "A Discussion: The Friant Division and Water Marketing." Sacramento, Calif.: U.S. Fish and Wildlife Service, 1988.

Sylvester, Marc A., et al. "Preliminary Results of the Department of the Interior's Irrigation Drainage Studies." *Proceedings on Planning Now for Irrigation and Drainage,* IR Div/ASCE, Lincoln, Neb., July 18–21, 1988, 665–77.

U.S. Congress, House. *Agricultural Drainage Problems and Contamination at Kesterson Reservoir*. Hearing before the Subcommittee on Water and

Power Resources of the Committee on Interior and Insular Affairs, House of Representatives, 99th Cong., 1st sess., 1985.

U.S. Congress, House. *Agricultural Drainage in the San Joaquin Valley, California.* Hearing before the Subcommittee on Water and Power Resources of the Committee on Interior and Insular Affairs, House of Representatives, 99th Cong., 1st sess., 1985.

U.S. Congress, House. *Chemical Contamination from Federal Irrigation Projects.* Hearing before the Subcommittee on Water and Power Resources of the Committee on Interior and Insular Affairs, House of Representatives, 99th Cong., 1st sess., 1985.

U.S. Department of the Interior, Office of the Inspector General. *Department of the Interior Irrigation Drainage Problems.* Audit report no. 93-I-1302, July 1993.

U.S. Department of the Interior, Office of the Inspector General. *Report of Investigation, Kesterson National Wildlife Refuge, Kesterson Reservoir, San Luis Drain, Merced County, California.* Case no. 5VI-025, September 4, 1985.

Chapter 5

Archival collections contributed greatly to this chapter, including the Floyd Dominy and William E. Warne papers at the University of Wyoming's American Heritage Center in Laramie, Wyoming; the National Archives collections on the Kendrick and Riverton projects and the U.S. Bureau of Reclamation's main library, both located at the Denver Federal Center; the Clinton P. Anderson collection at the Library of Congress in Washington, D.C.; unpublished transcripts of congressional hearings from the National Archives in Washington, D.C.; and the B. F. Sisk papers, which are stored not in the library but in disgraceful condition in an academic building attic at California State University, Fresno. The Central California Irrigation District provided microfiche copies of exhibits from its two 1960s-era lawsuits concerning the San Joaquin Valley drain; those documents proved to be extremely valuable in piecing together the story and verifying accounts of participants. The Bureau of Reclamation also provided valuable documents on the expansion of the San Luis Unit service area in response to a Freedom of Information Act request.

Bailey, John W., and Doyle R. Cardon. *Special Report: Land Classification and Related Studies, San Luis Unit.* Fresno, Calif.: U.S. Department of the Interior, Bureau of Reclamation, April 1962.

California, Department of Water Resources. *California State Water Project 200. Vol. 1, History, Planning and Early Progress.* Sacramento, Calif.: November 1984, 73–78.

California, Department of Water Resources. *Report of the Water Resources Task Force on the State Water Project.* Sacramento, Calif.: May 1967.

California, Department of Water Resources. *Response to the Governor's Water Resources Task Force.* Sacramento, Calif.: September 1967.

Central California Irrigation District. "Summary of Statements and Documents, San Luis Interceptor Drain and San Joaquin Master Drain." Unpublished document from district headquarters, Los Banos, Calif.

Central California Irrigation District et al. v. Stewart Udall et al., U.S. District Court case no. F-59-CIV, Eastern District of California, 1967.

Central California Irrigation District et al. v. Stewart Udall et al., U.S. District Court case no. 2356ND, Eastern District of California, 1962.

Cooper, Erwin. *Aqueduct Empire: A Guide to Water in California, Its Turbulent History and Its Management Today.* Glendale, Calif.: Arthur H. Clark, 1968.

O'Neill, Bill. *A Mountain Never Too High: The Story of J. E. O'Neill.* Fresno, Calif.: Valley Publishers, 1977.

Simmons, Ed. *Westlands Water District: The First 25 Years.* Fresno, Calif.: Westlands Water District, 1977.

Sisk, B. F. *A Congressional Record: The Memoir of Bernie Sisk.* Fresno, Calif: Panorama West, 1980.

University of California, Bancroft Library, Regional Oral History Office. *The California Water Project.* A series of oral histories of leading figures in the construction of the State Water Project. Interviews by Malca Chall.

U.S. Bureau of Reclamation. *Alternative Solutions for Drainage: San Luis Unit.* February 1964. California State University, Fresno, B. F. Sisk papers, box labeled "Box 1: Water files, to Fresno Metropolitan Flood Control District," file labeled "Water: San Luis Dam, drainage."

U.S. Bureau of Reclamation. *Definite Plan Report: San Luis Unit, Central Valley Project, California.* Sacramento, Calif.: December 1962.

U.S. Bureau of Reclamation. *Feasibility Report: San Luis Unit, Central Valley Project, California.* Sacramento, Calif.: May 1955.

U.S. Bureau of Reclamation. *Special Task Force Report on San Luis Unit.* Sacramento, Calif.: 1978.

U.S. Congress. *An Act to Authorize the Secretary of the Interior to Construct the San Luis Unit of the Central Valley Project, California.* P.L. 86-488, 86th Cong., 2nd sess., 1960.

U.S. Congress, House. *Policies, Programs and Activities—Interior.* Hearing before the Committee on Interior and Insular Affairs, House of Representatives, 88th Cong., 1st sess., 1963.

U.S. Congress. *Report on the San Luis Project, California, to Accompany HR 7155.* House report no. 399, 86th Cong., 1st sess., 1959.

U.S. Congress, Senate. *San Luis Unit—Central Valley Project, California.* Hearing before the Subcommittee on Irrigation and Reclamation, Committee on Interior and Insular Affairs, Senate, 84th Cong., 2nd sess., 1958.

U.S. Congress, Senate. Stenographic transcript of hearings on S1887, S4002, and S4009, June 20, 1958. National Archives, Washington, D.C. RG no. 46, Sen-85A-E9, Senate, 85th Cong., box 15.

U.S. Department of the Interior, San Joaquin Valley Drainage Program. *A Management Plan for Agricultural Subsurface Drainage and Related Problems on the Westside San Joaquin Valley: Final Report of the San Joaquin Valley Drainage Program.* Sacramento, Calif.: 1990.

Warne, William E., letter to Honorable Edmund G. Brown, July 29, 1967. University of Wyoming American Heritage Center, Warne collection, box 12.

Chapter 6

The material on wildlife deformities in the Tulare basin is derived largely from the author's reporting for the *Fresno Bee* between 1985 and 1994. Also helpful were a series of reports from the U.S. Department of the Interior's irrigation drainage study program, described above in the bibliographical notes to chapter 4.

California, Regional Water Quality Control Board, Central Valley Region.

Meeting agenda, August 6, 1993, Hanford, Calif., re: Agricultural Evaporation Basins in the Tulare Lake Basin.

California, Water Resources Control Board. *1990 Annual Report: Agricultural Drainage Water Management Loan Program.* Report no. 90-7-WQ, August 1990.

Corcoran Ranch Water Department. "Water Agencies That Concern the California Operating Division of J. G. Boswell Co." Unpublished document, 1986.

J. G. Boswell Co. v. *Family Farmers for Proposition 9 et al.,* Superior Court of California, County of Kern, case no. 179027, 1982.

"J. G. Boswell Leads Farm Crop 500 List," *Fresno Bee,* November 1, 1993.

J. G. Boswell Company, consolidated statements of changes in financial position for years ending February 29, 1988, February 28, 1987, February 28, 1986, February 28, 1985, February 29, 1984, February 28, 1983, and February 28, 1982.

Patuxent Wildlife Research Center. *Patuxent Research Review Panel Report.* Laurel, Md.: U.S. Fish and Wildlife Service, 1991.

Preston, William L., *Vanishing Landscapes: Land and Life in the Tulare Lake Basin.* Berkeley: University of California Press, 1981.

"Salyer American Principal Officers and Managers," undated news release.

U.S. Congress, Senate. *Report of the Secretary of War communicating, in compliance with a resolution of the Senate, a report of the Tulare valley, made by Lieutenant Derby.* Ex. doc. no. 100, 32d Cong., 1st. sess., 1852.

U.S. Fish and Wildlife Service. Memorandum to Deputy Regional Director and Regional Director, Region 1, Portland, Ore., from Drainwater Studies Coordinator, Sacramento, Calif., *re* Applicability of MBTA to Operation of Evaporation Ponds in the San Joaquin Valley, July 31, 1988.

U.S. Fish and Wildlife Service. Memorandum to Frank Dunkle, director, from Martin J. Suuberg, associate solicitor, conservation and wildlife, *re* Applicability of Migratory Bird Treaty Act to Bird Losses Caused by Agricultural and Industrial Activities, October 21, 1988.

Chapter 7

The backbone of this chapter was a series of Freedom of Information Act requests and declassification requests filed with the federal government by the author. The most fruitful were two FOI requests filed with the Department of State and the Department of the Interior for documents on the negotiations between the United States and Mexico on the Colorado River salinity problem. Additional material came from the Herbert Brownell collection at the Dwight D. Eisenhower Presidential Library in Abilene, Kansas, and from the Nixon Presidential Materials Project of the National Archives in Alexandria, Virginia. Some documents from those two archives were released as a result of the author's declassification review requests. In the Nixon archives, most of the documents came from the office files of John C. Whitaker and the White House subject files on water.

Ambrose, Stephen E. *Eisenhower, Vol. 2; The President.* New York: Simon & Schuster, 1983.

Ambrose, Stephen E. *Nixon, Vol. 2; The Triumph of a Politician, 1962–1972.* New York: Simon & Schuster, 1989.

Brownell, Herbert, and Samuel D. Eaton. "The Colorado River Salinity Problem with Mexico." *American Journal of International Law, 69* (1975): 255–71.

"Burec Taps Mammoth Desalting for Southwest Supplemental Water," *Water Desalination Report, 4* (2, January 11, 1968): 1–3.

"Central Arizona Project." *Arizona Republic,* October 24–31, 1993.

Chamberlin, Eugene Keith. "Mexican Colonization versus American Interests in Lower California." *Pacific Historical Review, 20* (1, February 1951): 43–55.

"Clouds Forming Over Yuma Plant Completion." *Water Desalination Report, 16* (4, January 24, 1980): 1–4.

Cummings, Ronald G., et al. *Waterworks: Improving Irrigation Management in Mexican Agriculture.* World Resources Institute Paper No. 5. Washington, D.C.: World Resources Institute, 1989.

Dailey, Joseph M. "The Reluctant Candidate: Dwight Eisenhower in 1951." In Joann P. Krieg, ed., *Dwight D. Eisenhower: Soldier, President, Statesman.* New York: Greenwood Press, 1987.

Dominy, Floyd. "Statement of Floyd E. Dominy, Commissioner of Reclamation, before the House of Representatives Committee on Interior and Insular Affairs, July 22, 1968." Unpublished paper in Dominy collection, box 9, American Heritage Center Archives, University of Wyoming.

Eisenhower, Dwight D. *Mandate for Change: 1953–1956*. Garden City, N.Y.: Doubleday, 1963.

Fernandez, Raul. *The Mexican-American Border Region: Issues and Trends*. Notre Dame, Ind.: University of Notre Dame Press, 1989.

Fernandez, Raul. "Twentieth Century Colonization: The Case of the Imperial (U.S.A.) and Mexicali (Mexico) Valleys." Unpublished paper presented at the 86th annual meeting of the Association of American Geographers, April 1990.

Fradkin, Philip L. *A River No More: The Colorado River and the West*. Tucson: University of Arizona Press, 1984.

Friedkin, Joseph F. "The International Problem with Mexico over the Salinity of the Lower Colorado River." In David H. Getches, ed., *Water and the American West: Essays in Honor of Raphael J. Moses*. Boulder: University of Colorado, 1988.

Glenn, Edward P. "Oasis in the Colorado Delta." *CEDO News,* 4 (1, Fall-Winter 1991–92): 14ff.

Gottlieb, Robert. *A Life of Its Own: The Politics and Power of Water*. San Diego: Harcourt Brace Jovanovich, 1988.

Gottlieb, Robert, and Peter Wiley. *Empires in the Sun*. New York: Putnam, 1982.

Gottlieb, Robert, and Irene Wolt. *Thinking Big: The Story of the Los Angeles Times, Its Publishers, and Their Influence on Southern California*. New York: Putnam, 1977.

Hundley, Norris, Jr. *Dividing the Water: A Century of Controversy Between the United States and Mexico*. Berkeley: University of California Press, 1966.

Hundley, Norris, Jr. *Water and the West: The Colorado River Compact and the Politics of Water in the American West*. Berkeley: University of California Press, 1975.

Mann, Dean E. "Politics in the United States and the Salinity Problem of the Colorado River." *Natural Resources Journal,* 15 (January 1975): 114–28.

McWilliams, Carey. *California: The Great Exception.* New York: Current Books, 1949.

Miller, Taylor O., et al. *The Salty Colorado.* Washington, D.C.: Conservation Foundation, 1986.

Pach, Charles, Jr., and Elmo Richardson. *The Presidency of Dwight D. Eisenhower.* Lawrence: University of Kansas Press, 1991.

"Senate Passes Yuma Plant Increases." *Water Desalination Report,* 15 (23, June 21, 1979): 1–4.

Snyder, N. W. "A North American Continental Water Transfer Plan." Unpublished paper presented at the Symposium on Southern California's Future: An Engineering Challenge, Pasadena, Calif., September 22, 1988.

U.S. Bureau of Reclamation. "Definite Plan Report Volume 1: Wellton-Mohawk Division, Gila Project, Arizona." Boulder City, Nev.: November 1950.

U.S. Bureau of Reclamation. "Executive Summary: West Texas and Eastern New Mexico Import Project." June 1973.

U.S. Bureau of Reclamation. "Land Classification Report: Wellton-Mohawk Division, Gila Project, Arizona." Yuma, Ariz.: July 1948.

U.S. Bureau of Reclamation. *1988 Joint Evaluation of Salinity Control Programs in the Colorado River Basin.* December, 1988.

U.S. Bureau of Reclamation. *Quality of Water Colorado River Basin.* Progress Report no. 14, March 1989.

U.S. Bureau of Reclamation. "Reconnaissance Report: Augmentation of the Colorado River by Desalting of Sea Water." January 1968.

U.S. Congress, General Accounting Office. "Colorado River Basin Water Problems: How to Reduce Their Impact." Report no. CED-79-11, May 4, 1979.

U.S. Congress, General Accounting Office. "Desalting Water Probably Will Not Solve the Nation's Water Problems, But Can Help." Report no. CED-79-60, May 1, 1979.

U.S. Congress, General Accounting Office. "Information on USDA's Water Quality Cost-Share Programs." Report no. RCED-92-139FS, March 1992.

U.S. Congress, House. *Colorado River Basin Project.* Hearings before the

Subcommittee on Irrigation and Reclamation of the Committee on Interior and Insular Affairs, 90th Cong., 1st sess., 1967.

U.S. Congress, House. *Relocate the Boundaries of the Gila Project.* Hearings before the Subcommittee on Irrigation and Reclamation of the Committee on Public Lands, 80th Cong., 1st sess., 1947.

U.S. Congress, Senate. *Colorado River Basin Salinity Control Program Development.* Hearing before the Subcommittee on Soil and Water Conservation, Forestry and the Environment of the Committee on Agriculture, Nutrition and Forestry, 98th Cong., 2d sess., 1984.

U.S. Congress, Senate. *Light on the Mexican Water Treaty from the Ratification Proceedings in Mexico.* Doc. no. 249, 79th Cong., 2d sess., 1946.

U.S. Congress, Senate. *Water Treaty of the Colorado River and Rio Grande Favors Mexico.* Doc. no. 98, 79th Cong., 1st sess., 1945.

U.S. Congress, Senate. *Water Treaty with Mexico.* Doc. no. 32, 79th Cong., 1st sess., 1945.

U.S. Department of the Interior, Office of the Inspector General. *Implementation of the Colorado River Basin Salinity Control Program, Bureau of Reclamation.* Report no. 93-I-810, March 1993.

U.S. Department of the Interior, Office of the Inspector General. *Operation and Maintenance Contracts, Colorado River Basin Salinity Control Program, Bureau of Reclamation.* Report no. 93-I-258, December 1992.

U.S. Department of the Interior, Office of the Inspector General. *Survey Report on the Review of the Colorado River Basin Salinity Control Program, Bureau of Reclamation.* Report no. 89-109, September 1989.

U.S. Water and Power Resources Service (Bureau of Reclamation). *Project Skywater Fiscal Year 1979 Report.* Office of Atmospheric Resources Research, March 1981.

Watkins, T. H. *The Grand Colorado: The Story of a River and Its Canyons.* Palo Alto, Calif.: American West Publishing, 1969.

"Yuma Desalting Plant." *Western Resources Wrap-Up,* 13 (50, December 15, 1977): 1–5.

Chapter 8

The government of Victoria and the Murray-Darling Basin Commission, a commonwealth-level agency based in Canberra, have published numerous documents on the salinity problem in southeastern Australia, where it is widely regarded as the region's most serious environmental problem, a sharp contrast to its low profile in the United States. These documents were extremely useful in the preparation of this chapter.

Alexandra, Jason. "ACF Response to the Draft Salinity Plan for Northern Victoria." Unpublished paper by the Australian Conservation Foundation, Melbourne, November 1989.

Davidson, B. R. *Australia Wet or Dry?* Carlton, Victoria: Melbourne University Press, 1969.

LaNauze, J. A. *Alfred Deakin: A Biography.* London: Melbourne University Press, 1965.

Murray-Darling Basin Commission. "A Pipeline to the Sea: Pre-Feasibility Study." Canberra, Australia: March 1990.

Pigram, John J. "Salinity and Basin Management in Southeastern Australia." *Geographical Review,* 76 (July 1986): 249–64.

Powell, J. M. *Watering the Garden State: Water, Land and Community in Victoria, 1834–1988.* Sydney: Allen and Unwin, 1989.

Royal Commission on Water Supply. "Irrigation in Western America So Far as It Has Relation to the Circumstances of Victoria." Victoria: Government of Victoria, 1885.

Chapter 9

Michel's book on the Indus is the definitive work on the Punjab and its rivers, though it is somewhat dated; the Sims book helps to place the subject in a more current perspective. Of the many international organizations that are working in the Punjab, the International Irrigation Management Institute, part of the Consultative Group on International Agricultural Research, appears to have the best handle on the complex situation there and would be the best place to start for additional information. The Reeves book is by far the best of a limited number of published guides to the cultural geography of Pakistan.

Ahmed, Nazir. "Pakistan Experience with Drainage Tubewells: Success and Failure." Paper presented at the International Seminar on Hydrological Aspects of Drainage in Irrigated Areas, March 28–30, 1988, Drainage and Reclamation Institute of Pakistan, Tando Jam, 1988.

Johnson, Robert. *Private Tube Well Development in Pakistan's Punjab: Review of Past Public Programs/Policies and Relevant Research.* International Irrigation Management Institute Country Paper, Colombo, Sri Lanka: Pakistan No. 1, 1989.

Kijne, Jacob W., and Edward J. Vander Velde. "Salinity in Punjab Watercourse Commands and Irrigation System Operations: The Imperative Case for Improving Irrigation Management in Pakistan." Paper prepared for the Internal Program Review, International Irrigation Management Institute, Colombo, Sri Lanka, December 3–5, 1990.

Lieftinck, Pieter, et al. *Water and Power Resources of West Pakistan: A Study in Sector Planning.* Baltimore: Johns Hopkins Press, 1969.

Michel, Aloys Arthur. *The Indus Rivers.* New Haven, Conn.: Yale University Press, 1969.

Pakistan, Ministry of Food and Agriculture. *Report of the National Commission on Agriculture.* Islamabad, Pakistan: 1988.

Pakistan, Water and Power Development Authority. "International Waterlogging and Salinity Research Institute, Pakistan: An Introduction."

Rathur, Anwarul Qadeer. "A Review of Salinity and Waterlogging in the Indus Basin Area of Punjab, Pakistan." In Prinya Nutalaya, et al., eds., *Proceedings of the First International Symposium on Soil, Geology and Landforms: Impact on Land Use Planning in Developing Countries.* Bangkok: Association of Geoscientists for International Development, 1982.

Reeves, Richard. *Passage to Peshawar: Pakistan, between the Hindu Kush and the Arabian Sea.* New York: Simon & Schuster, 1984.

Sims, Holly. "Issue Salience and Regime Responsiveness: The Politics of Reclamation in Two Punjabs." *Journal of Commonwealth and Comparative Politics,* 28 (2, July 1990): 183–200.

Sims, Holly. *Political Regimes, Public Policy and Economic Development: Agricultural Performance and Rural Change in Two Punjabs.* New Delhi: Sage Publications, 1988.

Trimmer, Walter L. "Partial Irrigation and Its Application to Pakistan." Report of a temporary duty assignment, University of Idaho, ISM Research Project, Pakistan, September 1988.

U.S. Bureau of Reclamation. "Subsurface Drainage Design Memorandum: Fourth Drainage Project, Lower Rechna Remaining Subproject, Faisalabad, Pakistan." October 1989.

U.S. White House–Department of the Interior Panel on Waterlogging and Salinity in West Pakistan. *Report on Land and Water Development in the Indus Plain.* Washington, D.C.: Government Printing Office, January 1964.

Vlotman, Willem F., et al. "Comparison of Three Subsurface Pipe Drainage Projects in Pakistan." Paper presented at the Symposium on Land Drainage for Salinity Control in Arid and Semi-Arid Regions, Cairo, February 25–March 2, 1990.

Chapter 10

The scientists, past and present, of the U.S. Salinity Laboratory were generous in granting multiple extended interviews for this chapter. The laboratory's backlist of published papers is freely available and useful in tracking the lab's progress; however, supplies of Handbook 60 were long ago exhausted. Sources listed in the bibliographical notes for chapter 7, most notably the FOI and archival documents on the Brownell mission, were also used heavily in preparing this chapter.

Bernstein, Leon, and L. E. Francois. "Leaching Requirement Studies: Sensitivity of Alfalfa to Salinity of Irrigation and Drainage Waters." *Soil Science Society of America Proceedings,* 37 (6, 1973): 931–43.

Rawlins, S. A., and P. A. C. Raats. "Prospects for High-Frequency Irrigation. *Science, 188* (1975): 604–10.

Rhoades, J. D. "Evidence of the Potential to Use Saline Water for Irrigation." Paper presented at the Symposium on Reuse of Low Quality Water for Irrigation, Water Research Center, Egypt, 1987.

Rhoades, J. D. "Intercepting, Isolating and Reusing Drainage Waters for Irrigation to Conserve Water and Protect Water Quality." *Agricultural Water Management, 16* (1989): 37–52.

Rhoades, J. D., et al., "Minimizing the Salt Burdens of Irrigation Drainage Waters." *Journal of Environmental Quality, 3* (4, October-December 1974): 311–16.

Rhoades, J. D., et al., "Salt in Irrigation Drainage Waters. Pt. 1, Effects of Irrigation Water Composition, Leaching Fraction and Time of Year on the Salt Compositions of Irrigation Drainage Waters." *Soil Science Society of America Proceedings, 37* (5, September-October 1973): 770–74.

Rhoades, J. D., et al. "Use of Saline Drainage Water for Irrigation: Imperial Valley Study." *Agricultural Water Management, 16* (1989): 25–36.

U.S. Salinity Laboratory. *Diagnosis and Improvement of Saline and Alkali Soils.* U.S. Department of Agriculture Handbook no. 60, February 1954.

U.S. Salinity Laboratory. "History." Unpublished document, October 1989.

Van Schilfgaarde, Jan, et al. "Irrigation Management for Salt Control." Paper presented at the Irrigation and Drainage Division Specialty Conference of the American Society of Civil Engineers, Fort Collins, Colorado, April 22–24, 1973.

Chapter 11

Scientists at Ben-Gurion University of the Negev and elsewhere in Israel were generous with their time in interviews for this chapter. Claude Phene and others at the U.S. Department of Agriculture's Agricultural Research Service station in Fresno, California, similarly answered repeated questions about their work. Phene was especially helpful in arranging interviews in Israel.

Brown, Lester R. "Facing Food Insecurity." In Lester R. Brown, ed., *State of the World 1994.* New York: Norton, 1994.

Brown, Lester R. *Seeds of Change: The Green Revolution and Development in the 1960s.* New York: Praeger, 1970.

Cooley, John K. "The War Over Water." *Foreign Policy, 54* (Spring 1984): 3–27.

Gelburd, Diane E. "Managing Salinity: Lessons from the Past." *Journal of Soil and Water Conservation* (July-August 1985): 329–31.

"General Review." Unpublished paper on the Ramat Negev Agricultural Experiment Station, Ramat Negev Regional Council, Israel, 1988.

Goldberg, S. Dan, and Menachem Schmueli. "Drip Irrigation: A Method Used under Arid and Desert Conditions of High Water and Soil Salinity." In Jules Janick, ed., *Classic Papers in Horticultural Science.* Englewood Cliffs, N.J.: Prentice-Hall, 1989.

Horiuchi, Shiro. "Stagnation in the Decline of the World Population Growth Rate During the 1980s." *Science, 257* (1992): 761–65.

Israel National Water Carrier: 50 Years of Mekorot. Tel Aviv: Mekorot Water Company, 1987.

Jacobsen, Thorkild. *Salinity and Irrigation Agriculture in Antiquity: Diyala Basin Archeological Projects, Report on Essential Results, 1957–58.* Malibu, Calif.: Undena Publications, 1982.

Jacobsen, Thorkild, and Robert M. Adams. "Salt and Silt in Ancient Mesopotamia." *Science, 128* (3334, 1958): 1251–58.

Lips, S. Herman, and Jiftah Ben-Asher. *Fertilization and Saline Water Irrigation.* Report on AID/CDR Project C5-001. Sde Boker, Israel: Center for Desert Agrobiology, Ben-Gurion University of the Negev, 1990.

Mann, Charles C. "How Many Is Too Many?" *Atlantic Monthly* (February 1993): 47–67.

Naff, Thomas, and Ruth C. Matson, eds. *Water in the Middle East: Conflict or Cooperation?* Boulder, Colo.: Westview Press, 1984.

Netafim Company Profile. Israel: Netafim, Kibbutz Hatzerim, 1989.

Norse, David. "A New Strategy for Feeding a Crowded Planet." *Environment, 34* (5, 1992): 6–11 ff.

Pasternak, Dov, and Yoel De Malach. *Saline Water Irrigation in the Negev Desert.* Beersheba, Israel: Publications Section of the Institutes for Applied Research, Ben-Gurion University of the Negev, 1987.

Ponting, Clive. "Historical Perspectives on Sustainable Development." *Environment, 32* (9, 1990): 4–9 ff.

U.S. Department of Agriculture, Agricultural Research Service. *Progress Report 1991.* Fresno, Calif.: USDA-ARS Water Management Research Laboratory, 1991.

Weiss, H., et al. "The Genesis and Collapse of Third Millennium North Mesopotamian Civilization." *Science, 261* (1993): 995–1004.

Index